Pathology

NOTICE

Medicine is an ever-changing science. As new research and clinical experience broaden our knowledge, changes in treatment and drug therapy are required. The editors and the publisher of this work have checked with sources believed to be reliable in their efforts to provide drug dosage schedules that are complete and in accord with the standards accepted at the time of publication. However, readers are advised to check the product information sheet included in the package of each drug they plan to administer to be certain that the information contained in these schedules is accurate and that changes have not been made in the recommended dose or in the contraindications for administration. This recommendation is of particular importance in connection with new or infrequently used drugs.

Pathology:
PreTest® Self-Assessment and Review

Fourth Edition

Edited by

Paul Harrison Duray, M.D.
Assistant Professor of Pathology
Yale University School of Medicine
New Haven, Connecticut

Instructor in Pathology
Boston University School of Medicine
Boston, Massachusetts

McGraw-Hill Book Company
Health Professions Division
PreTest Series

New York   St. Louis   San Francisco
Auckland   Bogotá   Guatemala   Hamburg
Johannesburg   Lisbon   London   Madrid
Mexico   Montreal   New Delhi   Panama
Paris   San Juan   São Paulo   Singapore
Sydney   Tokyo   Toronto

PATHOLOGY: Pretest Self-Assessment and Review
INTERNATIONAL EDITION

Copyright © 1986
Exclusive rights by McGraw-Hill Book Co. — Singapore
for manufacture and export. This book cannot be re-exported
from the country to which it is consigned by McGraw-Hill.

3rd Printing 1987

Copyright © 1986, 1983, 1980, 1976 by McGraw-Hill, Inc.
All rights reserved. No part of this publication may be reproduced
or distributed in any form or by any means, or stored
in a data base or retrieval system, without the prior
written permission of the publisher.

This book was set in Times Roman by Waldman Graphics, Inc.
The editors were Beth Kaufman Barry and Bruce MacGregor.
The production supervisor was Ave McCracken.
The cover was designed by Edward R. Schultheis.

Library of Congress Cataloging in Publication Data
Main entry under title:

Pathology: PreTest self-assessment and review.

    On t.p. the registered trademark symbol "R" is
superscript following "PreTest" in title.
    Bibliography: p.
    1. Pathology—Examinations, questions, etc.
I. Duray, Paul Harrison. [DNLM: 1. Pathology—
examination questions. QZ 18 P297]
RB119.P37 1986   616.07'076   85-16584
ISBN 0-07-051944-7

When ordering this title use ISBN 0-07-100177-8

PRINTED AND BOUND BY B & JO ENTERPRISE PTE LTD, SINGAPORE.

Contents

Preface	vii
Introduction	ix
General Pathology	
Questions	1
Answers, Explanations, and References	30
Hematology	
Questions	62
Answers, Explanations, and References	84
Cardiovascular System	
Questions	97
Answers, Explanations, and References	110
Respiratory System	
Questions	122
Answers, Explanations, and References	133
Gastrointestinal System	
Questions	140
Answers, Explanations, and References	156
Endocrine System	
Questions	166
Answers, Explanations, and References	172
Genitourinary System	
Questions	178
Answers, Explanations, and References	196
Nervous System	
Questions	215
Answers, Explanations, and References	222
Musculoskeletal System	
Questions	233
Answers, Explanations, and References	243

Skin and Breast
    Questions   249
    Answers, Explanations, and References   259

Bibliography   269

Preface

The study of pathology permits a "hand-in-glove" link between the sciences and the fields of clinical medicine, and the better prepared students of pathology will, by virtue of this linkage process, become more knowledgeable, efficient, and caring physicians. This study manual will tempt the undergraduate medical student who is advised to strengthen this desired link both in preparation for writing board examinations and for entering the wards and clinics. In addition, many questions and photomicrographs will challenge graduate physicians in their own assessment of development prior to licensure and board certifying examinations.

Since the last edition, new knowledge in cell and molecular biology has increased our understanding of the mechanisms of many human disorders. New findings surface daily. For example, when the third edition was in press, a new and mysterious disease we now call AIDS was first being reported by the Center for Disease Control. Breath-taking discoveries are occurring at a frantic pace because of technology like recombinant DNA, transection with retroviruses, hybridomas, monoclonal antibodies, and the demonstration of oncogenes, to name a few. One can only wonder what the fifth edition will need to take into account.

Paul Harrison Duray, M.D.

Introduction

Pathology: PreTest® Self-Assessment and Review provides medical students, as well as physicians, with a comprehensive and convenient instrument for self-assessment and review within the field of pathology. The 500 questions parallel the format and degree of difficulty of the questions contained in Part I of the National Board of Medical Examiners examinations, the Federation Licensing Examination (FLEX), and the Foreign Medical Graduate Examination in the Medical Sciences (FMGEMS).

Each question in the book is accompanied by an answer, an explanation, and specific page references to current textbooks, journal articles, or both. A bibliography, listing all the sources used, follows the last chapter.

Perhaps the most effective way to use this book is to allow yourself one minute to answer each question in a given chapter; as you proceed, indicate your answer beside each question. By following this suggestion, you will be approximating the time limits imposed by the board examinations previously mentioned.

When you finish answering the questions in a chapter, you should then spend as much time as you need verifying your answers and carefully reading the explanations. Although you should pay special attention to the explanations for the questions you answered incorrectly, you should read **every** explanation. The author of this book has designed the explanations to reinforce and supplement the information tested by the questions. If, after reading the explanations for a given chapter, you feel you need still more information about the material covered, you should consult and study the references indicated.

This book meets the criteria established by the AMA's Department of Continuing Medical Education for up to 22 hours of credit in category 5D for the Physician's Recognition Award. It should provide an experience that is instructive as well as evaluative; we also hope that you enjoy it. We would be very happy to receive your comments.

General Pathology

DIRECTIONS: Each question below contains five suggested answers. Choose the **one best** response to each question.

1. Which of the following provides an example of concomitant hyperplasia and hypertrophy?
   (A) Uterine growth during pregancy
   (B) Left ventricular cardiac hypertrophy
   (C) Athletic skeletal muscle enlargement
   (D) Breast enlargement at puberty
   (E) Cystic hyperplasia of the endometrium

2. All the following are examples of cellular adaptation EXCEPT
   (A) atrophy
   (B) hypertrophy
   (C) hyperplasia
   (D) dysplasia
   (E) metaplasia

3. Which group of factors is most important in the cellular pathogenesis of acute ischemia?
   (A) Mitochondrial hyperplasia, lysozyme release, membrane injury
   (B) Reduced ATP, increased calcium influx, membrane injury
   (C) Lipid deposition, reduced protein synthesis, nuclear damage
   (D) Ribosome detachment, glycolysis, nuclear damage
   (E) Mitochondrial condensation, glycolysis, sodium cell loss

4. Which of the following is most important in events leading to irreversible cell injury?
   (A) Cell membrane damage
   (B) Increased cell water
   (C) Myelin figure accumulation
   (D) Loss of ribosomes
   (E) Swelling of mitochondria

5. Antibacterial activity occurs within the phagolysosome of the cell in association with
   (A) neutral protease
   (B) serotonin
   (C) prostaglandin E
   (D) myeloperoxidase
   (E) bradykinin

6. Defects in chemotaxis resulting in increased susceptibility to infection can be demonstrated in all the following EXCEPT
   (A) diabetes mellitus, juvenile type
   (B) chronic granulomatous disease of childhood
   (C) chronic renal failure of any cause
   (D) Chédiak-Higashi syndrome
   (E) newborn infants of normal gestation

7. The cluster of cells in the photomicrograph below appeared in a cytologic specimen of sputum for a 57-year-old man with chest pain, hemoptysis, and a nonproductive cough of many years' duration. Which of the following is the most likely diagnosis?

(A) Squamous cell metaplasia of ciliated, bronchial epithelium
(B) Oat-cell (small-cell undifferentiated) carcinoma
(C) Adenocarcinoma
(D) Cytomegalic inclusion virus pneumonia
(E) Normal bronchial epithelium

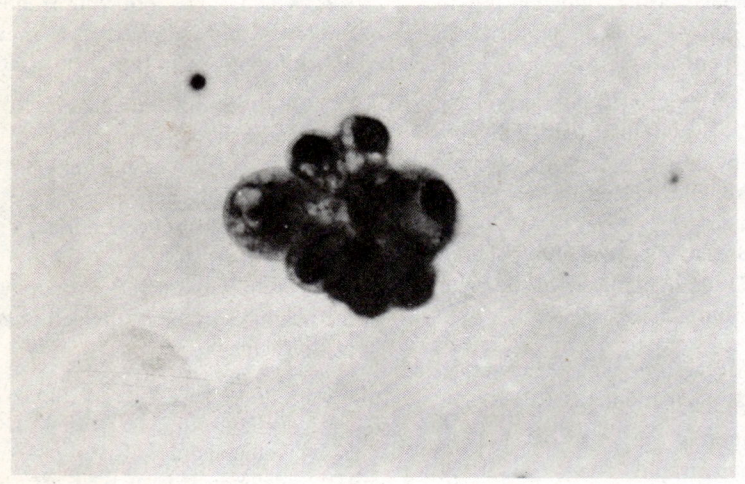

8. An understanding of complex disorders like hereditary spherocytosis, Chédiak-Higashi syndrome, and alcoholic liver disease has improved with molecular discoveries in

(A) lysosomal release
(B) recombinant DNA
(C) cytoskeleton makeup
(D) membrane phospholipids
(E) lipid accumulation

9. In hypovolemic shock, which of the following organs is most severely affected?

(A) Liver
(B) Lung
(C) Heart
(D) Kidney
(E) Adrenal gland

10. The cells in the photomicrograph shown below are from a drop of cerebrospinal fluid. The most likely diagnosis is

(A) subarachnoid hemorrhage
(B) viral meningitis
(C) tuberculous meningitis
(D) bacterial meningitis
(E) leukemic meningitis

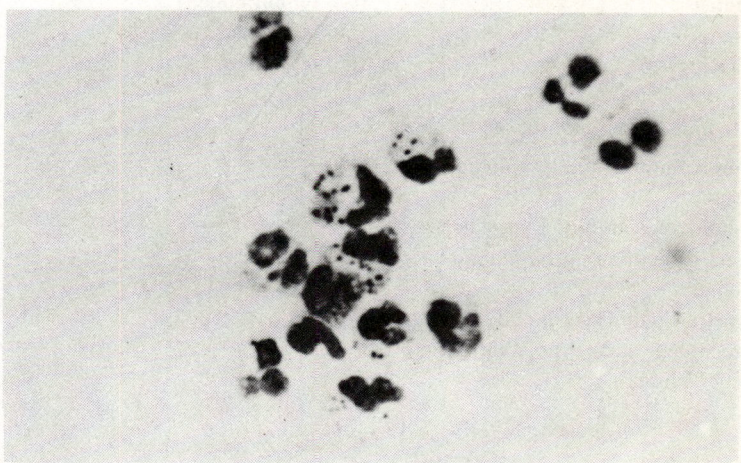

11. The chemical mediators of inflammation listed below often proceed in a cascade after activation EXCEPT

(A) complement
(B) kinin
(C) arachidonic acid
(D) fibrinopeptides
(E) neutral proteases

12. A middle-aged alcoholic woman with a history of heavy cigarette smoking is at risk of developing which of the following in the oral cavity?

(A) Adenocarcinoma
(B) Squamous cell carcinoma
(C) Malignant melanoma
(D) Necrotizing sialometaplasia
(E) Malignant lymphoma

13. Protothecosis infections occur in two clinically distinct forms: cutaneous infection and

(A) pulmonary abscesses
(B) renal abscesses
(C) fistulae
(D) bursitis
(E) cellulitis

14. Sarcomas often metastasize by

(A) embolization in the lymphatic system
(B) embolization in blood vessels
(C) direct growth along lymphatic channels
(D) direct growth along blood vessels
(E) detachment and reimplantation in body cavities

15. The exceedingly important cells of the mononuclear phagocyte system originate from the

(A) spleen
(B) liver
(C) lymph node
(D) bone marrow
(E) thymus

16. The histologic pattern of the lymph node section shown below is likely to support a diagnosis of

(A) sickle cell anemia
(B) carcinoma
(C) leukemia
(D) infectious mononucleosis
(E) rheumatoid arthritis

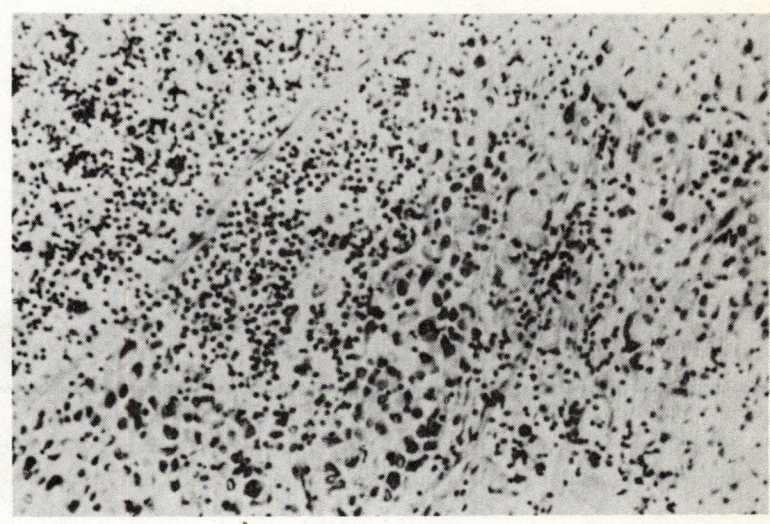

17. In tissues affected by the predominant form of Niemann-Pick disease, which of the following is found at abnormally high levels?

(A) Sphingomyelin
(B) Sphingomyelinase
(C) Kerasin
(D) Acetyl coenzyme A
(E) Ganglioside

18. The diseases of the Hand-Schüller-Christian complex all involve the

(A) skeleton
(B) reticuloendothelial system
(C) heart
(D) lungs
(E) teeth and nails

19. The lesion in the photomicrograph shown below was removed from a discrete mass in the retroperitoneum. It is a

(A) lymphoma
(B) neuroma
(C) fibroma
(D) fibrosarcoma
(E) carcinoma

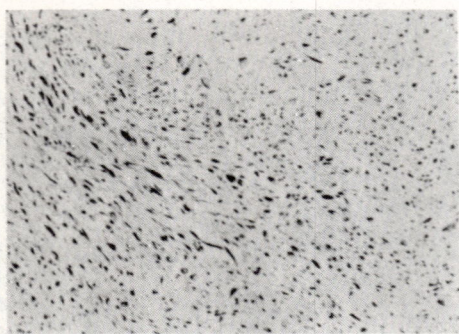

20. All the following symptoms are associated with Klinefelter's syndrome EXCEPT

(A) large, soft testes
(B) gynecomastia
(C) eunuchoidism
(D) azospermia
(E) elevated urinary gonadotropins

21. The biologic behavior of many types of malignant tumors can be generally predicted on the basis of

(A) nuclear chromatin
(B) cytoplasmic volume
(C) differentiation
(D) proximity to arteries
(E) in vitro growth rate

22. In an evaluation of an 8-year-old boy who had had recurrent infections since the first year of life, findings included enlargement of the liver and spleen, lymph node inflammation, and a superficial dermatitis resembling eczema. Microscopic examination of a series of peripheral blood smears taken during the course of a staphylococcal infection indicated that the bactericidal capacity of the boy's neutrophils was impaired or absent. Which of the following is the most probable diagnosis?

(A) Chronic granulomatous disease
(B) Congenital agammaglobulinemia
(C) Hereditary thymic dysplasia
(D) Chédiak-Higashi syndrome
(E) Wiskott-Aldrich syndrome

23. The irregular eosinophilic hyaline inclusions within the hepatocytoplasm shown below are

(A) Russell bodies
(B) parasites
(C) characteristic of chronic alcoholism
(D) characteristic of viral hepatitis
(E) characteristic of carbon tetrachloride poisoning

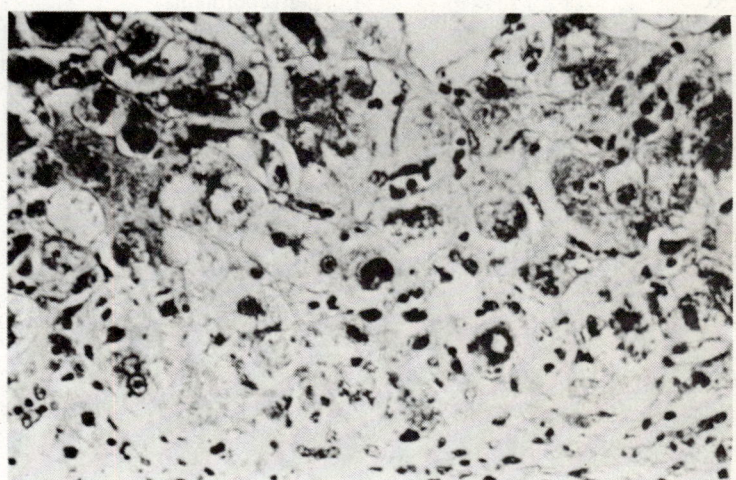

24. If a mutant gene is not expressed phenotypically in an individual, this is said to represent

(A) variable expressivity
(B) reduced penetrance
(C) codominance
(D) genetic heterogeneity
(E) nondisjunction

25. The autosomal recessive genetic disorders known as Fanconi's anemia, ataxia telangiectasia, and Bloom's syndrome are sometimes referred to as "chromosome-breakage syndromes." The reason for this is

(A) that they are associated with leukemia
(B) that they are autosomal recessive disorders
(C) excess chromosomal vulnerability to osmotic changes
(D) increased susceptibility to cell mutations
(E) lack of DNA repair systems

26. Interest is growing in recently discovered cell markers on neoplastic cells that are designated

(A) ADCC
(B) A1AT
(C) HTLV
(D) TSTA
(E) ARC

27. All the following cytologic and membrane alterations can generally be found in neoplastic cells EXCEPT

(A) changes in pseudopodia and microvilli
(B) changes in the cytoskeleton
(C) acquisition of surface-associated glycoproteins
(D) increased lectin agglutinability
(E) decreased membrane transport

28. The cells seen in the following photomicrograph were stained by ABC technique using OKT1 (Leu-1), OKT3 (Leu-4), and OKT11 (Leu-5). The result indicates that the cells are of what origin?

(A) T lymphocytes
(B) Oat cells
(C) Mesothelial cells
(D) EAC rosettes
(E) Melanoma cells

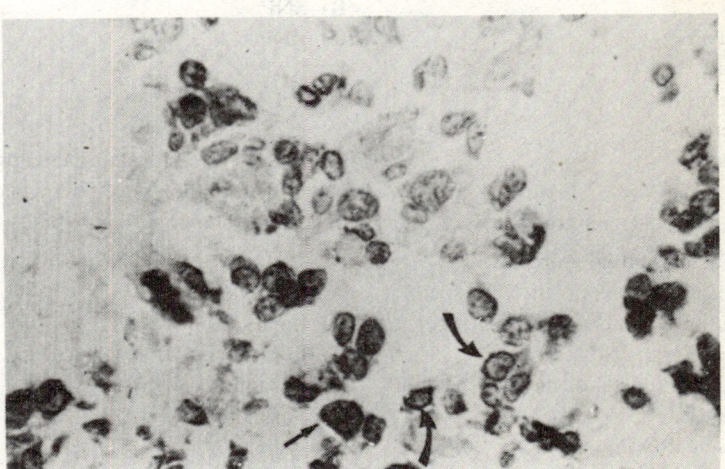

29. Which of the following best describes K cells?

(A) They have no Fc receptor and no surface Ig
(B) They have Fc receptors and surface Ig
(C) They have Fc receptors but no surface Ig
(D) They form EAC rosettes
(E) They have surface HLA-DR antigen

30. After receiving incompatible blood, a patient develops a transfusion reaction in the form of back pain, fever, shortness of breath, and hematuria. This type of immunologic reaction is classified as a

(A) systemic anaphylactic reaction
(B) systemic immune complex reaction
(C) delayed-type hypersensitivity reaction
(D) complement-mediated cytotoxicity
(E) T cell-mediated cytotoxicity

31. An industrial foundry worker who has been chronically exposed to heavy metal vapors has developed a radiographic pattern of pulmonary "honeycombing." Which of the following heavy metals is most likely responsible?

(A) Cobalt
(B) Lead
(C) Cadmium
(D) Mercury
(E) Arsenic

32. An allograft is a graft between

(A) a human and an animal
(B) two individuals of different species
(C) two individuals of the same species
(D) two individuals of the same inbred strain
(E) identical twins

33. Which of the following conditions is most likely to be associated with cancer?

(A) Systemic lupus erythematosus
(B) Hypertension
(C) Polymyositis
(D) Autoimmune thyroiditis
(E) Arteriosclerosis

34. A 19-year-old female college student with a history of arthropathy and a facial rash is found to have leukopenia. Which of the following types of antinuclear antigens should be assessed?

(A) SS-A
(B) SNP
(C) RNP
(D) RAP
(E) Scl-1

35. In systemic lupus erythematosus, which of the following findings has the highest correlation with morbidity and mortality?

(A) LE cells
(B) Lupus nephritis
(C) Lupus endocarditis
(D) Thrombocytopenia
(E) Skin lesions

36. In which of the following disorders is the incidence of positive tests for antinuclear antibody the highest?

(A) Systemic lupus erythematosus
(B) Chronic lymphatic leukemia
(C) Polyarteritis nodosa
(D) Rheumatic fever
(E) Cirrhosis of the liver

37. A patient with severe diabetic renal disease receives a donor cadaver kidney, following which a progressive rise in the serum creatinine occurs over a period lasting 5 months. In the photomicrograph below, what single finding is most characteristic for chronic rejection?

(A) Damaged glomeruli
(B) Interstitial fibrosis
(C) Interstitial inflammation
(D) Tubular atrophy
(E) Vascular changes

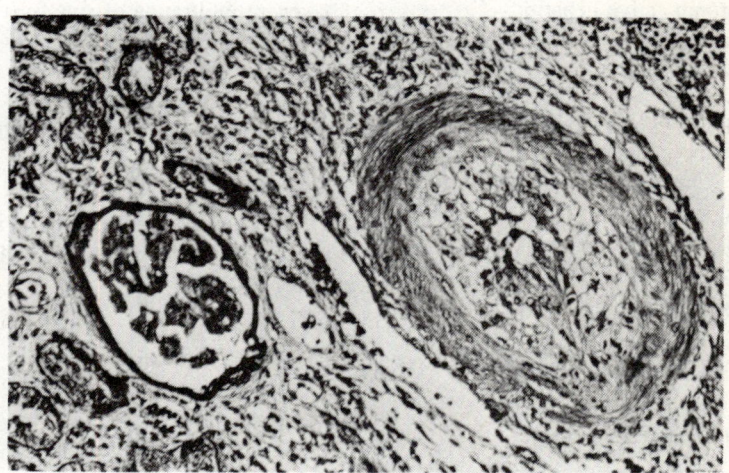

38. An adult patient in the summer months suffers a rash on one of the extremities followed several weeks later by arthritis of the knee. In addition to viral and bacterial disorders and rheumatoid joint disease, which of the following should also be considered in the differential diagnosis?

(A) Hemarthrosis
(B) Reiter's disease
(C) Lyme disease
(D) Charcot's joint
(E) Baker's cyst

39. One of the most important factors determining the growth of a malignant tumor is its

(A) parenchyma
(B) stroma
(C) periphery
(D) cell type
(E) center

40. In which of the following diseases or conditions would a negative immunofluorescent procedure for detection of serum antibodies to mitochondria be expected?

(A) Primary biliary cirrhosis
(B) Chlorpromazine-induced jaundice
(C) Acute viral hepatitis
(D) Chronic active hepatitis
(E) Systemic lupus erythematosus

41. A young woman of average intelligence and short stature who has never menstruated is under clinical investigation for Turner's syndrome. However, a buccal smear shows some cells having one Barr body. Which of the following best explains this finding?

(A) Laboratory error
(B) The patient is a male
(C) Classic XO
(D) Turner mosaic
(E) Klinefelter's syndrome

42. Normal levels of C-reactive protein (CRP) are most often observed in

(A) acute viral illness
(B) pneumococcal pneumonia
(C) active rheumatoid arthritis
(D) active pulmonary tuberculosis
(E) acute myocardial infarction

43. The most sensitive of the commonly used tests for diagnosing active syphilis is the

(A) rapid plasma reagin (RPR) test
(B) *Treponema pallidum* immobilization (TPI) test
(C) fluorescent treponemal antibody-absorption (FTA-ABS) test
(D) Venereal Disease Research Laboratory (VDRL) test
(E) Kolmer test

44. Features commonly seen in tuberculoid leprosy include all the following EXCEPT

(A) presence of large numbers of bacilli in involved tissues
(B) extension of epithelioid cell and lymphocyte infiltrates into the papillary dermis
(C) severe infiltration of small nerves by chronic inflammatory cells
(D) destruction of nerves early in the course of the disease
(E) proliferation of epithelioid cells arranged in clusters and cords

45. As visualized by the electron microscope, all the following are cell organelles EXCEPT

(A) lysosomes
(B) the Golgi complex
(C) the endoplasmic reticulum
(D) desmosomes
(E) microbodies

46. Spirochetal infections include all the following EXCEPT

(A) bejel
(B) yaws
(C) pinta
(D) Weil's disease
(E) lymphogranuloma venereum

47. An elevated IgG level in cerebrospinal fluid and an abnormal band on agar gel electrophoresis of cerebrospinal fluid are findings consistent with the diagnosis of

(A) secondary stage of syphilis
(B) muscular dystrophy
(C) tumor involvement of the spinal cord
(D) meningeal involvement by leukemia
(E) multiple sclerosis

48. Which of the following conditions is most likely to be associated with a negative result on routine pregnancy tests?

(A) Ectopic pregnancy
(B) Hydatidiform mole
(C) Polyhydramnios
(D) Eclampsia
(E) Choriocarcinoma

49. The texture and resilience of a given tumor grossly (macroscopically) are largely influenced by which of the following?

(A) Presence or absence of connective tissue stroma
(B) Degree of malignancy
(C) Normal tissue-tumor interface
(D) Type of epithelium present
(E) Relative blood supply

50. A 37-year-old woman who has a clinical picture of fever, splenomegaly, varying neurologic manifestations, and purplish ecchymoses of the skin is found to have a hemoglobin level of 10.0 g/dl, a mean corpuscular hemoglobin concentration (MCHC) of 48, peripheral blood polychromasia with stippled macrocytes, and spherocytes, with a blood urea nitrogen level of 68 mg/dl. The findings of coagulation studies and the patient's fibrin-degraded products are not overtly abnormal. Which of the following is most closely identified with these findings?

(A) Idiopathic thrombocytopenic purpura
(B) Thrombotic thrombocytopenic purpura
(C) Disseminated intravascular coagulopathy
(D) Submassive hepatic necrosis
(E) Waterhouse-Friderichsen syndrome

51. The "stat" laboratory sends the following electrolyte results to the ward concerning a new admission: Na^+, 142 mEq/L; K^+, 7.2 mEq/L; Cl^-, 101 mEq/L; and CO_2, 32 mEq/L. On the basis of these results, the physician should

(A) treat with sodium exchange resin
(B) institute peritoneal dialysis immediately
(C) inquire about a hemolyzed blood sample
(D) infuse insulin intravenously
(E) make a diagnosis of hyperkalemia

52. Parathyroid hormone, by its action on target organs, is known to cause all the following EXCEPT

(A) increased intestinal calcium absorption
(B) increased renal tubular reabsorption of calcium
(C) increased serum phosphate levels
(D) mobilization of calcium from bone
(E) decreased renal tubular reabsorption of phosphate

53. The enzyme activity curve labeled II, shown below, best represents the pattern for which of the following serum enzymes after an uncomplicated acute myocardial infarction?

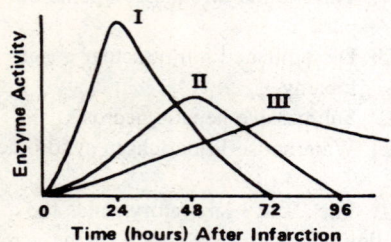

(A) Glutamic-oxaloacetic transaminase
(B) Creatine phosphokinase
(C) Lactic dehydrogenase
(D) Alkaline phosphatase
(E) 5'-Nucleotidase

54. A 65-year-old known diabetic male is admitted with fever, dehydration, and altered consciousness, with no perceptible odor of acetone on his breath. The serum Na^+ level is 146 mEq/L, the glucose level is 960 mg/dl, and the blood urea nitrogen level is 48 mg/dl. Calculate the serum osmolality.

(A) 280 mOsm
(B) 310 mOsm
(C) 318 mOsm
(D) 356 mOsm
(E) Insufficient data

55. Parkinsonism is associated with

(A) arbovirus encephalitis
(B) encephalitis lethargica
(C) St. Louis encephalitis
(D) equine encephalitis
(E) lymphocytic choriomeningitis

56. The most comprehensive determination of adrenocortical function can be obtained by measurement of

(A) urinary 17-hydroxysteroids
(B) urinary 17-ketosteroids
(C) urinary 17-ketogenic steroids
(D) plasma cortisol
(E) plasma aldosterone

57. A lower than normal serum amylase level is most typical of patients who have

(A) diabetes mellitus
(B) mumps
(C) renal insufficiency
(D) a ruptured ectopic pregnancy
(E) received morphine

58. What is the creatinine clearance of a person who passes 361 mg of creatinine in a 24-hour urine sample of 770 ml and whose plasma creatinine is 2.0 mg/100 ml?

(A) 12.5 ml/min
(B) 25.0 ml/min
(C) 50.0 ml/min
(D) 75.0 ml/min
(E) 100.0 ml/min

59. Which of the following would be contraindicated in an individual with hyperuricemia?

(A) Large amounts of citrus fruit
(B) Large volumes of cranberry juice
(C) A diet low in meat
(D) Large doses of salicylates
(E) Allopurinol

60. A 20-year-old student has an upper respiratory infection with severe sore throat and pain on swallowing. Her dormitory roommates make a diagnosis of infectious mononucleosis, thus saving her a trip to Student Health. Six weeks later, she develops a low-grade fever and back pain. A urinalysis finding of red blood cell casts

(A) reflects glomerular damage
(B) is insignificant if few casts are present
(C) is probably due to a menstrual "contaminant"
(D) suggests the presence of hemorrhagic cystitis
(E) is present in any instance of hematuria

61. While many factors come into play in a tumor's behavior, which of the following can be expected to influence the biology of a given tumor the **most**?

(A) Lack of a peripheral capsule
(B) Histologic differentiation
(C) Presence of inflammation
(D) Size of the tumor
(E) Nuclear cytoplasmic ratio

62. Elevated levels of alkaline phosphatase are typical findings in each of the following conditions EXCEPT

(A) cirrhosis
(B) obstructive jaundice
(C) hepatitis
(D) polycythemia vera
(E) myocardial infarction

63. An adult patient suffers from recurrent bleeding from the gums, intermittent GI bleeding, and excessive bleeding from minor trauma to the skin. A prolonged bleeding time is discovered. Which of the following levels or activities should be assessed to complete the diagnosis?

(A) Prothrombin time
(B) Plasma fibrinogen
(C) Factor VIII:R
(D) Factor VIII:C
(E) Factor VIII:Ag

64. The table below shows the normal serum values for the five isoenzymes of lactic dehydrogenase (LDH) and the values obtained for one patient. The diagnosis most compatible with the patient's values is

Isoenzyme	Normal % activity	Patient's % activity
LDH_1	20-35	18
LDH_2	30-40	24
LDH_3	20-30	13
LDH_4	5-15	26
LDH_5	1-15	19

(A) acute hepatitis
(B) pernicious anemia
(C) pulmonary infarct
(D) myocardial infarct
(E) cerebrovascular accident

65. An African boy with a rapidly expanding mass in the region of the jaw and cheek is thought to have Burkitt's lymphoma. These cells are growing rapidly because of

(A) their permanent nature
(B) shortening of the cell cycle
(C) nonsequencing of the EBV genome
(D) fewer G_0 cells entering the cycle
(E) delayed progression from G_2 to mitosis

66. Environmental and industrial pollutants are becoming increasingly relevant in human oncogenesis. Which of the following combinations is most closely allied with human neoplasia?

(A) Asbestos, silica, arsenicals
(B) Diethylstilbestrol, radioactive dusts, cyanide
(C) Aflatoxin, beryllium vapor, benzidine
(D) Polyvinyl chloride, nickel, chromium
(E) Carbon tetrachloride, lead, chloroform

67. Which of the following is physiologically the most active thyroid hormone?

(A) Thyroglobulin
(B) Monoiodotyrosine (MIT)
(C) Diiodotyrosine (DIT)
(D) Triiodothyronine (T_3)
(E) Thyroxine (T_4)

68. Most patients with primary hemochromatosis become symptomatic between the ages of

(A) 1 and 4 weeks
(B) 1 and 3 years
(C) 3 and 7 years
(D) 10 and 20 years
(E) 40 and 60 years

69. The low-power electron micrograph shown below depicts the presence of what type of cell?

(A) Chondrocyte
(B) Squamous
(C) Adenocarcinoma
(D) Liver
(E) Endocrine

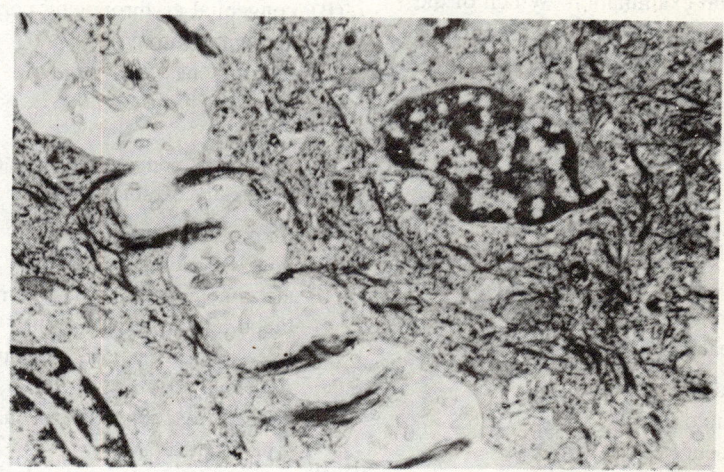

70. A diagnosis of adrenogenital syndrome with demonstrable adrenal hyperplasia is consistent with

(A) generalized calcium oxalate deposition similar to that occurring in oxalosis
(B) accumulation of glycolipids in tissues
(C) salt loss simulating Addison's disease
(D) symptoms similar to those occurring in phenylketonuria
(E) severe acidosis

71. In Tay-Sachs disease, the ganglioside that accumulates specific to the disease lacks

(A) sphingosine
(B) the terminal galactose unit
(C) the fatty acid moiety
(D) a hexosamine moiety
(E) the entire carbohydrate moiety

72. A 21-year-old female with recurrent painful crises in the extremities and an inability to sweat is found to have multiple abdominal and thigh vascular lesions and corneal opacity on slit-lamp examination. Which of the following conditions is suggested by these findings?

(A) Fabry's disease
(B) Fanconi syndrome
(C) Tay-Sachs disease
(D) Hand-Schüller-Christian disease
(E) Gaucher's disease

73. A chromosomal aberration that results in a disturbance in the normal gene balance is termed

(A) nondysjunction
(B) euploidy
(C) aneuploidy
(D) breakage
(E) variance

74. The major underlying defect in classical renal tubular acidosis (caused by gradient defect) appears to be

(A) an excessive back-diffusion of secreted hydrogen ions from tubular urine to blood
(B) an impairment of ammonia excretion
(C) a leakage of bicarbonate ions out of the proximal tubule
(D) a deficiency in the total hydrogen ion secretory capacity
(E) an impairment in the reclamation of filtered bicarbonate ions

75. Disorders of porphyrin metabolism associated with cutaneous photosensitivity include all the following EXCEPT

(A) erythropoietic porphyria
(B) congenital erythropoietic porphyria
(C) variegate porphyria
(D) intermittent acute porphyria
(E) protoporphyria

76. Relatively nonpathogenic pneumococci typically exhibit

(A) R (rough) genotypes
(B) positive quellung reactions
(C) alpha-hemolysis when grown on blood agar
(D) bile-solubility when grown in deoxycholate media
(E) positive reactions on exposure to type 3 antisera

77. Characteristically, T lymphocytes do all the following EXCEPT

(A) occur in the interfollicular portion of lymph nodes
(B) occur as the most common lymphocyte of peripheral blood
(C) secrete immunoglobulin G
(D) affect cell-mediated immunity
(E) contain the theta surface antigen

78. Which of the following organisms produces signs and symptoms that mimic acute appendicitis?

(A) Enteropathic *Escherichia coli*
(B) *Enterobius vermicularis*
(C) *Trichomonas hominis*
(D) *Yersinia enterocolitica*
(E) *Bacillus anthracis*

79. An adult migrant farm worker in the San Joaquin Valley of California has been hospitalized for 2 weeks on the medical service with progressing lassitude, fever of unknown origin, and skin nodules on the lower extremities. A biopsy of one of the deep dermal nodules shown in the photomicrograph below reveals the presence of

(A) Russell bodies
(B) malignant lymphoma
(C) coccidioides spherule
(D) lymphomatoid granulomatosis
(E) erythema nodosum

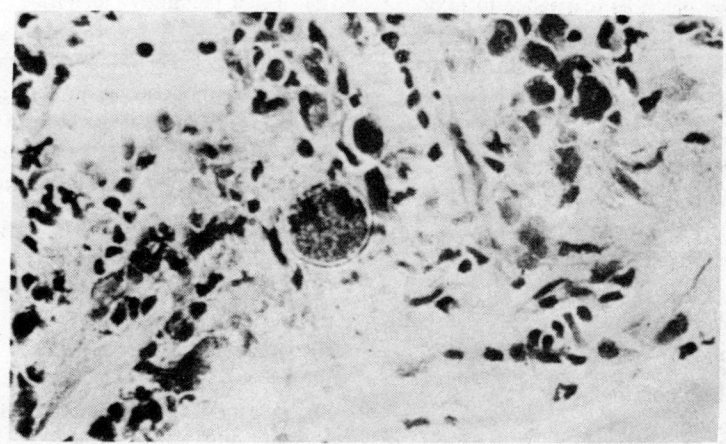

80. From a geographical standpoint, the prevalence of carcinoma of the stomach shares an inverse relationship with the prevalence of carcinoma of the

(A) lung
(B) colon
(C) rectum
(D) uterus
(E) gallbladder

81. Delayed-type hypersensitivity reactions of the tuberculin skin test type

(A) appear within 1 or 2 hours
(B) require an intact T lymphocyte population
(C) show dermal infiltrates of granulocytes
(D) are associated uniquely with small antigens
(E) do not require previous exposure to the antigen

82. Large amounts of antigen are required to produce

(A) serum sickness
(B) an Arthus reaction
(C) generalized anaphylaxis
(D) cutaneous anaphylaxis
(E) atopic responses

83. Unusual characteristics of mycobacteria, such as resistance to toxic agents, environmental viability, and unusual stain reactions, can be attributed to their

(A) acid fastness
(B) aerobic requirements
(C) high lipid content
(D) peptidoglycan content
(E) plasma membrane

84. Picornaviruses typically cause all the following conditions EXCEPT

(A) the "common cold"
(B) poliomyelitis
(C) keratoconjunctivitis
(D) aseptic meningitis
(E) herpangina

85. Under aerobic conditions, which of the following organisms will NOT grow on heat-treated chocolate agar unless another organism such as *Staphylococcus aureus* is growing in its vicinity?

(A) *Bordetella bronchiseptica*
(B) *Bordetella pertussis*
(C) *Hemophilus ducreyi*
(D) *Hemophilus influenzae*
(E) *Streptococcus (Diplococcus) pneumoniae*

86. All the following statements about *Mycobacterium tuberculosis* are true EXCEPT

(A) it has a long doubling time
(B) its cell wall contains large amounts of lipid
(C) it frequently infects silica miners
(D) it is prone to drug-resistant mutation
(E) it is a facultative anaerobe

87. Which of the following organisms is highly pathogenic in humans, grows as an encapsulated yeast both in culture and in infected tissues, and often produces a chronic, exudative meningitis?

(A) *Aspergillus fumigatus*
(B) *Histoplasma capsulatum*
(C) *Coccidioides immitis*
(D) *Cryptococcus neoformans*
(E) *Blastomyces dermatitidis*

88. All the following diseases are associated with herpesviruses EXCEPT

(A) shingles
(B) chickenpox (varicella)
(C) influenza
(D) cytomegalic inclusion disease
(E) mononucleosis

89. A woman taking oral contraceptives during the reproductive years has a minimal but real risk of developing any or all of the following EXCEPT

(A) pulmonary infarction
(B) myocardial infarction
(C) vaginal adenosis
(D) venous thrombus
(E) liver cell adenoma

90. The presence in the serum of cold-reacting antibodies, as well as antibodies against specific alpha-hemolytic streptococci, is compatible with infection caused by

(A) *Mycoplasma pneumoniae*
(B) *Streptococcus (Diplococcus) pneumoniae*
(C) *Nocardia asteroides*
(D) influenza virus
(E) cytomegalovirus

91. That the human T cell lymphotrophic retrovirus (HTLV-III) is responsible for AIDS is supported by the fact that

(A) it is a retrovirus
(B) retroviruses are antigenically distinguishable
(C) it is associated with lymphadenopathy
(D) antibodies to HTLV-III appear with onset of AIDS
(E) helper/suppressor ratios are less than 2.0 in AIDS

92. Alcohol may be the most significant cause of public health problems in the United States. All the following entities are correlated with alcohol abuse EXCEPT

(A) subdural hematoma
(B) esophageal carcinoma
(C) elevated creatine phosphokinase
(D) primary biliary cirrhosis
(E) portal vein thrombosis

DIRECTIONS: Each question below contains four suggested answers of which **one or more** is correct. Choose the answer:

A	if	**1, 2, 3**	are correct
B	if	**1 and 3**	are correct
C	if	**2 and 4**	are correct
D	if	**4**	is correct
E	if	**1, 2, 3, and 4**	are correct

93. A 54-year-old woman with a 30 pack-year history of cigarette smoking underwent a bronchial biopsy after a central mass was seen on x-ray. The photomicrograph below shows the biopsy result. This disorder is demonstrated in which of the following paraneoplastic syndromes?

(1) Cushing's syndrome
(2) Hyponatremia
(3) Carcinoid syndrome
(4) Hypercalcemia

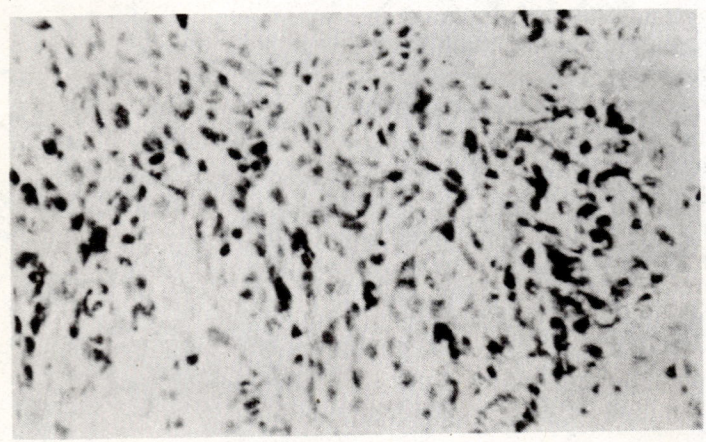

94. Epstein-Barr virus (EBV) infections can be associated with neoplastic states. In infectious mononucleosis, which of the following best accounts for control of the EBV infected cells?

(1) Immunoregulatory mechanisms
(2) Macrophage migration inhibitory factor
(3) Activation of T cells
(4) Lack of EBV replication

95. Mononuclear phagocytes of the reticuloendothelial system include

(1) Kupffer cells
(2) Langhans' giant cells
(3) heart-failure cells
(4) plasma cells

96. A patient suffers from weight loss, fever, and persistent generalized lymphadenopathy and weakness. Severe diarrhea consisting of watery stools develops. A biopsy of the small bowel is stained by a tissue Ziehl-Neelssen technique (photomicrograph below). The patient **may** have which of the following?

(1) An underlying non-Hodgkin's lymphoma
(2) Anti-HTLV antibodies
(3) HLA-DR5 antigen
(4) Whipple's disease

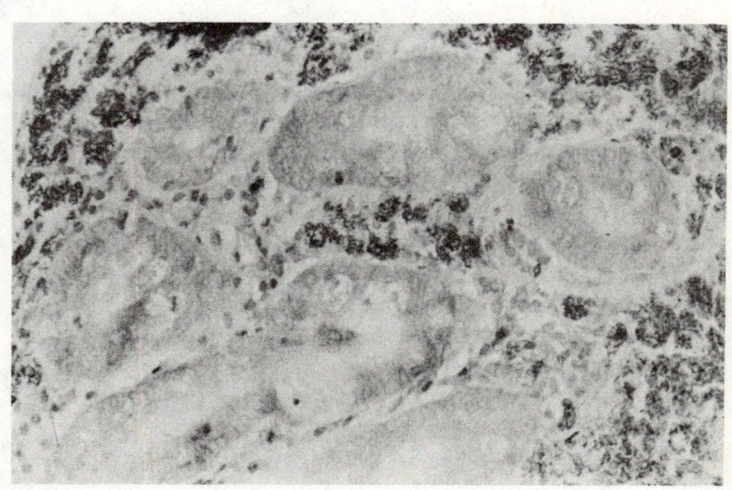

97. The photomicrograph below shows a labeling phenomenon of dark cytoplasmic granules within select cells. This staining technique

(1) relies on neutral polysaccharides for a positive reaction
(2) relies on antigen-antibody binding
(3) stains neutral and acid mucopolysaccharides
(4) may be used to identify tumor cell markers

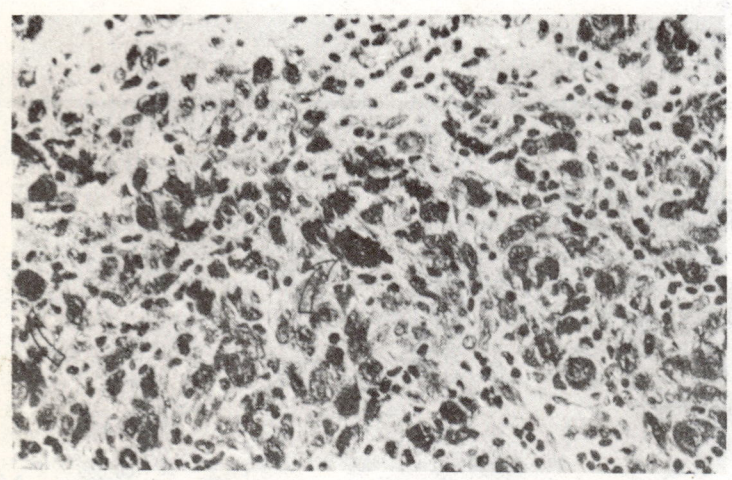

98. Fat necrosis is a characteristic histologic change associated with

(1) acute pancreatitis
(2) hyperlipidemia
(3) traumatized breast tissue
(4) hibernomas

99. Secondary gout may be seen in association with

(1) polycythemia
(2) psoriasis
(3) hemolytic anemias
(4) myeloproliferative diseases

100. Atherosclerosis, the most prevalent form of arterial disease in humans, is first manifested by an innocuous fatty streaking of the intima and is characterized by

(1) formation of essential lesions in the intima
(2) disintegration of the internal elastic lamina in advanced lesions
(3) relatively numerous lesions in larger arteries and fewer in smaller arteries
(4) plaque formations that cause little reduction in the lumen size of large arteries

101. Vitamin D deficiency might be expected to lead to a
(1) relative excess of osteoid tissue in bone
(2) decreased production of bone matrix
(3) decreased absorption of calcium
(4) reduced collagen formation

102. Glycogen storage diseases include which of the following?
(1) Von Gierke's disease
(2) Pompe's disease
(3) McArdle's disease
(4) Tay-Sachs disease

103. Morphologic alterations observed in women taking oral contraceptives include
(1) formation of ovarian follicular cysts
(2) intimal fibrosis and endothelial proliferation of small pulmonary arteries
(3) deep vein thrombosis
(4) hepatocellular necrosis and bile duct hyperplasia

104. Increased deposition of hemosiderine, as shown below in a liver section stained with Prussian blue, may
(1) result from excessive dietary intake
(2) be associated with bronze diabetes
(3) occur in pulmonary macrophages in chronic heart failure
(4) be associated with cirrhosis

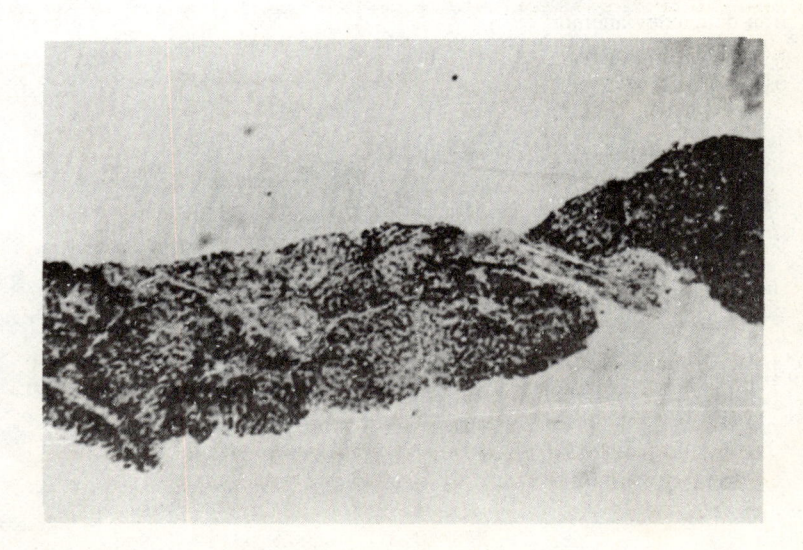

SUMMARY OF DIRECTIONS

A	B	C	D	E
1, 2, 3 only	1, 3 only	2, 4 only	4 only	All are correct

105. As a result of active world travel, parasitic infestations are far from being considered exotic diseases in the United States today. A pulmonary phase is part of the development of which of the following helminths?

(1) *Necator americanus*
(2) *Strongyloides stercoralis*
(3) *Ascaris lumbricoides*
(4) *Wuchereria bancrofti*

106. Taking patient discomfort and expense into account, bone marrow aspiration and trephine examination are indicated to document

(1) metastatic carcinoma
(2) iron deficiency anemia
(3) sideroblastic anemia
(4) osteoporosis

107. Evidence that depressed immunocompetence leads to an increased risk of developing malignancy is found in

(1) patients of advanced age
(2) genetic immunodeficient states
(3) immunosuppressed transplant recipients
(4) male homosexuals

108. Organisms that can cause summertime infections around coastal areas of the United States and are characterized microscopically by a curved bacillus include

(1) *Mycobacterium avium*
(2) *Mycobacterium bovis*
(3) *Mycobacterium marinum*
(4) *Vibrio cholerae*

109. Which of the following functions can be attributed to the cell depicted in the electron photomicrograph below?

(1) Production of thromboplastin
(2) Degranulation in type I reactions
(3) Production of interleukin I
(4) factor VIII synthesis

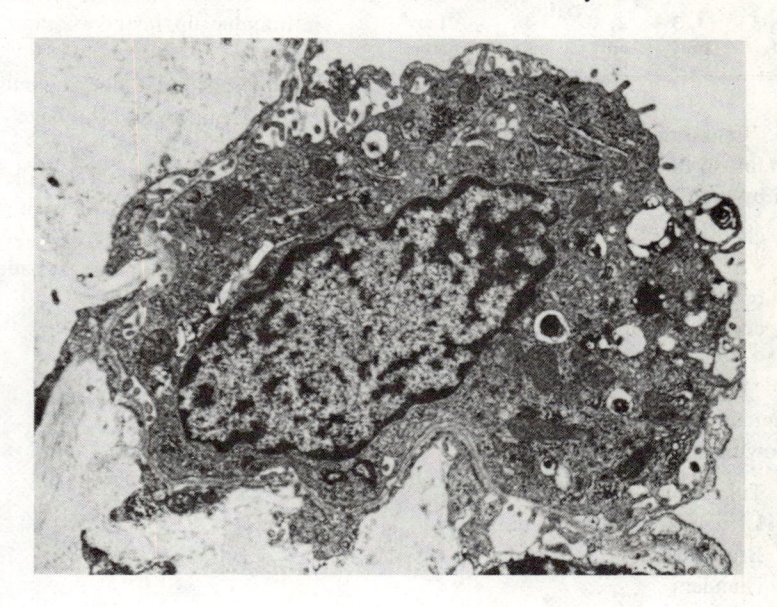

SUMMARY OF DIRECTIONS

A	B	C	D	E
1, 2, 3 only	1, 3 only	2, 4 only	4 only	All are correct

110. Leukotrienes differ from prostaglandins in the mediation of inflammation by their more potent actions of

(1) chemotaxis
(2) vasoconstriction
(3) bronchoconstriction
(4) edema formation

111. Diseases characterized by granulomatous lesions include which of the following?

(1) Tularemia
(2) Lymphogranuloma inguinale
(3) Brucellosis
(4) Glanders

112. Which of the following observations can support the contention that host immunity plays a role in cancer?

(1) The increased incidence of cancer in immunosuppressed allograft recipients
(2) The presence of "blocking antibodies" in patients who have cancer
(3) The presence of tumor-specific antibodies in patients who have cancer
(4) The presence of anergy in patients who have cancer

General Pathology

DIRECTIONS: The groups of questions below consist of lettered choices followed by several numbered items. For each numbered item select the **one** lettered choice with which it is **most** closely associated. Each lettered choice may be used once, more than once, or not at all.

Questions 113-115

Assays of circulating hormones, enzymes, proteins, and other products often can be helpful in diagnosing a specific type of tumor. For each of the following tumors, select the circulating product that is most likely to assist in diagnosis.

(A) Acid phosphatase
(B) Carcinoembryonic antigen
(C) α_1-Fetoprotein
(D) β-Fetoprotein
(E) β_2-Microglobulin

113. Prostatic carcinoma

114. Gastrointestinal carcinoma

115. Hepatoma

Questions 116-119

For each phenomenon that follows, choose the immune agent responsible.

(A) T lymphocytes
(B) IgA
(C) IgD
(D) IgE
(E) IgM

116. Allograft rejection

117. Tuberculin reaction

118. Hay fever

119. Anaphylaxis

Questions 120-123

Match each immunoglobulin with the characteristic with which it is most likely to be associated.

(A) Cytophilic for mast cells
(B) Secretory piece
(C) Appears first in a primary immune response
(D) Constitutes 80 percent of the circulating gamma globulin in adults
(E) A component of HLA histocompatibility antigen

120. IgG

121. IgM

122. IgA

123. IgE

General Pathology Answers

1. **The answer is A.** *(Robbins, ed 3. pp 31-33.)* In uterine growth during pregnancy, both cell proliferation involving the endometrial glands and muscle enlargement of the uterine wall occur. These processes offer models of both hyperplasia and hypertrophy. When both are present, DNA synthesis is markedly accelerated. Hyperplasia is an increase in the number of cells, whereas hypertrophy is an increase in cell size, as in cardiac muscle hypertrophy in response to volume overload or peripheral vascular hypertension. Breast tissue enlargement resulting from hormonal influences is due solely to an increase in cell numbers.

2. **The answer is D.** *(Robbins, ed 3. pp 2, 29-33.)* Cellular adaptation reflects a cell's capacity to undergo change in response to an external influence, be it a stimulant for growth, such as endocrine influences, or a stressor, such as chemical vapors on the respiratory mucosa. Metaplasia refers to replacement of an adult cell by another cell, usually of a more primitive and less vulnerable type. The specialized ciliated pseudostratified columnar epithelium of the respiratory tract undergoes squamous cell metaplasia in response to inhaled irritants, such as tobacco smoke. Dysplasia can also be associated with inflammation or irritation but results in abnormal cell proliferation, which may progress to malignant transformation in some instances.

3. **The answer is B.** *(Robbins, ed 3. pp 5-9.)* Cell membrane injury, the loss of cell ATP, and the influx of CA^{2+} into the mitochondria are thought to be the most critical of multiple cellular events after experimental ischemia in animals. A major detriment following reduction of cell oxygen tension is the cessation or reduction in ATP because of falling oxidative phosphorylation; this occurs early in hypoxia. While increasing anaerobic glycolysis subsequently occurs, the pivotal step is loss of the energy producing ATP, which leads to cell NA^+ accumulation, K^+ efflux, and Ca^{2+} influx, by reduced effectiveness of the active transport NA^+ pump. Cells greatly enlarge as a consequence of isoosmotic water accumulation. These changes are still reversible if oxygen tension is restored. Continuing hypoxia results in mitochondrial damage (vacuole formation), which is irreversible. Cell death will occur when lysosomes break down and release proteases, RNA and DNAases, and cathepsins. Central nervous system cells are most susceptible to ischemia (5 minutes or less), while liver and kidney cells survive up to 2 hours with epidermal cells tolerating several hours of hypoxia.

4. **The answer is A.** *(Robbins, ed 3. pp 9-10.)* Reversible changes in cell injury include mild changes in pH, brief electrolyte imbalance, water uptake by dissociation

General Pathology

of lipoproteins (myelin figures in cytoplasm), detachment of ribosomes from rough endoplasmic reticulum, and enlargement of mitochondria. These are changes indicative of injury, especially hypoxia-induced, but do not correlate with inevitable cell necrosis and death. The cell membrane, composed of a bilipid-glycoprotein coat, is essential for cell volume regulation and if damaged may result in phospholipid loss with a reduction in continued biosynthesis of the bilipid layer. Membrane damage probably also results from the accumulation of breakdown products such as lysophospholipids and acyl carnitine, free radical formations, and reduction of ATP. It is postulated that Ca^{2+} ingress through damaged cell membranes into mitochondria may be responsible for ultimate cell death.

5. **The answer is D.** *(Robbins, ed 3. pp 26, 50.)* The enzyme myeloperoxidase is found in especially high concentrations in the neutrophilic granulocyte and exerts its strong antibacterial effects by combining with chloride and hydrogen peroxide. Neutral proteases are mainly extracellular enzymes with action on collagen, elastin, fibrin, and cartilage. Prostaglandins are hormones that are involved in the mechanisms of vasodilation occurring during inflammation. The biogenic amines bradykinin and serotonin are also vasoactive, but they have no direct antibacterial activity.

6. **The answer is B.** *(Robbins, ed 3. pp 51-52.)* The enzymatic defect that exists in chronic granulomatous disease of childhood does not impair chemotaxis or the cell's ability to engulf bacteria, but rather involves a failure to produce hydrogen peroxide after engulfment. Chemotactic defects resulting in inhibition of the capacity of leukocytes to infiltrate an area of infection or injury may be due to intracellular defects, as found in Chédiak-Higashi syndrome, in other genetic defects, and in diabetes mellitus. Chronic renal failure and other liver disease may be associated with factors in the circulation that impair chemotaxis. Whether they are full-term or immature, neonatal leukocytes have a temporary chemotactic defect that is corrected with increasing age.

7. **The answer is C.** *(Takahashi, ed 2. pp 305-306.)* In the cluster of cells shown, marked variation in cell size, nuclear hyperchromatism, and prominent nuclear membranes can be seen and are diagnostic characteristics of malignancy. The tendency of cells to cluster and overlap, the prominent nucleoli, and the vacuolated cytoplasm are signs that strongly support a diagnosis of adenocarcinoma rather than oat-cell carcinoma.

8. **The answer is C.** *(Robbins, ed 3. pp 20, 28-29, 51-52.)* Cytoskeletal filament proteins compose the framework of cells involved in cell functions, such as pinocytosis, structural stability, contractility, organelle movement, and cell motility. The cytoskeleton is seen ultrastructurally as microtubules (25 nm diameter) of tubulin protein, intermediate filaments (8 to 10 nm) of keratins, desmin, vimentin, glial and neurofilaments, thin filaments of actin (6 to 8 nm), and thick filaments (15 nm) of myosin. Every cell has tubulin and actin, while most have some myosin. Epithelial

cells have any of the many types of cytokeratins, with a few having the mesenchymal filament vimentin. Muscle cells and fibroblasts have desmin. Glial cells and neurons contain glial and neurofilament protein, respectively. Phagocytosis is impaired in the Chédiak-Higashi syndrome because of a defect in the polymerization of microtubules. Alcoholic "hyaline" (Mallory's bodies) in alcoholic liver disease appears to be composed of prekeratins. Red cells have a membrane skeleton made up of spectrin, ankyrin, actin, and protein 4.1. In hereditary spherocytosis a genetic defect is responsible for abnormal spectrin that is unable to bind protein 4.1 required for the stability of the red cell membrane.

9. The answer is D. *(Robbins, ed 3. pp 113-116.)* The kidney is usually the organ most severely damaged by shock. The cortices become pale, and the pyramids become cyanotic and congested. Microscopically, the cells of the distal convoluted tubules can be seen to be swollen or dead. These changes are called acute tubular necrosis.

10. The answer is D. *(Henry, ed 17. p 474.)* In a patient who is suspected of having meningitis, microscopic examination of cerebrospinal fluid is of immediate importance. In the photomicrograph shown, all the cells are polymorphonuclear leukocytes and bacteria are visible in the cytoplasm. Neutrophils may be present in viral or tuberculous meningitis, but lymphocytes are more common. Demonstration of bacteria by Gram stain of the cerebrospinal fluid is the most valuable aid in establishing a diagnosis of early bacterial meningitis and is possible in more than 90 percent of cases.

11. The answer is E. *(Robbins, ed 3. pp 52-58.)* Lysosomes contain many substances involved in inflammation including alkaline and acid phosphatase, collagenases, lysozymes, lactoferrin, myeloperoxidase, cationic proteins, and acid proteases. Of these, the neutral proteases (elastase, collagenase, cathepsin G) function in stages of inflammatory confinement and wound healing by degrading tissue matrix like collagen, fibrin, cartilage, elastin, and basement membranes. The other mediators cascade as follows: complement cascade starts classically by an antigen-antibody complex or alternately by nonimmunologic stimuli. C5a leads to chemotaxis while the complement complex C5b-9 leads to cell lysis. The kinins are activated by Hageman factor (XIIA), via prekallikrein into bradykinin. The fibrinopeptides of the clotting system can also be activated by Hageman factor, or by extrinsic tissue thromboplastin to eventuate into a polymerized fibrin clot. The important cascades of arachidonic acid metabolites (cyclooxygenase, lipoxygenase), leading to functioning vasodilators (prostaglandins) and membrane permeability factors (leukotrienes), are the most complex of all, beginning with the actions of phospholipase.

12. The answer is B. *(Robbins, ed 3. pp 783-784.)* Ninety-seven percent of oral cavity malignancies are squamous cell carcinomas, of which about half arise in the tongue. The prognosis depends on the degree of cellular differentiation, the extent of spread, and the presence of lymph-node metastases. Generally, metastases are confined to nodes above the clavicles, but lung, liver, and bone may be involved later in the disease.

13. The answer is D. *(Anderson, ed 8. pp 379-380.)* Prototheca algae are related to the green algae, *Chlorella*, and are capable of causing disease in humans as a result of penetrating injuries. Cutaneous protothecosis is characterized by verrucous or papulonodular lesions of the hands, wrists, feet, and scalp. Infected subcutaneous nodules near the elbow joint constitute olecranon bursitis, the second form of infection. The algae are not responsive to chemotherapy, and local excision appears to be the only effective remedy. Disseminated protothecosis, successfully treated with amphotericin-B and transfer factor, has been reported. Spherules with endospores are seen in tissue section.

14. The answer is B. *(Robbins, ed 3. p 226.)* Carcinomas tend to spread via the lymphatic system, whereas sarcomas seem to use the blood vessels. (These generalizations are not, however, absolutes.) Regional lymph nodes are frequently excised at the time of removal of the primary tumor in the case of a carcinoma but not in the case of a sarcoma. Hematogenous tumor emboli most frequently involve the liver and lungs because embolization follows the pathway of venous drainage from the affected site.

15. The answer is D. *(Robbins, ed 3. pp 59-61.)* There is evidence that most, if not all, macrophages originate from a committed bone marrow stem cell, which differentiates into a monoblast, then a promonocyte, which matures into a monocyte in the circulating peripheral blood. When called upon, the circulating monocyte can enter into any organ or tissue bed as a tissue macrophage (previously called a histiocyte). Examples of tissue macrophages are Kupffer cells (liver), alveolar macrophages (lung), osteoclasts (bone), Langerhans cells (skin), microglial cells (central nervous system), and possibly the dendritic immunocytes of the dermis, spleen, and lymph nodes. The entire system, including the peripheral blood monocytes, constitutes the mononuclear phagocyte system.

16. The answer is B. *(Rosai, ed 6. pp 1212-1214.)* The lymph-node section shown in the photomicrograph contains metastatic carcinoma cells and was probably excised from a patient who has carcinoma. The tumor cells are clustered in small nests within the node and are separated by stromal tissue. The cellular clustering is characteristic of carcinomas that have metastasized to lymph nodes.

17. The answer is A. *(Stanbury, ed 5. pp 831-839.)* Sphingomyelin, a lipid composed of phosphocholine and a ceramide, characteristically is found in abnormally high concentrations throughout the body tissues of patients who have any one of the forms of Niemann-Pick disease. Division of this disease into five categories is generally accepted; type A, the acute neuronopathic form, is the one that has the highest incidence. The lack of sphingomyelinase in type A is the metabolic defect that prevents the hydrolytic cleavage of sphingomyelin, which then accumulates in the brain. Patients who have the type A form usually show hepatosplenomegaly at 6 months of age, progressively lose motor functions and mental capabilities, and die during the third year of life.

18. The answer is B. *(Robbins, ed 3. pp 694-696, 1272-1273.)* The Hand-Schüller-Christian (HSC) disease is a complex of three syndromes affecting the reticuloendothelial system: Letterer-Siwe syndrome, Hand-Schüller-Christian syndrome, and eosinophilic granuloma. An unknown etiology and an abnormal production of histiocytes are characteristics common to all three syndromes and provide the basis for the designation of HSC disease as histiocytosis X (the alternate term is Langerhans cell granulomatosis, since the cells have the Birbeck granules ultrastructurally, as do Langerhans cells).

19. The answer is D. *(Robbins, ed 3. pp 269-270.)* Interlacing bundles of anaplastic spindle cells characterize fibrosarcoma. The extreme variations in nuclear size and shape, mitoses, and lack of fibrocollagenous areas help to differentiate this tumor from a benign fibroma. Hypoglycemia may be associated with fibrosarcoma.

20. The answer is A. *(Anderson, ed 8. p 794.)* The findings of small, firm testes, eunuchoidism, gynecomastia, and mental retardation constitute the classic manifestations of Klinefelter's syndrome, a type of hypogonadism. The seminiferous tubules may be sclerosed and hyalinized. Urinary levels of gonadotropin are usually elevated; the elevation is thought to result from the absence of controlling testicular hormones, not from pituitary dysfunction.

21. The answer is C. *(Robbins, ed 3. pp 218-222.)* The extent to which malignant tumor cells reproduce the cytologic appearance of the normal parent tissue from which they arise is referred to as the degree of differentiation. Tumors that resemble the tissue of origin to a high degree are called well-differentiated. The other end of the spectrum is referred to as poorly differentiated. An undifferentiated carcinoma means that the cell of origin is unknown, because there are no recognizable features of the defined normal tissue types within the tumor. All conceivable grades of differentiation exist between the two extremes. In general, the better-differentiated tumors have a more favorable clinical course and poorly differentiated tumors are found to be aggressive in their behavior.

22. The answer is A. *(Robbins, ed 3. pp 50-51, 52, 208.)* The classic form of chronic granulomatous disease usually afflicts boys and causes their death before they reach the age of 10 years. Key findings in chronic granulomatous disease include lymphadenitis, hepatosplenomegaly, eczematoid dermatitis, pulmonary infiltrates that are associated with hypergammaglobulinemia, and defective ability of neutrophils to kill bacteria. The last finding is thought to be caused by a delay in the release of neutrophilic lysosomal enzymes responsible for intracellular bactericidal action. Although defective neutrophilic bactericidal action also is associated with the Chédiak-Higashi syndrome, this syndrome is distinguished by photophobia and oculocutaneous albinism. Thrombocytopenia is a feature of Wiskott-Aldrich syndrome.

23. The answer is C. *(Robbins, ed 3. pp 29, 919-930.)* Hyaline inclusions, as shown in the illustration, may appear in liver cells injured by chronic alcoholism and have been shown by ultrastructure studies to result from the close packing of fibrils. The appearance of these inclusions is not a morphologic expression of cell injury. Alcoholic hyaline inclusions (Mallory's bodies) are nonspecific and occur in Wilson's disease, Indian childhood cirrhosis, bypass operations for morbid obesity, and alcoholic hepatitis. They react with antibodies to cytokeratins, which suggests they are related to the intermediate filament, keratin.

24. The answer is B. *(Robbins, ed 3. pp 123, 134-135.)* Mendel's laws deal with single-gene mutations that may be inherited or acquired de novo, with expression of the abnormality highly variable. In autosomal dominance inheritances, if a mutant gene is unexpressed, this is called reduced penetrance and it may vary by a percentage that reflects the degree of expression. Variable expressivity refers to expression of the trait in all who harbor the mutant gene, but with different expressions of the abnormality. Nondisjunction refers to a failure of disjoining of a homologous pair of chromosomes during meiosis (may result in aneuploidy). Codominance refers to the full expression of both alleles of a gene pair. Genetic heterogeneity applies to multiple-loci mutations (each in a different location, reflecting multiple different mutations), which can result in the same or similar expressed abnormality.

25. The answer is D. *(Robbins, ed 3. pp 122, 241.)* Mutations are alterations in the genetic code. The incidence of these alterations normally increases with age and is especially high in certain autosomal recessive disorders—e.g., Fanconi's anemia, ataxia telangiectasia, and Bloom's syndrome ("chromosome-breakage syndromes"). Individuals with such disorders are highly susceptible to mutations due to environmental influences, such as sunlight, ionizing radiation, drugs, viruses, and possibly elements in the diet (e.g., nitrite additives). It is thought that one mechanism operative in genetic code alterations is the binding of mutagenic substances directly to DNA guanine.

26. The answer is D. *(Robbins, ed 3. pp 166, 208-209, 233-234, 930-931.)* Newly discovered membrane surface antigens on the surfaces of neoplastic cells have stimulated interest and research. These tumor-associated antigens are largely glycoproteins (proteoglycans, chondroitins, heparan) that are at least anchored in the bilipid cell membrane with polypeptide chains emerging "into space" on the surface. Monoclonal antibodies can be raised against certain epitopes on the external portions of these surface antigens. Also the host may mount specific immunoglobulins against these sites. These antigens are membrane-associated, induce transplantation immunity, and are distinct from histocompatibility antigens; they are called tumor-specific transplantation antigens (TSTA) or tumor-associated rejection antigens (TARA). TSTA are found on tumor cells that were transformed by viral oncogenes. TSTA resemble differentiation antigens in normal cells of some animal strains. Most TSTA are carcinogen or oncogene related and are usually absent in spontaneous tumors. ADCC is antibody-dependent cell-mediated cytotoxicity; A1AT is alpha-1-antitrypsin. HTLV is the designation of the AIDS-related agent, human T leukemia virus, while ARC is the AIDS-related complex.

27. The answer is E. *(Robbins, ed 3. pp 235-236.)* Generally tumor cells, by virtue of their transformation, exhibit ultrastructural alterations as visualized by electron microscopy as well as physiologic changes. Membrane projections (microvilli, filopodia, pseudopodia) may become blunted, or lost altogether. Neoplastic transformation may be associated with formation of projections in some cells, but the loss of attenuation of surface projections is more characteristic of neoplastic cells. Cytoskeletal microfilaments and tubules become disorganized, while intermediate filaments (keratins, desmin, vimentin) may increase. In addition to formation of membrane-associated glycoproteins (tumor antigens), there is increased "shedding" and loss of surface antigens. Fibronectin, for instance, is lost from tumor cell surfaces and may be measured in the patient's plasma as cold-insoluble globulin. Surface glycolipids (many are receptor sites) are diminished or lost in some neoplastic cells, theoretically enabling tumor cells to escape the growth inhibitory effects of chalones. Plant lectins can agglutinate cells because their property of divalency cross-links sugars on neighboring cells. This lectin agglutinability is increased in many malignant cells. Fundamental to the biologic behavior of neoplastic cells is the increased demand for cell nutrients, which is aided by an observed increase in neoplastic cell membrane transport.

28. The answer is A. *(Robbins, ed 3. pp 158-159.)* With the advent of monoclonal antibodies derived from hybridomas it is now possible to identify cells of certain specificity. These antibodies recognize epitopes of antigens found on the cell surfaces that have been used to induce immunity within the mouse. Using an immunoperoxidase technique, the OKT (Leu series) identifies T cells. In addition specific markers will identify subsets of T cells: For example all peripheral blood T cells react with OKT1, OKT3, and OKT11; OKT4 (Leu-3) reacts with mature T cells; OKT4 identifies helper T cells; and OKT8 reacts with suppressor cells. The normal T helper/suppressor ratio in humans is about 2. These antibodies do not label cells other than those in the T lymphocyte system. T cells as a group function in immune regulation and act in concert with B lymphocytes and macrophages. T helper cells aid the cellular immune response in reaction to antigens, while T suppressor cells help in turning the immune response off. EAC rosette cells refer to B lymphocytes that have surface receptors (C3b) that bind to sheep erythrocytes that have been coated with IgM antibody and complement. B lymphocytes also express surface immunoglobulin.

29. The answer is C. *(Robbins, ed 3. pp 160-161.)* The presence of Fc receptors on the cell surfaces with no surface Ig and no evidence for T cell derivation is the characteristic finding in K cells. Since they lack the usual markers for B and T lymphocytes as well as macrophages, they may be thought of as "null cells." However, their morphologic appearance is that of medium-sized lymphocytes. The Fc receptors on the surfaces exist for IgG, enabling them to lyse antibody-coated target cells. This cytotoxicity ability is referred to as antibody-dependent cellular cytotoxicity. A related cell is the NK cell (natural killer), which has the capacity to cause lysis of tumor cells, nonsensitized normal cells, and cells infected with viruses. The NK cells differ from K cells because previous antibody coating is not a requirement for cell lysis. They resemble larger lymphocytes more than the K cells and have more T cell surface antigens than the K cells. The HLA-DR antigens are found on the surfaces of macrophages, Langerhans cells, and dendritic immunocytes. These cells function in overall cell immunity by presenting and processing the foreign antigen(s) to the immune system. They belong to the mononuclear phagocytic system. Dendritic cells have no phagocytic function, unlike macrophages.

30. The answer is D. *(Robbins, ed 3. pp 163-171.)* The type of reaction in the question is a type 2 hypersensitivity reaction that is mediated by antibodies reacting against antigens present on the surface of cells, in this case blood group antigens or irregular antigens present on the donor's red blood cells. Type 2 hypersensitivity reactions result from attachment of antibodies to changed cell surface antigens or to normal cell surface antigens. Complement-mediated cytotoxicity occurs when IgM or IgG binds to a cell surface antigen with complement activation and consequent cell membrane damage or lysis. Blood transfusion reactions and autoimmune hemolytic anemia are examples of this form. Systemic anaphylaxis is a type 1 hypersensitivity reaction in which mast cells or basophils that are bound to IgE antibodies are reexposed to an allergen, which leads to a release of vasoactive amines that cause edema and broncho- and vasoconstriction. Sudden death can occur. Systemic immune complex reactions are found in type 3 reactions and are due to circulating antibodies that form complexes upon reexposure to an antigen, such as foreign serum, which then activates complement followed by chemotaxis and aggregation of neutrophils leading to release of lysosomal enzymes and eventual necrosis of tissue and cells. Serum sickness and Arthus' reactions are examples of this. Delayed-type hypersensitivity is type 4 and is due to previously sensitized T lymphocytes, which release lymphokines upon reexposure to the antigen. This takes time—perhaps up to several days following exposure. The tuberculin reaction is the best known example of this. T cell-mediated cytotoxicity leads to lysis of cells by cytotoxic T cells in response to tumor cells, allogenic tissue, and virus-infected cells. These cells have OKT5/T8 antigens on their surfaces.

31. The answer is C. *(Anderson, ed 8. p 231.)* Heavy metal poisoning may occur via the respiratory route owing to contaminated inhalant and vapors. Such poisoning is usually industrially related, as with mercury (calomel workers), arsenic (pesticides), and lead (batteries and paints). Cadmium has been implicated in producing not only an acute form of pneumonia, but, with chronic exposure to small concentrations of cadmium vapors, diffuse interstitial pulmonary fibrosis and an increased incidence of emphysema as well. The "honeycomb" radiologic pattern is indicative of an interstitial fibrotic process and may be the result of repeated pneumonitis and bronchitis. Cadmium can also be found in tobacco smoke. Cobalt poisoning leads to myocardiopathy, mercury poisoning leads to renal tubular damage, and lead poisoning leads to liver necrosis and cerebral edema, whereas arsenic poisoning in addition to carrying an increased risk of lung and skin cancer, may produce death caused by inhibition of respiratory enzymes and cardiac subendocardial hemorrhages complicated by gastroenteritis with shock.

32. The answer is C. *(Anderson, ed 8. pp 483-484.)* An allograft is also called a homograft and refers to a graft between members of the same species. An autograft refers to a tissue graft taken from one site and placed in a different site in the same individual. Isografts are grafts between individuals from an inbred strain of animals. A graft between individuals of two different species is a xenograft or heterograft.

33. The answer is C. *(Robbins, ed 3. pp 193-194.)* Fifteen to twenty percent of cases of polymyositis are associated with underlying visceral malignancies of virtually any organ. Although the cause of this association remains unknown, it has been postulated that some cancers either produce products that are toxic to skeletal muscles or contain antigens that are cross-reactive with skeletal muscle.

34. The answer is B. *(Henry, ed 17. pp 926-931.)* Since the original identification of antinuclear antibodies occurring in systemic lupus erythematosus (SLE), numerous specific subtypes have been defined. Although they are collectively referred to as antinuclear antibodies, at least 13 subtypes have been described that are found in other autoimmune states; these are measured by radioimmunoassay, agar gel immunodiffusion, or counterimmunoelectrophoresis. Although it is not very sensitive, the fraction SNP (the deoxynucleoprotein-soluble subtype extracted from calf thymus nuclei) is highly specific for SLE, especially if the nonhistone Sm antigen also reacts with antibody from the patient's serum. Antibodies to nuclear acidic protein SS-A antigens occur in Sjögren's syndrome, antibodies to RAP occur in rheumatoid arthritis, antibodies to RNP occur in mixed connective tissue disease, and antibodies to Scl-1 occur in systemic sclerosis.

35. The answer is B. *(Robbins, ed. 3, pp 185-188.)* While lupus erythematosus is a multisystem disease, the most ominous prognostic sign is the development of nephritis. In addition to renal failure, causes of death include cardiac failure, central nervous system disease, hemorrhage, and bacterial infections, which are probably related to the immunosuppressive therapy used to control the primary disease. Tissue damage results from DNA-anti-DNA immune complexes that are deposited in tissues and cell-directed autoantibodies.

36. The answer is A. *(Henry, ed 17. pp 926-931.)* A positive test for antinuclear antibody (ANA) can be obtained in virtually all patients who have systemic lupus erythematosus (SLE). A substantially lower incidence of positive tests for ANA has been demonstrated in cases of chronic lymphatic leukemia, polyarteritis nodosa, and cirrhosis of the liver; in rheumatic fever, ANA tests are negative. A diagnosis of SLE without a positive test for ANA is probably subject to doubt.

37. The answer is E. *(Robbins, ed 3. pp 171-175.)* Histocompatible antigens (HLA) are responsible for rejection of transplanted organs in humans. Organ rejection requires both humoral and cell-mediated immunologic reactions involving T cells both from the donated organ and the patient's own OKT4 T helper cells and OKT5/8 cytotoxic T cells. Hyperacute rejection occurs within minutes after transplantation and consists of neutrophils within the glomerulus and peritubular capillaries. Acute rejection occurs within days after transplantation and is marked by vasculitis and interstitial lymphocytic infiltration. Subacute rejection vasculitis occurs during the first few months after transplantation and is characterized by the proliferation of fibroblasts and macrophages in the tunica intima of arteries. In chronic rejection tubular atrophy, mononuclear interstitial infiltration and vascular changes are encountered, with the vascular changes being characteristic and probably reflecting an end stage of arteritis. The vascular obliteration leads to interstitial fibrosis and tubular atrophy with loss of renal function. However, the histologic picture is complicated by secondary ischemic damage, and it may be difficult to discern inflammation, fibrosis, and vascular changes as cause or effect.

38. The answer is C. *(Robbins, ed 3. pp 334, 574, 1348-1349, 1355-1356, 1362.)* A localized skin rash in the summertime followed within a period of weeks by arthritis, especially involving less than three joints, should arouse suspicion of Lyme disease. This disorder was first described in the mid 1970s in Connecticut when small clusters of cases of children suffering from an illness resembling juvenile rheumatoid arthritis were first noted. The disease has now been shown to be caused by a spirochete, *Borrelia burgdorferii*, through the bite of a tick belonging to the genus *Ixodes*. The spirochete-infested ticks reside in forested areas where there are deer and small rodents present. The deer act as a wintering-over reservoir for the ticks. In the spring the tick larval stage emerges and evolves into a nymph, which is infective for humans if they are bitten. Adult ticks are also capable of transmitting the spirochete as well during questing. The bite is followed by a rash called erythema chronicum migrans, which may resolve spontaneously. However, many patients have a transient phase of spirochetemia which may allow the spread of the spirochete to the meninges, heart, and synovial tissue. Originally thought to be confined to New England, Lyme disease has now been shown to be present in Europe and in Australia as well. The spirochetes are sensitive to penicillin, erythromycin, and tetracycline. Reiter's disease does not present with a spreading rash, and a Baker's cyst produces swelling in the popliteal fossa behind the knee rather than joint effusions anteriorly.

39. The answer is B. *(Robbins, ed 3. pp 221-223.)* Experimentation with in vitro cell culture systems has greatly increased understanding of the behavior of ordinary healthy cells, such as fibroblasts and lymphocytes, and of benign and malignant tumors. All cells need nutrients, oxygen, and a medium for support and transport of nutrients and oxygen. No matter how malignant a given tumor is, and regardless of its cell type (mesenchyme, sarcoma; epithelium, carcinoma; lymphocyte, lymphoma), if it is not provided with a vascularized stroma (fibroconnective tissue support), its capacity to grow beyond a given size is severely limited. A heavily collagenized stroma gives a tumor its palpable hardness. Infiltrating duct carcinoma of the breast is characteristically very hard on palpation because of the presence of a densely collagenized fibrous stroma that may accompany the tumor in metastatic sites as well as in the primary focus. Tumors without much stroma are soft (even to the cutting block). Soft tumors include lymphomas and adenocarcinoma of the colon.

40. The answer is C. *(Henry, ed 17. pp 236-237.)* Antibodies to mitochondria are not present in the serum of patients who have acute viral hepatitis when immunofluorescent techniques are used. Serum antibodies to mitochondria are present, however, in 87 percent of patients who have primary biliary cirrhosis, 69 percent of patients who have chlorpromazine-induced jaundice, 66 percent of patients who have chronic active hepatitis, and 18 percent of patients who have systemic lupus erythematosus. Immunofluorescent detection techniques for antibodies to mitochondria are not specific for one particular disease, but, when evaluated in conjunction with tests for antinuclear antibodies and antibodies to smooth muscle, they can be helpful in differential diagnosis.

41. The answer is D. *(Henry, ed 17. pp 129-131, 132-133.)* The Barr body represents a sex chromatin clump attached to the nuclear membrane that originates from an entire X chromosome and can easily be seen by using light microscopy to examine scrapings of the epithelium of the inside buccal mucosa. According to the formula $M = n - 1$, the total number of X chromatin masses equals the number of cellular X chromatin masses seen in the nucleus minus 1. Hence, normal males are $0 = 1 - 1$ (no Barr body), and normal females are $1 = 2 - 1$ (one Barr body). In

General Pathology   41

classic Turner's syndrome (XO), the expected buccal smear would be $0 = 1 - 1$ (no Barr bodies seen), as in a normal male. Karyotyping is necessary when the Barr body screening test is ambiguous or inconclusive. In a young woman of short stature and average intelligence who has never menstruated, there is a strong indication that one of the forms of Turner's syndrome exists, and the presence of one Barr body indicates that the patient has XX in some percentage of cells. About 10 percent of all Turner syndrome patients show a mosaic pattern, with some cells having XO/XX or XO/XXX patterns. In this example, the patient is likely to be XO/XX by the formula $1 = 2 - 1$. In Turner mosaics, the likelihood of developing a seminoma or gonadoblastoma is higher than expected, and gonadectomy may be indicated.

42. The answer is A. *(Henry, ed 17. pp 212-213.)* C-reactive protein (CRP) elevations, as well as elevations in the erythrocyte sedimentation rate, are nonspecific markers of inflammatory conditions. The CRP rises faster and returns to normal earlier than the erythrocyte sedimentation rate in most inflammatory diseases. Most bacterial infections, rheumatoid arthritis, rheumatic fever, and diseases leading to necrosis and tissue damage will elevate the CRP. CRP elevations do not occur in most viral illnesses.

43. The answer is C. *(Henry, ed 17. pp 1140-1142.)* Although the rapid plasma reagin (RPR) test, Kolmer test, and Veneral Disease Research Laboratory (VDRL) test are rapid and easily performed tests that can help confirm a diagnosis of active syphilis, these tests, because of their low specificity for antibodies against treponemal or cardiolipin antigens, are associated with false-positive reactions. Therefore, RPR tests, Kolmer tests, and VDRL tests usually are used for screening programs. The *Treponema pallidum* immobilization (TPI) test and the fluorescent treponemal antibody-absorption (FTA-ABS) test have greater specificity for treponemal antigen but are technically more difficult to perform. The FTA-ABS test is generally the most sensitive and most specific of the syphilis testing procedures.

44. The answer is A. *(Anderson, ed 8. pp 322-334.)* The histopathologic findings of epithelioid cells organized into clusters of cords extending into the papillary stroma and of chronic lesions occupied by few (or no) bacilli are characteristic of tuberculoid leprosy and help to differentiate it from lepromatous leprosy. The extension of epithelioid cell infiltration into epidermal basal cells that occurs in tuberculoid leprosy is evidence for strong host resistance and contrasts with the histologic character of lepromatous lesions. Lepromatous lesions show not only a clear zone between infiltrating epithelioid cells and the overlying epidermis, but also numerous bacilli within small skin nerves.

45. The answer is D. *(Robbins, ed 3. pp 1, 26-27.)* The cytoplasmic matrix contains numerous organelles with highly specialized functions. Whereas mitochondria are the "power" units of the cell involved with the Krebs cycle and anaerobic metabolism, the endoplasmic reticulum is a complex network of rodlike tubules containing ribosomes and is involved in protein synthesis (rough endoplasmic reticulum). Lysosomes are round bodies containing enzymes involved in inflammation. These include the sulfatases, desoxyribonucleases, hydrolases, and acid phosphatates. The Golgi apparatus (complex) is made up of tiny vesicles, membranes, and vacuoles and is also involved in protein synthesis, as it receives the synthesized proteins from the endoplasmic reticulum. The Golgi complex appears to collect, segregate, and export protein. Microbodies are membrane-bound spheres that contain catalase, oxidases, and uric acid oxidase. Epithelial cells, especially surface-lining cells, are held together by connections referred to as intercellular junctions. Desmosomes (squamous cells), tight junctions (zonula occludens), and gap junctions (nexuses) are examples of such membrane connectors.

46. The answer is E. *(Henry, ed 17. pp 1139-1144, 1312-1314.)* Lymphogranuloma venereum, usually transmitted by sexual contact, is caused by obligate intracellular parasites that contain both RNA and DNA and belong to the genus *Chlamydia (C. trachomatis)*. Chlamydial agents, originally thought to be viruses because they form inclusion bodies in infected cells, also cause trachoma, inclusion conjunctivitis, and psittacosis-ornithosis. The other infections listed are caused by spirochetes and are nonvenereal.

47. The answer is E. *(Henry, ed 17. p 947.)* Elevations in cerebrospinal fluid globulins often occur in multiple sclerosis and other demyelinating diseases. An abnormal band on electrophoresis may occur even in the absence of elevated globulins. Late tertiary syphilis may cause these findings, but they would not occur in the secondary stage. Tumor or meningeal leukemia can also produce elevated cerebrospinal fluid globulin levels, but the presence of tumor cells and absence of an electrophoretic band would lead to the proper diagnosis.

48. The answer is A. *(Henry, ed 17. p 497.)* Although human chorionic gonadotropin (HCG) levels characteristically are elevated in all the conditions listed, up to 50 percent of patients with an ectopic pregnancy may have urine levels of HCG less than 1.0 IU/ml. Since many of the pregnancy tests used do not detect levels in this range, a negative test for urinary HCG does not rule out an ectopic pregnancy.

49. The answer is A. *(Robbins, ed 3. pp 214, 215.)* All tumors whether benign or malignant have a supporting stroma composed of varying amounts of connective tissue and blood supply. The cellularity can range from that of a highly cellular lesion, such as oat-cell carcinoma of the lung or Burkitt's lymphoma, to that of a relatively hypocellular lesion, such as a hyalinized neurilemmoma, but the cellularity of the tumor per se does not usually influence the texture. Firmness and even hardness of tumors are a function of the amount of collagenous stroma present. The term *desmoplasia* refers to a collagenized and fibroblastic stroma; an example is carcinoma of the breast, which has the texture of a water chestnut because of the concurrent proliferation of the fibrous stroma with the carcinoma. Tumors that lack a collagenized fibrous stroma tend to be softer regardless of the tumor cellularity per se. Malignant tumors of mesenchyme have a fleshy character because of very little connective tissue stroma; examples include fibrosarcoma, liposarcoma, and leiomyosarcoma. There are a few exceptions to the desmoplastic rule, and an obvious example is a tumor of cartilage in which the hyaline cartilage matrix accounts for the firmness; some chondrosarcomas, however, may be soft and friable.

50. The answer is B. *(Anderson, ed 8. pp 691, 1044.)* A fulminating septic state should always be considered and excluded whenever the constellation of fever, deteriorating mental status, skin hemorrhages, and shock develops. Such conditions can be seen in gram-negative rod septicemia caused by any of the coliforms (gram-negative endotoxic shock) or fulminant meningococcemia (Waterhouse-Friderichsen syndrome). However, a form of nonbacterial vasculitis termed thrombotic thrombocytopenic purpura (TTP) is notorious for producing a clinical syndrome very similar to fulminating infective states. It is characterized by arteriole and capillary occlusions by fibrin and platelet microthrombi and is usually unassociated with any of the predisposing states seen in disseminated intravascular coagulopathy (DIC), such as malignancy, infection, retained fetus, and amniotic fluid embolism. Macrocytic hemolytic anemia, variable jaundice, renal failure, skin hemorrhages, and central nervous system dysfunction are all seen in TTP and are related to the fibrin thrombi, which can be demonstrated with skin, bone marrow, and lymph node biopsies. The vasculitis usually shows no inflammatory cells, which distinguishes TTP from other forms of vasculitis. There is less coagulopathy in TTP than is found in DIC, and hemolytic anemia is generally not found in idiopathic or autoimmune thrombocytopenic purpura. The condition of patients with TTP may be temporarily improved by plasmapheresis, but the outcome is usually grim.

51. The answer is C. *(Henry, ed 17. p 126.)* The type of blood sample sent to the laboratory, the type of container used to collect blood, the manner in which the blood specimen was collected, and the preparation of the patient (appropriate fasting, drug history, exercise) prior to venipuncture are just as important to the final laboratory result as the analytic method used by the laboratory to arrive at the result. All the above factors can cause laboratory result deviations, and these factors should be considered before accepting abnormal laboratory results. Red blood cells can readily lyse because of alcohol left on the arm while swabbing the skin, use of unclean or poorly dried syringes or too large a needle bore (17 gauge, for example), or a traumatic venipuncture. Since red blood cells contain a higher concentration of K^+ than does serum or plasma, even moderate hemolysis of red cells can cause spurious elevation of serum K^+. If the serum clot tube is seen to be slightly pink, most laboratories will notify the ward that an improper sample has been obtained. Once the laboratory result is confirmed as being valid, the next step is to exclude intravascular hemolysis within the patient before making a diagnosis of hyperkalemia.

52. The answer is C. *(Henry, ed 17. p 147. Robbins, ed 3. pp 1226–1229.)* Parathyroid hormone (PTH), by affecting the kidneys, bones, and intestinal mucosa, is the principal regulator of plasma levels of phosphate and calcium. PTH, by its action on renal tubular cells, not only causes decreased phosphate reabsorption, it causes increased calcium reabsorption; these reciprocal processes result in a decrease in serum phosphate and a corresponding increase in extracellular calcium levels. Extracellular levels of calcium are also maintained by the release of calcium during PTH-induced osteocytic and osteoclastic osteolysis, a process that is regarded as the mobilization of calcium from bone. PTH also may induce the intestinal mucosa to absorb calcium derived from dietary sources.

53. The answer is A. *(Henry, ed 17. pp 263-264, 275-277.)* Serum glutamic-oxaloacetic transaminase (SGOT) levels (curve II) become elevated within 12 hours after nearly all acute myocardial infarctions; they generally reach a peak level within 48 hours and return to normal within 4 to 5 days. After myocardial infarctions, creatine phosphokinase levels (curve I) rise and fall more rapidly than do SGOT levels. Lactic dehydrogenase levels (curve III) also become elevated within 1 day after infarctions, but they remain elevated for about 10 days. Alkaline phosphatase and 5'-nucleotidase levels, normal during infarctions, usually show marked increases in patients who have obstructive jaundice.

54. The answer is D. *(Henry, ed 17. pp 37-38, 394.)* Although most laboratories are capable of directly measuring the serum or urine osmolality with accurate osmometers, it is useful to remember the following formula:

$$\text{Osmolality (mOsm/kg) H}_2\text{O} = \frac{2(Na^+)}{1} + \frac{(glucose)}{20} + \frac{(BUN)}{3}$$

This formula gives an approximation of the serum osmolality in a given patient, since Na^+, glucose, and blood urea nitrogen account for at least 95 percent of the dissolved solutes composing the osmolality. The normal serum osmolality falls within the range of 285 to 310 mOsm/kg H_2O. An often overlooked cause of profound water loss with dehydration (in osmotic diseases) in elderly diabetic patients is nonketotic, hyperosmolar coma. These patients enter a phase of coma and dehydration with vascular collapse owing to hypovolemia caused by profound osmotic diuresis owing to the striking hyperglycemia. The serum acetoacetic acid and ketone levels may be normal or mildly elevated in contrast to the ketoacidosis of diabetic coma in younger patients.

55. The answer is B. *(Robbins, ed 3. pp 1385, 1417-1418.)* Encephalitis lethargica spread from the Orient in successive epidemics from 1915 to 1926 and first appeared in the United States in 1918. The neurologic sequelae of this epidemic encephalitis include parkinsonian states, dementias, spasticities, dystonias, and oculogyric crises. The consequences were seen in some patients immediately following recovery from the acute encephalitis, whereas in other individuals a latent period of 10 years or more passed before the onset of the chronic sequelae. This fact led to speculation that either a continuing chronic infection by the encephalitic virus was the cause or neuronal degeneration had occurred. Neither of these explanations has been proved.

56. The answer is C. *(Henry, ed 17. p 68.)* The urinary 17-ketogenic steroid determination measures 17-hydroxysteroids and additional metabolites. The measurement of urinary 17-ketosteroids gives information about androgen metabolites but not about glucocorticoid activity. Plasma cortisol and aldosterone levels fluctuate widely, and although they are useful for some purposes, they do not reflect cumulative daily activity.

57. The answer is A. *(Henry, ed 17. pp 538-539.)* Low levels of serum amylase usually are found in patients who have diabetes mellitus, congestive heart failure, gastrointestinal cancer or obstruction, fractures, or pleurisy. High levels of serum amylase usually are found in patients who have mumps, renal insufficiency, or ruptured ectopic pregnancy; who have received morphine; or who develop obstruction, strangulation, or perforation complications after abdominal surgery.

58. The answer is A. *(Henry, ed 17. pp 135-136.)* The renal plasma clearance of any substance (X) is expressed as the volume of plasma from which X is removed by renal activity per unit of time, usually 1 minute. In the clearance formula shown below, U_x represents the concentration of X in mg per ml of urine; V represents urine volume per minute and usually is derived from a 24-hour urine volume; P_x represents the plasma concentration of X in mg per ml; and C_x represents the volume of plasma cleared of substance X per minute.

$$C_x = \frac{(U_x)(V)}{P_x}$$

By interpolation of the given data into appropriate units and by substitution, the equation becomes

$$C_x = \frac{(0.469 \text{ mg/ml})(0.535 \text{ ml/min})}{0.02 \text{ mg/ml}}$$

The answer is 12.5 ml/min. For males, normal creatinine clearance values range from 107 to 139 ml/min; for females, the range is 87 to 107 ml/min.

59. The answer is B. *(Henry, ed 17. pp 137-138.)* An alkaline urine would be preferred in a patient with severe hyperuricemia, since the uric acid would then remain in solution. Consumption of a large amount of cranberry juice will acidify urine and promote formation of uric acid calculi from uric acid, which is relatively insoluble at low pH values. Acid urine may also be produced by a diet high in meat protein, but citrus fruits, paradoxically, will produce alkaline urine.

60. The answer is A. *(Henry, ed 17. pp 425-428, 1085-1088.)* If bilirubinuria and pyridium therapy are excluded, the presence of pink-orange-brown casts with contained granular debris or intact red cells within the casts always implies the presence of significant glomerular damage, usually in the form of immune complex glomerulonephritis (poststreptococcal, lupus, Goodpasture's) or owing to renal infarction. Damage to the glomerular capillary loops or the basement membrane allows the leakage of red cells and protein, which condense into casts in the distal tubules, are subsequently passed into the urine, and become directly visible under the microscope in urinalysis. Whereas renal biopsies are usually necessary to categorize the nature of the glomerulonephritis completely, poststreptococcal glomerulonephritis may be implicated if the antistreptolysis titer (ASO titer) or anti-DNAse-B titers are elevated.

61. The answer is B. *(Robbins, ed 3. pp 221-230.)* As all medical oncologists and students of oncology are painfully aware, tumors do not read textbooks and cannot be expected to follow predicted courses in every clinical circumstance. Thus, many exceptions and deviations from the expected occur. An important predictor of a given tumor's outcome, however, is the differentiation, which is a histologic parameter that gives some index as to the degree of resemblance of the tumor to the cell of origin; that is, differentiation states to what degree the tumor resembles its parent cell or tissues. Well-differentiated tumors resemble their cells of origin to a great extent, while poorly differentiated tumors do not resemble their origins to an appreciable extent. With some exceptions tumors may be expected to behave according to their differentiation. Furthermore, the growth rate of tumors appears to correlate with their level of differentiation, with the less-differentiated tumors growing faster than well-differentiated ones. The term *grade* implies differentiation and in some cases may be synonymous; for example, grade I tumors are well differentiated, while grade III tumors are poorly differentiated. Higher grade tumors tend to have more mitoses, which generally correlate with aggressiveness and final outcome.

62. The answer is E. *(Henry, ed 17. pp 260–262.)* Normal alkaline phosphatase levels are common in patients who have myocardial infarctions. Elevated levels of this nonlipid esterase are usually demonstrable in patients who have hepatitis, infectious mononucleosis, cirrhosis, or obstructive jaundice. In polycythemia vera, marked elevation of alkaline phosphatase is considered a classic sign and has been demonstrated in 80 percent of cases of this myeloproliferative syndrome.

63. The answer is C. *(Henry, ed 17. pp 775-777.)* Von Willebrand's disease is not as rare as once thought, and numerous subtypes, which are delineated by two-dimensional electrophoresis, have been described. The disease is characterized clinically by mucocutaneous bleeding, menorrhagia, and epistaxis. Milder forms of the disease may not be diagnosed until the patient is older. Factor VIII is a complex of several components that can be discerned electrophoretically. Of all the factor VIII components, factor VIII:R, or ristocetin cofactor, is most apt to be abnormal in von Willebrand's disease. The coagulant (C) and the related antigen (Ag) forms of factor VIII may sometimes be normal in various autosomal dominant types. Most patients even with the milder forms will have decreased factor VIII:R. Prothrombin time and fibrinogen levels are not affected in this disorder.

64. The answer is A. *(Henry, ed 17. pp 236-237.)* The patient described probably has hepatitis, according to the values given for the five isoenzymes of lactic dehydrogenase (LDH). Liver cells contain higher proportions of LDH_4 and LDH_5 than do myocardium or red blood cells, both of which contain greater relative amounts of LDH_1 and LDH_2. Lung tissue is high in LDH_3, and brain tissue contains only small amounts of LDH_5.

65. The answer is B. *(Robbins, ed 3. pp 233, 245, 662-663.)* Burkitt's lymphoma is one of the most rapidly growing tumors known to oncologists. Most tumors grow without inhibition by means of a decrease in the time spent within the cell growth cycle itself, a reduction in the total numbers of cells dying, and/or many more stable cells leaving G_0 to enter the cycle at G_1. One or all of these mechanisms may be in effect, along with a lack of cell growth inhibition. Cell growth inhibition is not completely understood, but cells are known to be delayed in progressing to mitosis from G_2. Permanent cells are essentially nondividing and usually die. In African Burkitt's lymphoma, but not necessarily in American Burkitt's lymphoma, high titers of serum antibody to Epstein-Barr viral capsid antigen have been described, along with incorporation of the viral genome.

66. The answer is D. *(Nicholson, Cancer 39:1792, 1977. Postkanzer, Cancer 39:1892, 1977. Robbins, ed 3. pp 238, 248-250.)* The association of the chemical and physical environment (with its implied hazards of toxic wastes, mainly from industrial pollution) with the development of tumors in humans is becoming a specialty field in itself. Major legislation and public health efforts are just beginning to place emphasis on these hazards. A major clue to the implication of environmental (therapeutic and dietary) substances lies in the clustering of rare tumor types in populations in which such an incidence is unexpected. For example, cases of angiosarcoma of the liver (a relatively rare tumor) were identified in employees of a rubber company and in a few residents living near the plant where the monomer vinyl chloride was present in the atmosphere. Exposure to asbestos in shipyard, roofing, and insulation workers has led to the development of not only pleural and peritoneal malignant mesotheliomas, but solid malignant tumors of the lung and viscera as well. Although increasing the risk of associated tuberculosis, silicosis has not, by itself, increased the risk of developing cancer. Similarly, beryllium vapor (fluorescent light bulb manufacture) causes marked granulomatous disease but has not been identified as a carcinogen. Cyanide is lethal if ingested. Also potentially lethal owing to hepatic necrosis are carbon tetrachloride and chloroform, but neither is implicated in tumorigenesis. Foundry workers are at risk of developing pulmonary and nasal sinus cancers when they are regularly exposed to nickel or chromium compounds.

67. The answer is D. *(Henry, ed 17. pp 305-307.)* Triiodothyronine (T_3) is the thyroid hormone with the greatest physiologic activity, although thyroxine (T_4) is present in greater quantities and thus is usually the best measure of thyroid activity. Monoiodotyrosine (MIT) and diiodotyrosine (DIT) are not released from the gland and have little activity. Thyroglobulin is the carrier protein for binding stored thyroid hormones.

68. The answer is E. *(Stanbury, ed 5. p 1282.)* Since excessive amounts of iron require several decades to accumulate, 80 percent of patients with primary hemochromatosis become symptomatic only after the age of 40. Patients with this disease may accumulate 20 to 60 g of iron in their tissues during a 50-year period.

69. The answer is B. *(Anderson, ed 8. pp 18-19, 152.)* Whereas cells from very dedifferentiated and primitive tumors may not show specific features, many different kinds of cells and tumors do demonstrate tell-tale features ultrastructurally, making possible recognition of tumor types via the electron microscope when the light microscopic pattern is vague. Seen in this example is an epithelial cell at relatively low magnification with characteristic desmosomes containing tonofilaments protruding from the cell surface. The cell surface desmosomes are a form of intercell junction, and together with tonofibrils and tonofilaments, they permit recognition of cells of squamous origin regardless of organ site. Chondrocytes have a unique scalloped outer membrane, whereas adenocarcinoma cells demonstrate characteristic intracytoplasmic lumina. Parenchymal cells such as hepatocytes reveal bile canaliculi and a prominent endoplasmic reticulum, whereas endocrine cells (pancreas, thyroid, and pituitary) have intracellular dense-core granules.

70. The answer is C. *(Stanbury, ed 5. pp 973, 977-978.)* A tendency to lose salt and water often appears in adrenogenital syndrome with adrenocortical hyperplasia. There is general agreement that in the salt-losing form of this syndrome aldosterol and cortisol production is deficient, a consequence of genetically impaired biosynthesis of adrenal corticoids. Adrenogenital syndrome also may be known as "congenital virilizing adrenocortical hyperplasia," a generic term that probably should be discarded because it paradoxically includes forms not associated with virilization.

71. The answer is B. *(Anderson, ed 8. pp 102, 106. Stanbury, ed 5. pp 946, 950, 957.)* Tay-Sachs disease (G_{M2} gangliosidosis type 1), first recognized in 1881 by

Warren Tay, is a storage disease in which the G_{M2} ganglioside accumulates in neurons because of a deficiency in β-N-acetylhexosaminidase. The G_{M2} ganglioside structurally lacks a terminal galactose unit. Tay-Sachs disease, the major form of gangliosidosis, afflicts thousands of patients. Major clinical features of Tay-Sachs disease include macrocephaly caused by cerebral gliosis, mental-motor deterioration, and lipidosis of cortical, autonomic, and rectal mucosal neurons.

72. The answer is A. *(Stanbury, ed 5. pp 906-915, 946, 950.)* Fabry's disease, first described by Anderson and Fabry independently, may be hemizygous or heterozygous and is caused by a deficiency in alpha-galactosidase A, which leads to abnormal accumulations of glycosphingolipid (trihexosylceramide) within the lysosomes of vascular-endothelial and smooth muscle cells of the heart and kidney, ganglion cells, and epithelial cells of the cornea. Multiple angiokeratoma of the skin in a patient with tortuous conjunctival vessels and corneal opacity are highly suggestive of the disease. Death usually ensues from progressive renal failure and uremia. Birefringent lipid bodies (Maltese crosses) may be seen in the urine sediment with polarized light.

73. The answer is C. *(Stanbury, ed 5. pp 11-13.)* Any deviation from the normal number of chromosomes, from their normal structure, or any combination of the two is an aberration that, if unbalanced, is termed aneuploidy. If the alterations remain balanced (balanced translocations), the condition is termed euploidy. Aneuploidy can result from the addition of a single chromosome to a pair (trisomy) from translocations, inversions, duplications, and deletions.

74. The answer is A. *(Stanbury, ed 5. pp 1812-1815.)* Renal tubular acidosis (RTA) can be either due to a gradient defect (the classic form) or due to bicarbonate wastage. In the classic form of this syndrome, too many hydrogen ions diffuse back from tubular urine to blood. This "back-diffusion" occurs in the distal tubules and prevents the formation of a steep pH gradient between blood and tubular urine. Ammonia excretion is normal in both forms of RTA. In RTA caused by bicarbonate wastage, the depressed reabsorption of bicarbonate ions in the proximal tubules leads to the spillage of these ions into urine.

75. The answer is D. *(Stanbury, ed 5. pp 1301-1302.)* Various degrees of cutaneous photosensitivity are associated with all forms of porphyrin metabolism disturbances except acute intermittent porphyria. Abdominal pain, often the first and most prominent symptom, is accompanied by constipation; and this combination mimics the symptomatology of intestinal obstructions. Remissions occur between acute attacks that last from several days to several months. Respiratory paralysis, with uremia and cachexia as contributing factors, usually causes death.

76. The answer is A. *(Davis, ed 3., pp 595-605.)* The rough or unencapsulated strains of *Streptococcus (Diplococcus) pneumoniae* are not thought to be pathogenic for humans. A capsule protects the bacteria and confers pathogenicity; the degree of virulence varies among antigenic types. Testing encapsulated species (e.g., type 3) with the appropriate antiserum leads to a positive quellung test (capsular swelling or refractivity).

77. The answer is C. *(Davis, ed 3. pp 391-392, 416-417.)* T lymphocytes do not secrete IgG as do plasma cells; this differentiates T from B lymphocytes. T lymphocytes can help to suppress or suppress functions of B lymphocytes or of other effector lymphocytes. T lymphocytes constitute the majority of lymphocytes in the immediate subcapsular and mantle zones surrounding follicles in lymph nodes, as well as in the periarteriolar regions (white pulp) of the spleen.

78. The answer is D. *(Davis, ed 3. pp 683-684.)* The Yersiniae are an important group of gram-negative bacilli (formerly called Pasteurellae), which cause a wide variety of human and animal disease, ranging from plague (*Y. pestis*) to acute mesenteric lymphadenitis (*Y. enterocolitica*) in older children and young adults. *Y. enterocolitica* infections also occur in the terminal ileum in young adults, causing an ileitis that produces inflammation not at all unlike that seen in some stages of Crohn's disease (regional enteritis). Since the organisms grow slowly on enrichment media, they may be overgrown by other coliforms at 37°C. The organisms may be isolated by means of cold enhancement at 4°C.

79. The answer is C. *(Davis, ed 3. pp 839-841.)* In the approximate center of the photomicrograph is the classic refractile double-walled spherule of the deep fungus *Coccidioides immitis*, which is several times the diameter of the largest inflammatory cell nearby. Coccidioidomycosis is endemic in California, Arizona, New Mexico, and parts of Nevada, Utah, and Texas, where it resides in the arid soils and is contracted by direct inhalation of airborne dust. If inhaled, it produces a primary pulmonary infection that is usually benign and self-limiting in immunologically competent individuals, often with several days of fever and upper respiratory flulike symptoms. However, certain ethnic groups, such as some blacks, Asians, and Filipinos, are at risk of developing a potentially lethal disseminated form of the disease that can involve the central nervous system. If the large, double-walled spherule containing numerous endospores can be demonstrated outside the lungs (e.g., in a skin biopsy), this is evidence for dissemination. Antibodies of high titers are detectable by means of complement fixation studies in patients undergoing spontaneous recovery. Amphotericin B is usually reserved for treating high-risk and disseminated infection. Persons traveling through the southwestern United States may contract the primary pulmonary form of the disease through exposure to contaminated dust. The cultured mycelia of the organism on Sabouraud's agar present a hazard for laboratory workers.

80. The answer is B. *(Anderson, ed 8. pp 1084-1086.)* Adenocarcinoma of the stomach has an inverse relationship in terms of incidence and prevalence with adenocarcinoma of the colon, but not of the rectum. This relationship is maintained throughout the world, but is seen strikingly in comparison of the United States and Japan. Gastric carcinoma was more prevalent in the United States 50 years ago than it is now, whereas the incidence of colon carcinoma has increased. Similarly, in Japan, where gastric carcinoma is notoriously prevalent, colon carcinoma is quite rare. Curiously, while colon carcinoma is uncommon in Japan, rectal cancer rates approach those found in the United States. Carcinoma of the stomach and carcinoma of the gallbladder are both more common in American Hispanics and in the native Americans of New Mexico than in other ethnic groups in the United States.

81. The answer is B. *(Davis, ed 3. pp 494-495, 732.)* Delayed-hypersensitivity reactions are mediated by T lymphocytes and other mononuclear cells. The reaction requires previous exposure to antigen, frequently a large protein, and takes from 1 to 3 days to develop fully. Only true palpable induration is considered a positive reaction.

82. The answer is A. *(Davis, ed 3. pp 486-489.)* Serum sickness is associated with antigen-antibody complexes produced and cleared in an environment of antigen excess. The complexes induce focal vascular lesions in many arterial and capillary beds. The other "allergic" responses listed in the question are associated with much smaller amounts of antigen.

83. The answer is C. *(Davis, ed 3. pp 724-727.)* Pathogenic mycobacteria, including *M. tuberculosis,* have a known propensity for resistance to drying in the environment, survival for extended periods of time on inanimate surfaces, resistance to alkali and acids, and impermeability to routine tissue and Gram stains. Many of these features are thought to be related to the very high lipid and wax content of the bacilli, which makes up some 60 percent of the total dry weight. Mycolic acid is only one of many fatty acids present. Virulence is thought to be related to the presence of the mycoside 6,6-dimycolytrehalose (cord factor).

84. The answer is C. *(Davis, ed 3. pp 1096-1116.)* Picornaviruses, a class of small, icosahedral, single-stranded RNA viruses, include polioviruses, coxsackieviruses (aseptic meningitis and herpangina), rhinoviruses (common cold), and echoviruses (viral meningitis). The etiologic agent of epidemic keratoconjunctivitis is usually the type 8 adenovirus, an icosahedral, double-stranded DNA virus.

85. The answer is D. *(Davis, ed 3. pp 63, 694-697.)* Aerobic growth of *Hemophilus influenzae* requires a rich medium that includes two growth factors known as X factor and V factor. X factor is heat-stable, whereas V factor is not. *Staphylococcus aureus* can grow on heat-treated chocolate agar and, as a growth product, produces V factor (NAD or NADP), which allows *H. influenzae* to grow nearby.

This phenomenon is called satellite phenomenon. The other four organisms listed in the question are capable of growth in the absence of V factor.

86. The answer is E. *(Davis, ed 3. pp 724-734.)* *Mycobacterium tuberculosis* is an obligate aerobe—thus its predilection for pulmonary infection. The high content of lipids in its cell wall is in part responsible for its acid-fast response to Ziehl-Neelsen staining. The frequency of occurrence of drug-resistant mutants in this organism has necessitated simultaneous use of multiple chemotherapeutic agents against it. Individuals who have silicosis have a high incidence of infection with *M. tuberculosis*, which on culture requires several weeks to grow.

87. The answer is D. *(Davis, ed 3. pp 833-840.)* *Cryptococcus neoformans* is a true pathogen. It is not dimorphic, as are *Coccidioides immitis*, *Histoplasma capsulatum*, and *Blastomyces dermatitidis*. *Aspergillus fumigatus* is also not dimorphic but grows as a mycelium and not as an encapsulated yeast. All the organisms listed in the question can cause systemic disease, but except for *C. neoformans*, respiratory involvement is the major clinical problem they cause. Although *C. neoformans* usually enters via the lung, pulmonary involvement is often minimal, and the meningeal involvement is the most serious common aspect of infection.

88. The answer is C. *(Davis, ed 3. pp 1062, 1071-1075, 1120-1121.)* Influenza is caused by small RNA viruses, classified as myxoviruses. All the other viral illnesses listed in the question are caused by herpesviruses, which are relatively large, double-stranded DNA viruses. Shingles and chickenpox are caused by herpes zoster, which is identical to varicella. Cytomegalovirus causes cytomegalic inclusion disease, and Epstein-Barr (EB) virus causes mononucleosis.

89. The answer is C. *(Robbins, ed 3. pp 446-448.)* Despite current controversy, most researchers agree that women taking oral contraceptives are at risk, however small, of developing myocardial infarction, especially if the woman is a cigarette smoker, and vascular thrombi that may lead to strokes and pulmonary embolism and infarction. Also very minimal in terms of numbers of cases are hepatic adenomas, which have been recorded in patients taking oral estrogens over a protracted period of time. Conflicting evidence is found concerning the risk of developing endometrial carcinoma. Some researchers have shown a definite risk of developing uterine cancer, but not all series have demonstrated a positive correlation. The same problem exists in estimation of the risk of developing breast cancer. Vaginal adenosis develops not in the women taking estrogens themselves, but rather in the female offspring of mothers who received diethylstilbestrol (DES) while pregnant. Some of these daughters have also developed clear cell carcinoma of the cervix, an adenocarcinoma that carries a rather poor prognosis. DES binds to cell nuclear DNA and hence may act as a cocarcinogen rather than as a mere promoter.

90. The answer is A. *(Davis, ed 3. p 793.)* In diagnosing *Mycoplasma pneumoniae* infection, the classic bedside test was the presence of cold agglutinins (antibodies reacting with red blood cells at 4°C but not at 37°C). This test is nonspecific but can be suggestive of *M. pneumoniae* infection; the same statement is true for antistreptococcal MG antibodies. Specific tests now are available that measure antimycoplasmal titers in acute phase and convalescent serum, but these tests give retrospective identification. Culture growth of the organism is slow, and the diagnosis of *M. pneumoniae* infection is largely made by the clinician on the basis of suspicion and exclusion.

91. The answer is D. *(Evatt, N Engl J Med 312:483, 1985.)* Evidence that the human T cell lymphotrophic retrovirus (HTLV-III)—also called the lymphadenopathy associated virus (LAV)—is associated with the cause of AIDS has come from the National Institutes of Health (NIH), the Pasteur Institute in France, and subsequent experience in the study of antibodies to these retroviruses through banked blood at the Center for Disease Control in Atlanta. These studies showed that antibodies to viral proteins p25 and p41 of LAV in hemophiliacs did not appear until the onset of the AIDS epidemic. Antibody to LAV was not detected in banked serum from patients during the years 1968 and 1969 and was seen in only 5 percent of patients tested before 1980 in California. Seropositivity occurred during the years 1981 through 1984 in California and Georgia in clinics treating hemophilia. It appears that LAV is spread by factor VIII concentrate.

92. The answer is D. *(Anderson, ed 8. pp 188-189, 1086, 1141-1143, 1151-1153, 1175, 1886-1888.)* The seemingly innumerable deleterious effects of alcohol abuse are recognized as constituting a major public health problem even in non-Western locations, such as Africa and Asia. The effects may be purely socioeconomic (divorce, absenteeism, and automobile mortality, with concomitant high insurance rates), political, moral, or organic. Indeed, it is difficult to think of an organ or organ system that does not develop a physical dysfunction, either reversible or irreversible, in response to excessive intake of ethanol. Subdural hematomas are commonly seen in alcoholics. Portal vein thrombosis is rarely seen in the absence of nutritional or Laennec's cirrhosis. Levels of the muscle and cardiac enzyme creatine phosphokinase may be elevated in states of alcoholic myocardiosis, cardiomyopathy, alcoholic rhabdomyolysis, or trauma to skeletal muscles while the patient is in an alcoholic toxic state. Primary biliary cirrhosis occurs predominantly in middle-aged women and its etiology is unknown, although marked immunologic factors have been described, as well as marked copper deposition in the liver, with normal serum ceruloplasmin.

93. The answer is A (1, 2, 3). *(Robbins, ed 3. pp 752, 842-843. Rosai, ed 6. pp 265-266.)* Small cell (oat-cell) carcinoma of the lung occurs in 80 to 85 percent of cases of lung carcinoma in cigarette smokers and is populated by a cell that is characterized by endocrinelike features. Ultrastructurally, the cytoplasm contains neurosecretory granules similar to other cells of the APUD system—e.g., carcinoid and Kultschitzky cells, which are associated with the elaboration of hormones and enzymes such as ACTH, calcitonin, histaminase, serotonin, ADH, and L-dopa decarboxylase. Owing to the release of substances into the circulation, endocrinelike syndromes are manifested symptomatically. For example, if the tumor secretes ACTH, the patient becomes frankly cushingoid. Other tumors produce ADH, which causes hyponatremia owing to vascular volume expansion (syndrome of inappropriate ADH). Elaboration of parathormone or parathormonelike hormones in lung carcinoma, with consequent hypercalcemia, is usually associated with squamous carcinoma of the lung rather than oat-cell carcinoma. The carcinoid syndrome, complete with episodic facial flushing, vasomotor responses, and bronchoconstriction, has been identified in oat-cell carcinoma and is due to the release of biogenic amines, such as serotonin.

94. The answer is B (1, 3). *(Robbins, ed 3. pp 288-289, 669)* Epstein-Barr virus (EBV) is contracted by contact with infected saliva, which then enters the epithelial cells of the salivary gland and thereupon enters the B lymphocytes with subsequent viral replication. The viral genome is incorporated into the transformed B lymphocyte DNA. Such transformed lymphocytes are capable of long-term growth in vitro. A virus-related membrane antigen then is found on these transformed B cells that elicits the formation of killer T lymphocytes, which dispose of the latent B cells. Viremia resulting from lysis of B cells is dealt with by virus-neutralizing antibodies that peak 10 to 14 days following infection and are life-long. In Burkitt's lymphoma a suppression or defect in a killer T-cell response to EBV results in a sustained B-cell proliferation, which, if it remains persistent, increases the risk for such changes as chromosomal translocations, which may then result in the neoplastic state. This emergence of monoclonal B-cell proliferation from a polyclonal response to the virus may also explain the lymphomas seen in X-linked lymphoproliferative syndrome and in angioimmunoblastic lymphadenopathy.

95. The answer is A (1, 2, 3). *(Robbins, ed 3. pp 58-61.)* The reticuloendothelial system consists of a dispersed system of phagocytic cells capable of taking up dyes or particles from the blood. These cells are most abundant in the spleen, liver, bone marrow, and lymph nodes, but they also are present as alveolar macrophages in the lung. They can participate in inflammatory reactions and may form giant cells. Kupffer cells are the phagocytic cells that line liver sinusoids. Langhans' cells are multinucleated giant cells seen in granulomatous reactions. Heart-failure cells are large mononuclear cells that contain phagocytized hemosiderin granules and are found in the sputum or lungs of patients who have chronic pulmonary congestion as the result of left-sided heart failure. Plasma cells are not phagocytic and thus are not considered to be a part of the reticuloendothelial system.

96. The answer is A (1, 2, 3). *(Robbins, ed 3. pp 208-210, 346, 849-850.)* Acquired immune deficiency syndrome (AIDS) is a new disorder that was first reported in 1981 when *Pneumocystis carinii* pneumonia was seen in homosexual men in Los Angeles. The spread and recognition of the disease is well known and is characterized as a clinical and pathologic syndrome with acquired T-cell deficiency reflected by an inversion of the ratio of T helper/inducer cells (OKT4) to cytotoxic/suppressor T cells (KT8). The ratio is ordinarily 2; the ratio in AIDS patients may be less than 0.5. This inversion is caused by a marked reduction in T helper cells, which appear to be a target in the disorder. While many viruses are associated with this syndrome, including Epstein-Barr, cytomegalovirus (CMV), and herpes simplex, an important finding was the discovery of anti-human T-leukemia virus antibodies and viral structures consistent with the human T-leukemia virus. This is a retrovirus that is horizontally transmitted. Up to 40 percent of patients may have anti-antibodies. This virus is known to be associated with the development of T-cell malignancies or non-Hodgkin's lymphomas. AIDS patients may be overwhelmed by opportunistic infections, which include almost any microorganism, but especially *Mycobacterium avium-intracellulare*, which is depicted in the lamina propria in the photomicrograph. The development of Kaposi's sarcoma in AIDS patients is significantly associated with the frequency of HLA-DR5 antigen, the class II major histocompatibility complex antigen, which is also increased in these patients.

97. The answer is C (2, 4). *(Robbins, ed 3. pp 267-268.)* The photomicrograph in the question shows an immunoperoxidase reaction, a technique fostered by Sternberger in the early 1970s to identify antigens within cells by the use of an antibody specific for the antigen sought. Following incubation with a specific antibody directed against the target antigen (primary antibody incubation), a secondary antibody incubation is conducted using heterologous immune sera directed against the first antibody. For example, the primary antibody may be rabbit antihuman IgG. If human IgG is present on or within a given cell, binding occurs. Secondary antibody could then be goat antirabbit, which now binds to the rabbit IgG. Then horseradish peroxidase-antiperoxidase conjugate is applied, which links to the antibody complexes. The last step is a chromagen substrate, in this case rust-brown diaminobenzidine. Rust-brown granules indicate a positive reaction. This useful technique (or a modification of it, such as the use of highly specific and sensitive monoclonal antibodies with avidin-biotin conjugate rather than peroxidase-antiperoxidase) is used to identify tumor-associated antigens, viruses, and other microorganisms, proteins, and hormones.

98. The answer is B (1, 3). *(Robbins, ed 3. pp 15-17, 963, 1168-1169.)* Necrosis of fat cells occurs in the stromal and peripancreatic fat, in fat depots within the abdominal cavity, and in traumatized breast tissue. Fat necrosis, perhaps the most characteristic histologic change of acute pancreatic necrosis, is thought to take place by the enzymatic hydrolysis of fat, in which one of the end products (fatty acids) is saponified with calcium and deposited as an insoluble granular material. Fat necrosis in traumatized breast tissue is without clinical significance, except that the calcifications may be mistaken for a sign of malignancy during mammographic evaluation.

99. The answer is E (all). *(Robbins, ed 3. pp 1356-1358.)* Diseases that lead to continued tissue synthesis and breakdown may produce hyperuricemia and clinical gout because of the resulting increase in nucleic acid turnover. This form of secondary gout may be seen in polycythemia vera, myeloid metaplasia, chronic leukemia, extensive psoriasis, and sarcoidosis. Cytologic drugs, used in the chemotherapy of cancer, may augment hyperuricemia. Decreased renal excretion of uric acid may also lead to secondary gout.

100. The answer is E (all). *(Anderson, ed 8. pp 687-696.)* In atherosclerosis, primarily a disease of the arterial intima, disintegration of the internal elastic lamina is typical in advanced lesions, and necrosis commonly occurs at the base of the thickened intima. Essential lesions, occurring in the intima, are more numerous in larger than in smaller arteries. Although plaque formations cause little reduction in the size of the lumen of large arteries, atherosclerosis can lead to arterial dilatation and aneurysms.

101. The answer is B (1, 3). *(Robbins, ed 3. pp 406-411.)* Vitamin D deficiency results in inadequate serum phosphorus and calcium levels and, therefore, in the impaired deposition of these minerals into the osteoid matrix. Insufficient mineralization of osteoid leads to the creation of soft, easily deformed bones. In vitamin D deficiency there is no failure of osteoid formation. This results in a relative excess of osteoid in bone.

102. The answer is A (1, 2, 3). *(Robbins, ed 3. pp 22, 150-153.)* Seven well-defined syndromes resulting from genetic defects in enzymes responsible for glycogen metabolism have been described. Six of these diseases, including von Gierke's, Pompe's, and McArdle's, are associated with excess accumulation of glycogen. The seventh disease is characterized by a lack of glycogen. Patients with Tay-Sachs disease have excessive accumulations of a ganglioside.

103. The answer is A (1, 2, 3). *(Anderson, ed 8. pp 164-165.)* The first three changes described in the question have been documented in women taking oral contraceptives. Liver changes are also described but consist of portal triad inflammatory reactions without necrosis or bile duct proliferation. In addition, endocervical microglandular hyperplasia is well documented.

104. The answer is E (all). *(Robbins, ed 3. pp 25, 924-928.)* Hemosiderin may be seen in pulmonary macrophages as a result of red blood cell breakdown in a chronically congested lung. In idiopathic hemochromatosis, hemosiderin deposition is frequently associated with cirrhosis, diabetes, and skin pigmentation. (The skin pigment is, however, melanin.) Excess iron intake also may lead to hemosiderin deposition.

105. The answer is A (1, 2, 3). *(Anderson, ed 8. pp 428, 433.)* Eggs of the roundworm *Ascaris* are found in contaminated soil in the southeastern United States. When swallowed, these eggs hatch, reach the small intestinal vessels, and travel to the lungs, where they may produce clinical bronchial asthma and pneumonitis. The New World hookworm, *Necator americanum*, penetrates exposed skin through exposure to larvae-containing soil; these infective filariform larvae reach the pulmonary circulation via the lymphatic and vascular systems and cause alveolar hemorrhages and temporary bronchopneumonia. Rhabditiform *Strongyloides* soil larvae also gain access to the vascular system and pulmonary circuit through penetration of exposed skin and also cause intraalveolar pneumonitis and hemorrhages. *Wuchereria bancrofti* filariae gain access to the human lymphatics (endolymphangitis, elephantiasis) via bites of the *Culex* mosquito; this organism is not noted for producing a pulmonary phase, but it does produce characteristic spermatic cord granulomas.

106. The answer is B (1, 3). *(Henry, ed 17. pp 655-656, 665-667.)* Since the advent of the Jamshidi biopsy needle in the 1960s and proof that iliac crest marrow accurately reflects the state of the erythron, clinicians have not hesitated in performing or requesting bone marrow examinations of the iliac crest. The procedure's safety records are unquestioned. The practice of using bone marrow biopsy to define and document involvement of bone marrow by both solid and hematopoietic tumors has great value in the staging of patients. Similarly, documenting sideroblastic anemia by demonstrating the presence of ringed sideroblasts in the marrow has great value in clarifying anemias refractory to treatment. However, some clinicians injudiciously order bone marrow examinations in the investigation of iron-deficiency anemia to identify stainable iron. In iron deficiency, the serum iron level is low, the iron-binding capacity is high, and the circulating serum transferrin level is high. After treatment with iron, the serum transferrin level will decrease. Evidence for osteoporosis can be established by simple x-rays.

107. The answer is E (all). *(Gottlieb, N Engl J Med 305:1425, 1981. Robbins, ed 3. pp 258-259.)* Research into the relationship of host immunocompetence and the development of malignant tumors offers an exciting new field of inquiry. Many factors may act to compromise the T-cell system, with its direct tumor cytolytic properties; the B-cell system, with its humoral antibody production and antigen processing; activated macrophages; and general immunologic surveillance. Inherited immunodeficiency states definitely cause predisposition to development of malignant tumors, if the patient does not first succumb to an infectious process. Examples of these states are the Wiskott-Aldrich syndrome and ataxia telangiectasia. Elderly patients have reduced immunocompetence for many reasons, such as reduced humoral antibody production, reduced T-cell function, coexisting degenerative disease (such as diabetes), and poor nutrition. Patients who have received donor organs (e.g., a renal transplant) have reduced immunocompetence because of treatment with prednisone, azathioprine, or antilymphocyte globulin and are well known for developing such malignancies as malignant melanoma, lymphomas, and even sarcomas. Public health studies from New York and California have demonstrated that male homosexuals show an increased incidence of Kaposi's sarcoma, which heretofore has been a relatively rare neoplasm in the United States. Active research into the mechanisms of immunodepression in male homosexuals is currently under way; preliminary data point toward T-cell dysfunction. The incidence of pneumocystis pneumonitis has also been shown to be increased in male homosexuals.

108. The answer is D (4). *(Henry, ed 17. p 1130. Morris, N Engl J Med 312:343, 1985.)* The *Vibrio* genus, including *V. cholerae*, is associated with gastrointestinal disease in the Far East, especially India, but is capable of inducing disease in the United States, as in pandemics occurring here around 1832 and in 1849. Along the coasts, especially the northeast and Gulf coasts of the United States, the vibrios increase in numbers in seawater and in seafood and are more likely to cause infections during the late summer and early autumn months. Patients with underlying liver disease, such as alcoholics, and those with immunosuppressive disorders are advised not to ingest raw shellfish during these months because of an increased incidence of disease with the vibrio organisms in these patients. The mycobacteria are acid-fast bacilli associated with tuberculosis and tuberculosislike diseases; *M. avium* intracellularae is known to be a frequent organism in AIDS. These organisms are not curved as the vibrios are.

109. The answer is B (1, 3). *(Robbins, ed 3. pp 59-60, 163-165, 648.)* The electron photomicrograph in the question shows a macrophage, the workhorse of the mononuclear phagocyte system. This wondrous cell is quite possibly the most active cell in the body. It certainly qualifies for the honor if multiple, varied functions are used to judge the competition. A partial list includes endocytosis (phagocytosis of particulate matter including injured cells and bacteria; pinocytosis of molecules in solution), antigen presentation and immunologic trafficking with sensitized T lymphocytes, and lysis of tumor cells. The macrophage also synthesizes and/or elaborates plasminogen activator, elastase, collagenase, some coagulation factors other than factor VIII (such as thromboplastin), neutrophilic chemotactic factor, mediators of inflammation, cyclooxygenase, lipoxygenase glycerol phosphocholine, components of complement, growth factors for wound healing, and endogenous pyrogen (interleukin I), and probably others. Its internal machinery includes the work of acid hydrolytic enzymes in phagolysosomes. Mast cells and basophils degranulate in anaphylactic reactions. Factor VIII is a complex of coagulant (factor VIII-C, probably made in the liver) and von Willebrand's factor (factor VIII-R) that is synthesized in megakaryocytes and vascular endothelium.

110. The answer is A (1, 2, 3). *(Robbins, ed 3. pp 56-57.)* Leukocytes, including basophils, are involved with the production of derivatives of a very important polyunsaturated fatty acid, arachidonic acid. By a complex two-path cascade system, the metabolites of arachidonic acid eventually yield prostaglandins (vasodilators) and leukotrienes (vasoconstrictors). The biosynthesis begins by activation of cell phospholipase A_2 and C and proceeds either by action of fatty acid cyclooxygenase on arachidonic acid to form prostaglandins, or by the action of lipoxygenase to yield leukotrienes (hydroperoxyeicosatetraenoic acid in platelets, mast cells, and leukocytes). While many substances can be chemotactic, few are known to be as potent as several of the leukotrienes. Leukotriene B_4 as a chemotactic agent is involved in neutrophil aggregation, while leukotrienes TC_4, TD_4, and TE_4 are involved with increased vascular permeability, bronchoconstriction, and vasoconstriction. Prostaglandin E and prostacyclin probably account for most vasodilatation seen in inflammation. Thus both leukotrienes and prostaglandins contribute to edema. Aspirin and indomethacin can block the actions of cyclooxygenase, thereby inhibiting the biosynthesis of prostaglandin.

111. The answer is E (all). *(Robbins, ed 3. pp 64-65, 330-331.)* A granuloma consists of a small collection of modified macrophages surrounded by a rim of mononuclear cells that are principally lymphocytes. The modified macrophages are called "epithelioid" because their abundant cytoplasm and plump appearance cause them to resemble epithelial cells. Often Langhans' giant cells also are present in granulomas. Granulomas are seen in tularemia, lymphogranuloma inguinale, brucellosis, glanders, and other disorders.

112. The answer is E (all). *(Robbins, ed 3. pp 258-259.)* Circulating, tumor-specific antibodies can assist in tumor destruction or can sometimes interfere with tumor killing by sensitized lymphocytes (so-called "blocking antibodies"). Depressed cellular immunity, as in immunosuppressed allograft recipients, leads to an increased incidence of cancer. The complex interaction between the humoral and cellular immune responses to tumor neoantigens may prove to be of crucial importance in the progression of a cancer.

113-115. The answers are: 113-A, 114-B, 115-C. *(Robbins, ed 3. pp 267-268.)* Procedures to detect or determine levels of circulating hormones, enzymes, proteins, and other products that are produced by carcinomas can aid in the diagnosis of cancer.

A high level of acid phosphatase in the presence of prostatic enlargement is a basis for suspicion of prostatic carcinoma. A normal level of acid phosphatase is not helpful because only radioimmunoassay procedures are sensitive enough to detect minor elevations. The prostatic isoenzyme of acid phosphatase should be used in instances of elevation in order to enhance specificity, although up to 20 to 30 percent of patients with stage II or III disease will not determine elevations.

In about 70 percent of cases of gastrointestinal carcinoma, carcinoembryonic antigen (CEA), a glycoprotein, is elaborated. But CEA has little specificity, since elevations are found in benign conditions such as ulcerative colitis, Crohn's disease, chronic obstructive pulmonary disease, and cirrhosis, as well as in carcinoma of the lung, pancreas, and liver. Its usefulness is in following a patient for recurrence.

α_1-Fetoprotein (AFP), an intrauterine α-globulin not normally present in the serum after birth, is elaborated in about 66 percent of cases of hepatoma. The clinical usefulness of AFP is in following the patient for recurrence of tumor following treatment. High levels of AFP in the serum generally correlate with recurrence.

116-119. The answers are: 116-A, 117-A, 118-D, 119-D. *(Robbins, ed 3. pp 163-164.)* Thymus-dependent lymphocytes (T lymphocytes) play a critical role in both the rejection of allograft tissues and the tuberculin skin reaction (delayed hypersensitivity).

An allograft is a transplantation of genetically unlike tissue onto a host of the same species. The immune response that follows is termed rejection (as in a rejected donor kidney transplant) and is based on genetically determined histocompatibility antigens (H genes) that lymphoid cells of the recipient recognize as foreign. The HLA complex makes up the histocompatibility complex and is termed "the HLA haplotype." Thus tuberculin sensitivity and allograft rejection are cell-mediated phenomena.

Anaphylaxis, bronchial asthma, and hay fever are anaphylactic reactions mediated by mast cell degranulation caused by IgE antibody attachment by the Fc portion. The causative allergen in hypersensitivity anaphylaxis stimulates the lymphocytes and plasma cells to produce IgE, which exists in small amounts prior to allergen exposure but is rapidly synthesized after exposure because of cell memory of the antigen. The IgE then forms a complex with the allergen, the Fc fragment, and cross-links with other complexes. Eventually, mast cell and basophil degranulation ensues. Histamine and other vasoactive compounds, such as serotonin and kinins, are released.

120-123. The answers are: 120-D, 121-C, 122-B, 123-A. *(Anderson, ed 8. pp 457-459.)* The majority (80 percent) of the circulating gamma globulins in humans are of the IgG class. IgG is composed of two FAB (antigen-binding sites) and one FAC (crystallizable) fragments and is the only immunoglobulin with Fc receptors. IgG fixes complement and crosses the placental barrier.

IgM appears first in phylogeny and ontogeny, is the first immunoglobulin secreted after the initial antigen encounter, and is the largest immunoglobulin, with a molecular weight of 900,000. IgM also fixes complement and is the first immunoglobulin to respond to an antigenic stimulus. Because of its shorter half-life, IgM is less effective against bacterial infection than IgG is.

IgA is synthesized by plasma cells of the mucosae of the GI tract, lung, and urinary tract, thus making it the immunoglobulin of "secretion," being found in saliva, sweat, and tears. It is composed of two 7s monomers bound to a glycoprotein secretory component.

IgE exists at very low concentrations in normal serum. IgE mediates allergic reactions by fixation to mast cells. It is the reagin antibody of anaphylaxis and binds to Fc fragments with complexes of allergens in the various hypersensitivity states of allergy, asthma, and parasitic infestations. These complexes cause mast cells and basophils to degranulate.

Another immunoglobulin, IgD, exists in minute amounts. Along with IgM, IgD binds antigen receptors onto B lymphocyte surfaces.

All five immunoglobulins are polypeptides with light and heavy chains. Light chains are either kappa or lambda. The classes are separable by immunoelectrophoresis owing to the heavy chains that account for the antigenic differences. All five immunoglobulins can be found in the cell membrane wherever there is free movement within the membrane.

Hematology

DIRECTIONS: Each question below contains five suggested answers. Choose the **one best** response to each question.

124. The photomicrograph below was taken from a soft tissue swelling in the cheek and mandible of a 17-year-old female patient. The cytoplasmic vacuoles would react with which one of the following?

(A) Myeloperoxidase
(B) Oil red O
(C) Nonspecific esterase
(D) Chloracetate esterase
(E) Periodic acid Schiff (PAS)

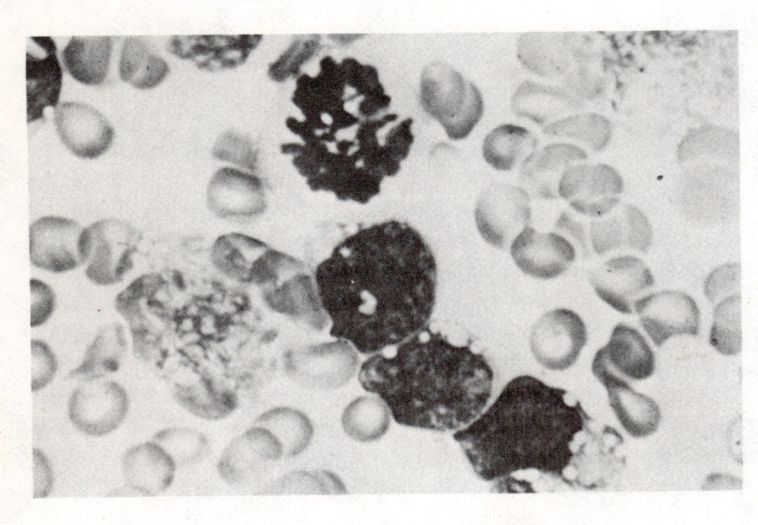

Hematology

125. The neutrophil in the photomicrograph shown below was obtained from peripheral blood and is most likely to be found in association with

(A) folic acid deficiency ✓
(B) infection
(C) iron deficiency
(D) malignancy
(E) ingestion of a marrow-toxic agent

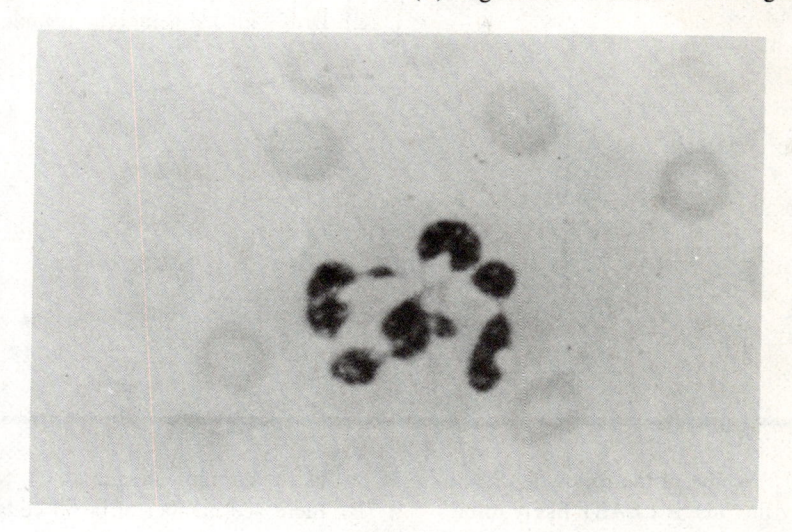

126. The graph below depicts the results of a red cell osmotic fragility test. The broken-line curve represents which of the following?

(A) Glucose 6-phosphate dehydrogenase deficiency
(B) Thalassemia
(C) Hereditary spherocytosis ✓
(D) Normal response
(E) Drug-induced hemolytic anemia

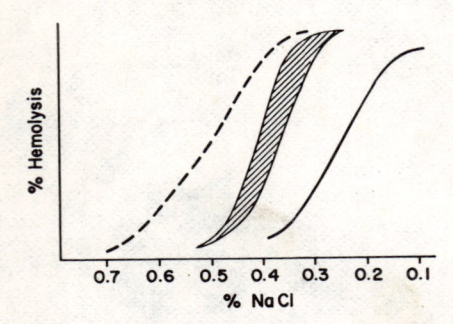

127. Which of the following laboratory findings is LEAST likely to be present in a patient with sickle cell anemia?

(A) Normochromic anemia
(B) Increased number of target cells
(C) Elevated reticulocyte count
(D) Elevated erythrocyte sedimentation rate ✓
(E) Increased hemoglobin F

128. In the photomicrograph below, the nucleated cell that is located next to the neutrophil has a gray-pink cytoplasm and is

(A) a polychromatophilic megaloblast
(B) a plasma cell
(C) an orthochromophilic normoblast
(D) a myelocyte
(E) a myeloblast

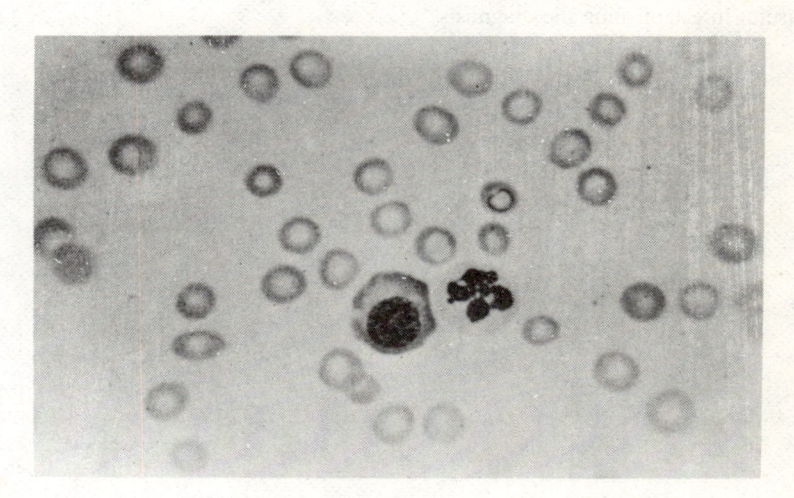

---

129. Patients with sickle cell trait have which of the following genotypes?

(A) $\alpha^s\alpha\beta\beta$
(B) $\alpha^s\alpha^s\beta\beta$
(C) $\alpha\alpha\beta\beta^s$
(D) $\alpha\alpha\beta^s\beta^s$
(E) $\alpha\alpha^s\beta\beta^s$

130. All the following causes of megaloblastic anemia are usually associated with vitamin B_{12} deficiency EXCEPT

(A) blind-loop syndrome
(B) *Diphyllobothrium latum* infestation
(C) alcoholic liver disease
(D) gastric atrophy
(E) total gastrectomy

131. Vitamin K is required for the synthesis of all the following EXCEPT

(A) prothrombin
(B) clotting factor VII
(C) clotting factor VIII
(D) clotting factor IX
(E) clotting factor X

132. Which of the following substances inhibits platelet aggregation?

(A) Prostaglandin E_1
(B) Epinephrine
(C) Adenosine diphosphate
(D) 5-Hydroxytryptamine
(E) Thrombin

133. The photomicrograph below is of peripheral blood from a patient with splenomegaly, anemia, and pancytopenia. If hairy cell leukemia is suspected, which of the following would be useful in establishing the diagnosis?

(A) Myeloperoxidase stain
(B) Sudan black B
(C) Acid phosphatase stain
(D) Leukocyte alkaline phosphatase
(E) Nonspecific esterase

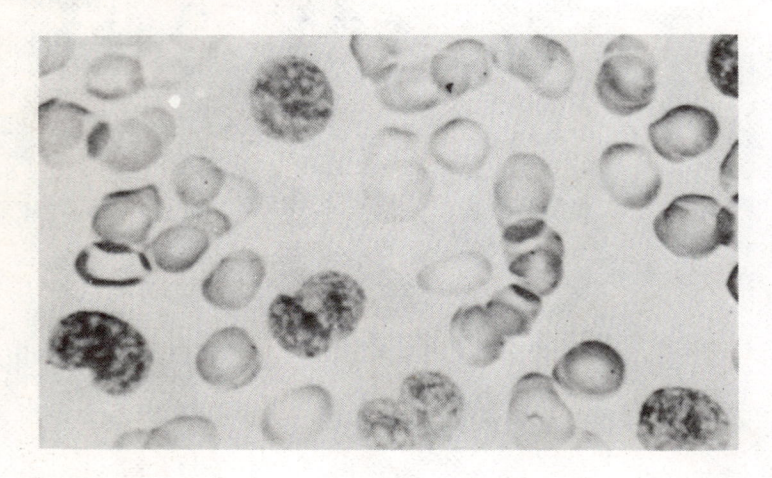

134. The photomicrograph below is of the spleen from an adult patient who had marked splenomegaly. Which of the following abnormalities is most compatible with the changes seen in the spleen?

(A) Reduced levels of glucocerebrosidase activity
(B) Glucose 6-phosphate dehydrogenase deficiency
(C) Glucuronidase deficiency
(D) Lysosomal glucosidase deficiency
(E) Trihexosylceramide alpha-galactosidase deficiency

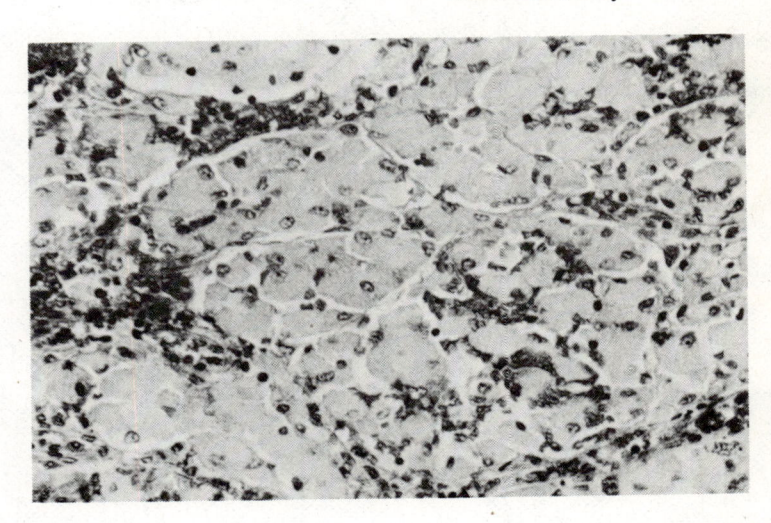

135. Excessive red blood cell lysis by complement in the presence of acidified serum suggests a diagnosis of

(A) hemolytic-uremic syndrome
(B) acute intermittent porphyria
(C) paroxysmal nocturnal hemoglobinuria
(D) pyruvate kinase deficiency
(E) Goodpasture's syndrome

136. An 11-year-old Jamaican boy develops a massive enlargement of the cervical lymph nodes associated with fever and leukocytosis. Which of the following nonmalignant lymph node disorders could account for these findings?

(A) Toxoplasmosis
(B) Histiocytic medullary reticulosis
(C) Burkitt's disease
(D) Sinus histiocytosis with massive lymphadenopathy
(E) Angioimmunoblastic lymphadenopathy with dysproteinemia

137. The photomicrograph below was taken after 30 minutes of incubation at 37°C of a mixture of one drop of blood and two drops of an aqueous 2-percent sodium metabisulfite solution. The appearance of the erythrocytes in this preparation shows that they contain

(A) hemoglobin A
(B) hemoglobin A_2
(C) hemoglobin C
(D) hemoglobin F
(E) hemoglobin S

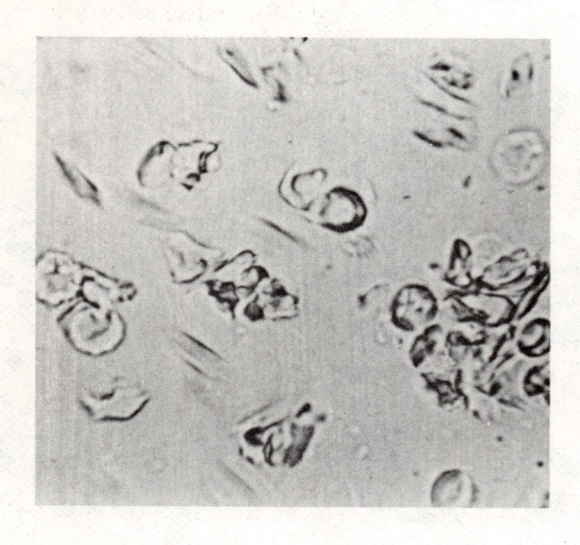

138. The photomicrograph below is from the bone marrow of a patient with weakness. All the following may be associated with this abnormality EXCEPT

(A) pernicious anemia
(B) hyperthyroidism
(C) celiac disease
(D) HTLV
(E) alcoholism

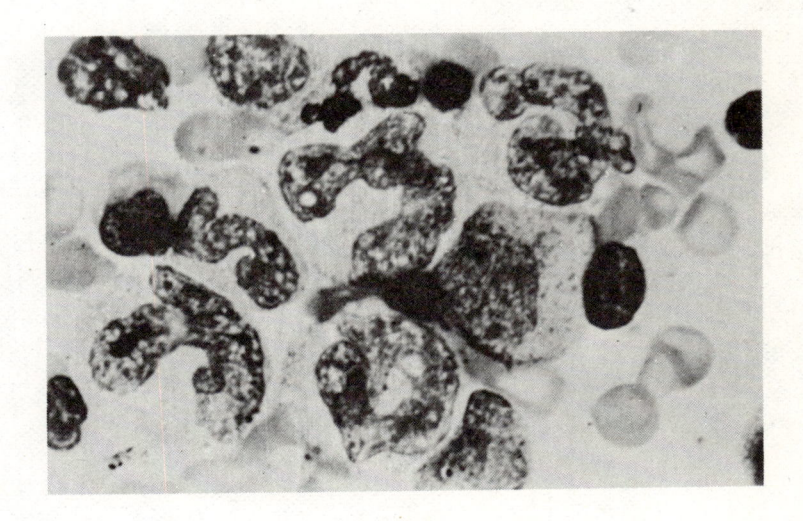

139. The cluster of cells shown in the photomicrograph below is from the bone marrow of a patient who has

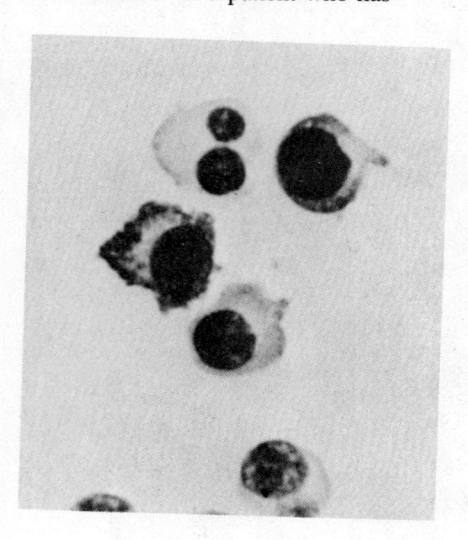

(A) Hodgkin's disease
(B) erythroleukemia
(C) Waldenström's macroglobulinemia
(D) multiple myeloma
(E) metastatic carcinoma

140. A bone marrow aspirate was obtained from a 70-year-old man whose symptoms included weakness, weight loss, and recurrent infections. Laboratory findings included proteinuria, anemia, and an abnormal component in serum proteins. A photomicrograph of the bone marrow aspirate is shown below. The most probable diagnosis is

(A) monomyelocytic leukemia
(B) histiocytic leukemia
(C) multiple myeloma
(D) Gaucher's disease
(E) leukemic reticuloendotheliosis

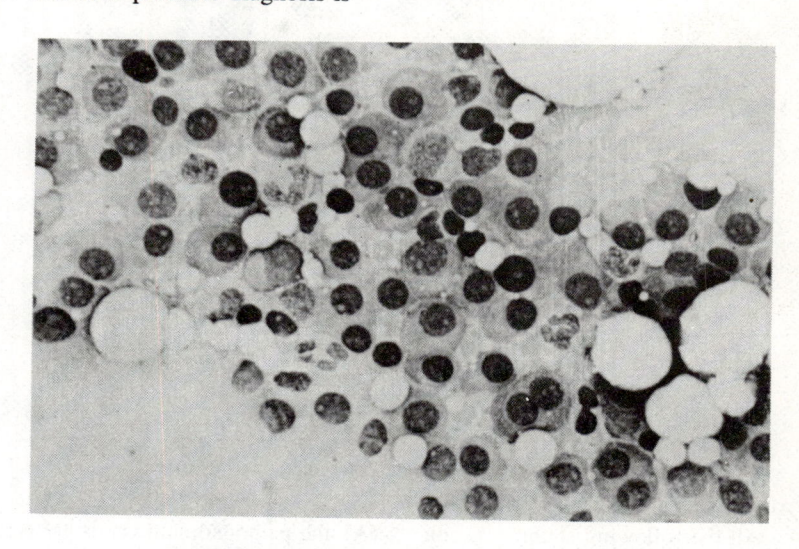

141. Typical findings in a patient with von Willebrand's disease include all the following EXCEPT

(A) decreased levels of factor VIII
(B) decreased glass bead adhesion of platelets
(C) prolonged bleeding time
(D) frequent hemarthrosis and spontaneous joint hemorrhage
(E) menorrhagia

142. δ-Aminolevulinic acid is excreted in increased amounts in the urine of patients with

(A) lead poisoning
(B) carcinoma of the pancreas
(C) chronic pyelonephritis
(D) vitamin C intoxication
(E) ulcerative colitis

Questions 143-144

143. The cell in the photomicrograph below was found in a bone marrow aspiration from a 25-year-old man. Such a cell is generally considered pathognomonic for

(A) Niemann-Pick disease
(B) histiocytic lymphoma
(C) megaloblastic anemia
(D) Gaucher's disease
(E) myelogenous leukemia

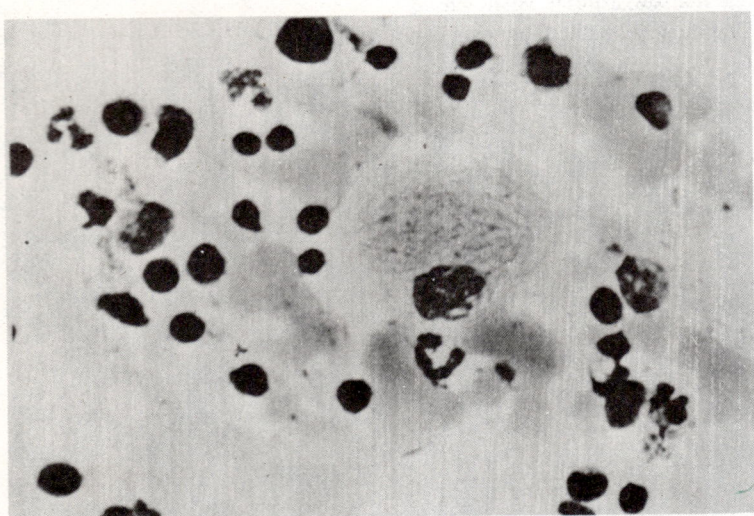

144. All the following statements concerning the disease associated with the cell shown above are true EXCEPT

(A) the pathognomonic cells are typically 20 to 100 μm in diameter and have a wrinkled, striated cytoplasm
(B) inheritance is autosomal dominant with variable penetrance
(C) the serum acid phosphatase level is frequently elevated
(D) an excess amount of sphingolipid is stored in body tissues
(E) three types of the disease can be differentiated genetically and clinically

Hematology

145. A woman who is 5 weeks postpartum (normal delivery, healthy child) develops bleeding episodes with oliguria and hematuria. No fever or neurologic manifestations are present. The blood urea nitrogen level is 65 mg/dl; a peripheral blood smear is represented in the photomicrograph below. This patient most likely has

(A) thrombotic thrombocytopenic purpura
(B) autoimmune thrombocytopenic purpura
(C) hemolytic uremic syndrome
(D) disseminated intravascular coagulopathy
(E) sickle cell crisis

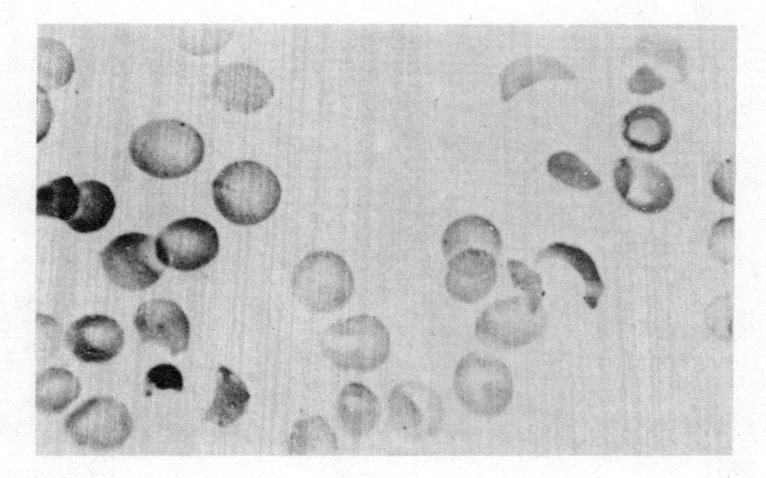

146. All the following are known to cause splenomegaly EXCEPT

(A) sickle cell disease
(B) Hodgkin's disease
(C) chronic lymphocytic leukemia (CLL)
(D) hairy cell leukemia
(E) polycythemia vera

147. A diagnosis of lymphocytic-predominant Hodgkin's disease was made after evaluation of biopsies of the left axillary and mediastinal lymph nodes of a young man whose symptoms included fever, weight loss, and night sweats. He had no other sites of Hodgkin's disease infiltration. His disease would be classed as stage

(A) IA
(B) IB
(C) IIB
(D) IIIB
(E) IVB

148. A 38-year-old man presents with a red, maculopapular rash, Coombs' positive hemolytic anemia, generalized lymphadenopathy, splenomegaly, hepatomegaly, fever, fatigue, and weight loss. The lymph node biopsy specimen seen in the photomicrograph below shows effacement and vascular proliferation. This constellation points to a diagnosis of

(A) lymphopathia venereum
(B) immunoblastic lymphadenopathy
(C) mucocutaneous lymph node syndrome
(D) acute leukemia
(E) malignant histiocytosis

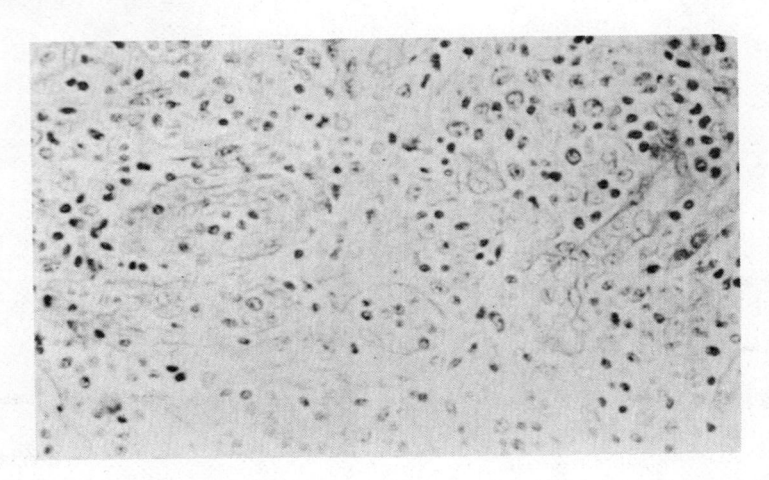

149. The cells seen in the photomicrograph below were stained with an iron stain and removed from a patient suffering from anemia. This patient is most likely to have

(A) iron deficiency anemia
(B) acute blood loss
(C) B_{12} deficiency
(D) B_2 deficiency
(E) pyridoxine deficiency

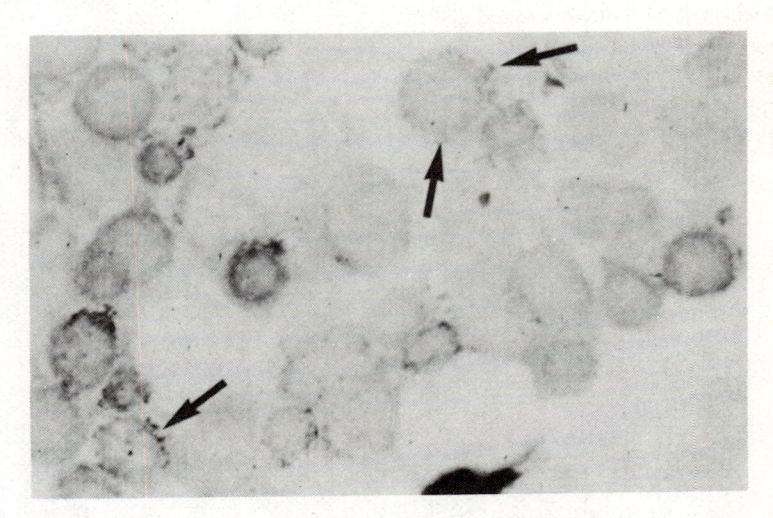

---

150. The presence in serum of a μ heavy-chain protein is a distinctive feature of which of the following diseases?

(A) Chronic lymphocytic leukemia
(B) Macroglobulinemia
(C) Lymphocytic lymphoma
(D) Plasma cell myeloma
(E) Multiple myeloma

151. An adult patient had a bone marrow trephine biopsy performed (see photomicrograph below) because of splenomegaly and anemia. On the basis of the appearance of the bone marrow core, select the characteristic red cell in the peripheral blood seen in this disorder.

(A) Acanthocyte
(B) Stomatocyte
(C) Tear drop cell
(D) Helmet cell
(E) Target cell

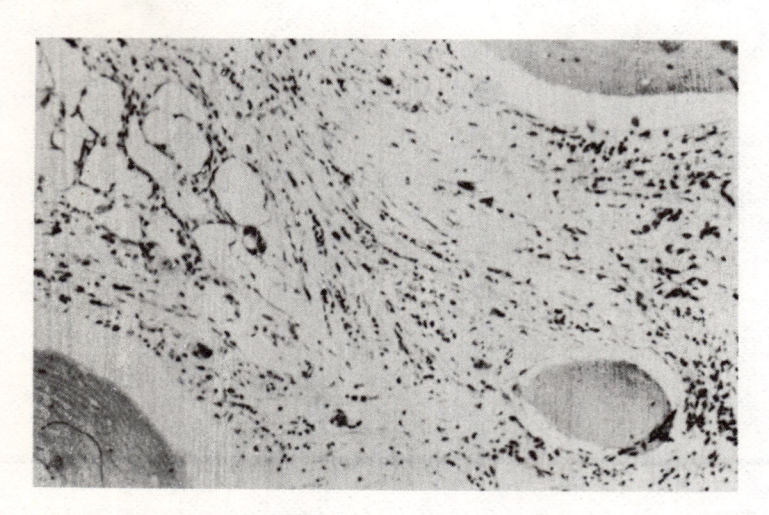

152. A 20-year-old man presents in the emergency room with a lymphoma involving the mediastinum that is producing respiratory distress. The lymphocytes are most likely to have cell surface markers characteristic of which of the following?

(A) B cells
(B) T cells
(C) Macrophages
(D) Dendritic reticulum cells
(E) Langerhans cells

153. Approximately what percentage of transferrin is saturated with iron in the serum of a normal individual?

(A) 10 percent
(B) 33 percent
(C) 50 percent
(D) 66 percent
(E) 90 percent

Hematology

154. An 84-year-old woman enters the hospital with an abdominal mass, anemia, and weakness. At surgery, an infiltrating mass in the retroperitoneum is seen that involves the mesenteric lymph nodes and the right kidney. A biopsy specimen taken from one of the lymph nodes is shown below. The cytology is compatible with

(A) renal cell carcinoma
(B) adrenal cortical carcinoma
(C) pheochromocytoma
(D) paraganglioma
(E) immunoblastic sarcoma

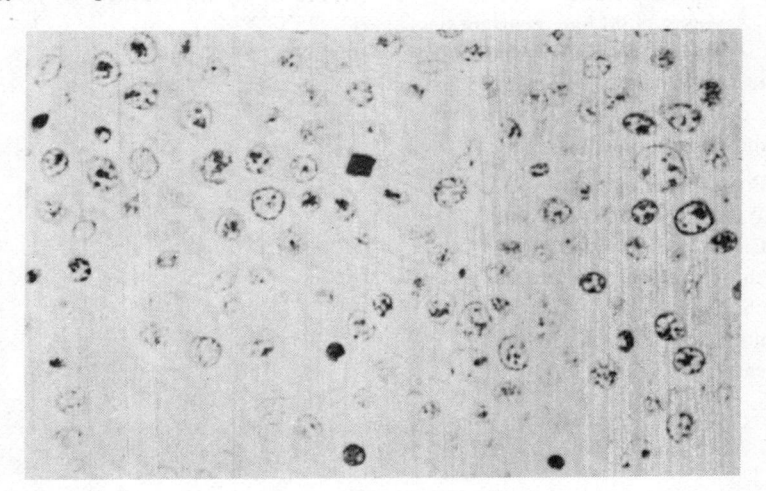

155. An anemic patient has the following red cell indexes: mean corpuscular volume, 70 μm^3 (normal: 90 ± 7); mean corpuscular hemoglobin, 22 g/100 ml (normal: 29 ± 2); and mean corpuscular hemoglobin concentration, 34 percent (normal: 34 ± 2). These values are most consistent with a diagnosis of

(A) folic acid deficiency anemia
(B) iron deficiency anemia
(C) pernicious anemia
(D) thalassemia minor
(E) sideroblastic anemia

156. Chronic granulocytic leukemia is LEAST likely to be associated with

(A) thrombocytopenia
(B) basophilia
(C) splenomegaly
(D) mild anemia (hemoglobin, 12 g/100 ml)
(E) a leukocyte count greater than 50,000/mm^3

157. During the induction of an immune response, which cell is thought to process the initiating antigen?

(A) Eosinophil
(B) Basophil
(C) Macrophage
(D) T cell
(E) B cell

158. A young child has recurrent bacterial infections, eczema, thrombocytopenia, lymphadenopathy, and the absence of delayed-type hypersensitivity. The most likely diagnosis is

(A) Pelger-Huët anomaly
(B) Wiskott-Aldrich syndrome
(C) Chédiak-Higashi syndrome
(D) chronic granulomatous disease of childhood
(E) nodular-sclerosing Hodgkin's disease

159. A 25-year-old woman with known systemic lupus erythematosus presents with jaundice, splenomegaly, peripheral blood schistocytes, and a reticulocyte count of 24 percent. The antibody most likely to be responsible for this complex reacts in vitro at

(A) 5°C
(B) 20°C
(C) 25°C
(D) 37°C
(E) 56°C

Hematology

DIRECTIONS: Each question below contains four suggested answers of which **one** or **more** is correct. Choose the answer:

A	if	**1, 2, and 3**	are correct
B	if	**1 and 3**	are correct
C	if	**2 and 4**	are correct
D	if	**4**	is correct
E	if	**1, 2, 3, and 4**	are correct

160. The binucleated or bilobed tumor giant cell with prominent acidophilic "owl-eye" nucleoli shown in the photomicrograph below

(1) is necessary but not sufficient for the diagnosis of Hodgkin's disease
(2) is sometimes referred to as the "lacunar cell"
(3) may be seen in benign conditions
(4) is a rapidly proliferating tumor cell seen in middivision

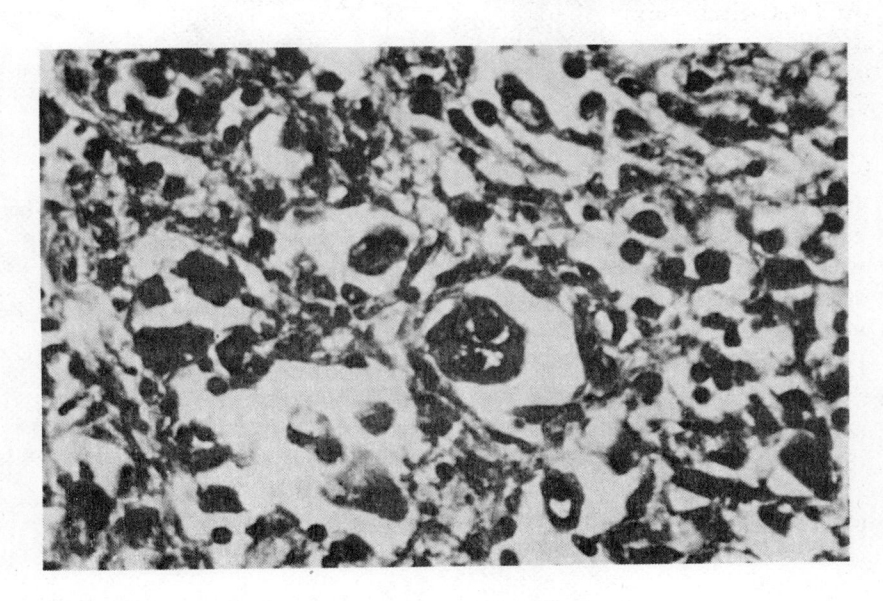

Questions 161-163

In the photomicrograph shown below, cells aspirated from bone marrow show megaloblastic erythroid changes.

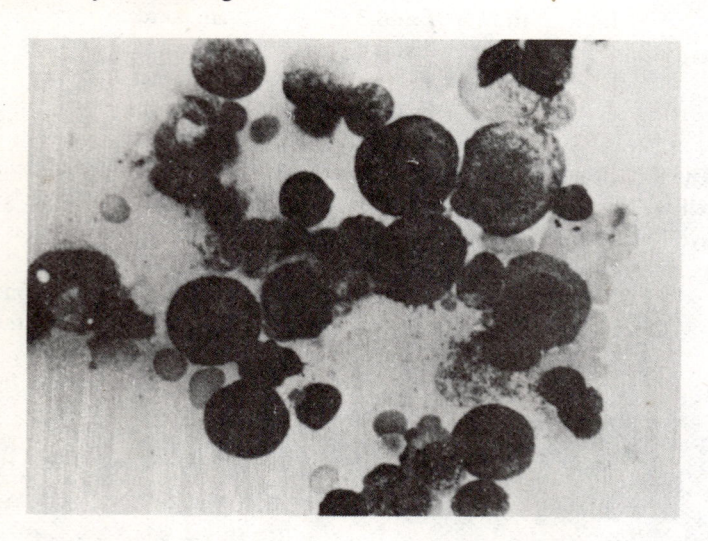

161. The cytologic features in *peripheral* blood that would be consistent with the megaloblastic bone marrow aspirate shown in the photomicrograph include

(1) macrocytes with mean corpuscular volumes exceeding 110 μm^3
(2) numerous myeloblasts
(3) neutrophils with more than the usual three to four segments
(4) secondary polycythemia

162. The megaloblasts shown could be found in bone marrow aspirates from patients who have

(1) erythroleukemia
(2) severe folate and B_{12} deficiency
(3) been treated with antifolates for leukemia
(4) vitamin A-responsive anemia

163. This bone marrow aspirate is an example of megaloblastic erythroid changes and reveals

(1) a decreased myeloid to erythroid ratio (1:1)
(2) giant band forms with maturation arrested in the granulocytic series
(3) increased mitotic figures in red cell precursors
(4) megaloblastic platelet precursors

164. Mechanisms that contribute to the decreased erythrocyte survival in autoimmune hemolytic anemia include which of the following?

(1) Complement-mediated lysis
(2) Decreased hemoglobin synthesis
(3) Increased phagocytosis of erythrocytes by the reticuloendothelial system
(4) Hemosiderin deposition

Questions 165-167

The amorphous material deposited in the section of tongue shown in the photomicrograph below stains pink with Congo red stain and in polarized light appears apple-green in color.

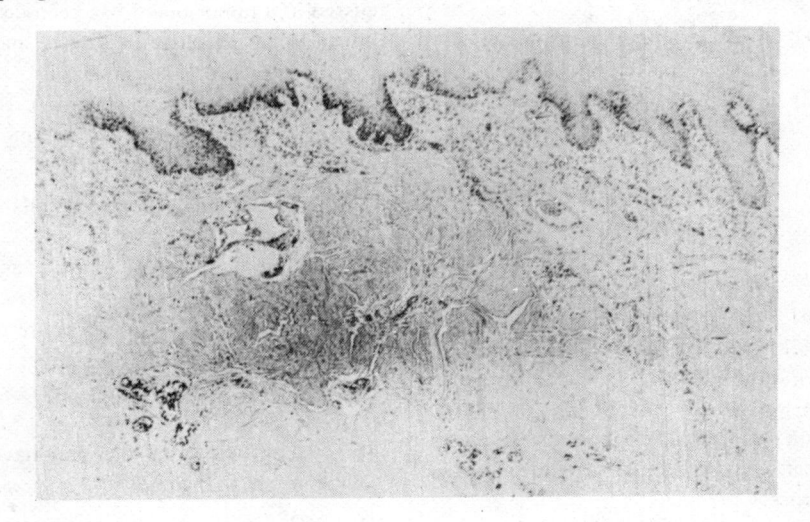

SUMMARY OF DIRECTIONS

A	B	C	D	E
1, 2, 3 only	1, 3 only	2, 4 only	4 only	All are correct

165. The presence of this material in an elderly man who has macroglossia and atypical marrow plasmacytosis would be

(1) unremarkable, occurring frequently in the geriatric population
(2) associated with the presence of M-type serum proteins or Bence Jones proteinuria
(3) almost invariably associated with an increased concentration of normal immunoglobulins
(4) associated with depositions of similar amorphous material in the heart, ligaments, skin, and peripheral nerves

166. Dependable laboratory studies that would aid in the diagnosis of this process include

(1) serum electrophoresis
(2) rectal biopsy or biopsy of clinically abnormal joint synovium
(3) increased absorption of Congo red and Evans blue dyes from the circulation
(4) immunoelectrophoresis on concentrated urine samples

167. Clinical features associated with primary distribution of this material include

(1) diarrhea and malabsorption
(2) cardiac failure unresponsive to digitalis administration
(3) polyarthritis with thickening of periarticular tissues
(4) peripheral neuropathy

168. A 21-year-old man being discussed at a tumor board has been determined to have Hodgkin's disease and lymphocyte predominance and is thought to be in clinical stage IIA. Statements that apply to his case include which of the following?

(1) There are Reed-Sternberg cells in the biopsies
(2) He may have fever, pruritus, and weight loss
(3) The involved lymph nodes are on the same side of the diaphragm
(4) The prognosis is fair to good

169. Neoplastic states that may have a leukemic phase include

(1) ALL
(2) mycosis fungoides
(3) T-cell lymphoma (other than mycosis fungoides)
(4) Hodgkin's disease

Hematology

DIRECTIONS: The group of questions below consists of lettered choices followed by several numbered items. For each numbered item, select the **one** lettered choice with which it is **most** closely associated. Each lettered choice may be used once, more than once, or not at all.

Questions 170-174

For each description below, choose the type of leukemia with which it is most likely to be associated.

(A) Acute lymphoblastic leukemia
(B) Acute myelogenous (granulocytic) leukemia
(C) Acute promyelocytic leukemia
(D) Chronic lymphocytic leukemia
(E) Chronic myelogenous leukemia

170. Auer rods are occasionally present in the cytoplasm of leukemic cells

171. Associated with low leukocyte alkaline phosphatase levels and the Philadelphia chromosome

172. High peripheral white cell counts with numerous promyelocytes, myelocytes, metamyelocytes, band forms, polymorphonuclear leukocytes, and eosinophilic and basophilic precursors

173. Characteristically associated with a short course and diffuse intravascular coagulation

174. Occurs in adults, produces the fewest symptoms of the group listed, and is associated with the longest survival

Hematology Answers

124. The answer is B. *(Henry, ed 17. pp 721, 737-738. Robbins, ed 3. pp 662-663.)* Burkitt's lymphoma, or undifferentiated lymphoma, is characterized by a rapid proliferation of primitive lymphoid cells with thick nuclear membranes, multiple nucleoli, and intensely basophilic cytoplasm when stained with Wright's stain. The cells are often mixed with macrophages in biopsy, giving a starry-sky appearance. The vacuoles contain lipid and this would be reflected by a positive oil-red-O reaction. PAS stain is nonspecific but does mark neutrophils and acute lymphoblastic leukemia cells. Nonspecific esterase is found predominantly within monocytes but also in megakaryocytes and to a minor extent in myelomonocytes. Chloracetate esterase and myeloperoxidase are primarily found within the lysosomes of granulocytes, includng neutrophils, promyelocytes, and faintly in rare monocytes.

125. The answer is A. *(Wintrobe, ed 8. pp 572-573.)* In contrast to a normal, mature neutrophil, which has from two to five nuclear lobes, the neutrophil shown has at least six lobes and is an illustration of neutrophilic hypersegmentation. Granulocytic hypersegmentation is a significant and among the first hematologic findings in the peripheral blood of patients who have megaloblastic anemia in its developmental stages. Neutrophilic hypersegmentation is generally considered a sensitive indicator of megaloblastic anemia, which can be caused by a deficiency either in vitamin B_{12}, in folate, or in both.

126. The answer is C. *(Henry, ed 17. pp 671-673. Robbins, ed 3. pp 29, 616-617.)* Spherocytes in a peripheral blood smear show a smaller diameter than normal and an apparent increase in hemoglobin concentration because of a decrease in cell surface, with consequent deeper staining for hemoglobin. Spectrin lacks the ability to bind protein 4.1 in this autosomal dominant disorder, yielding a red cell membrane skeleton defect. Other proteins that help maintain the shape of the red cell include protein 3 and ankyrin, which bridges the spectrin and the cell membrane protein 3. The disorder can be diagnosed in the laboratory by the osmotic fragility test (which the graph reflects, with the shaded area reflecting a normal response to a hypotonic solution). Spherocytes will lyse at a higher concentration of sodium chloride than normal red cells. Flat hypochromic cells, as those in thalassemia, have a greater capacity to expand in dilute salt solution and thus lyse at a lower concentration (which is seen in the unbroken curve to the far right). The longer the incubation of the red cells in these salt concentrations, the greater the response to osmotic change.

127. The answer is D. *(Henry, ed 17. pp 679-680. Isselbacher, ed 10. pp 1877-1880.)* Blood from patients who have sickle cell anemia exhibits a low erythrocyte sedimentation rate (ESR). The irregular shape of sickle cells prevents the rouleaux formation that is prerequisite for a normal ESR. Sickle cell anemia is classified as a normocytic, normochromic, and hemolytic anemia in which target cells, found in increased numbers, can compose up to 30 percent of peripheral blood cells, and in which reticulocytosis—as a reflection of an increased rate of erythropoiesis in the hyperplastic bone marrow—is persistently 10 percent above normal. In addition, electrophoretic findings reveal an elevation of hemoglobin F up to 40 percent, the presence of hemoglobin S in a range of 60 to 99 percent, and the absence of hemoglobin A.

128. The answer is A. *(Williams, ed 3. pp 268, 435-436.)* The cell in question is much larger than the other red cells and has an immature nucleus with coarse, clumped chromatin. These features help to identify it as a nucleated red cell exhibiting megaloblastic maturation. The cell might be confused with a plasma cell, but plasma cells exhibit clumped chromatin that stains a dark purple, a deep blue cytoplasm, and nuclei that are small and eccentric and often lie next to perinuclear clear zones.

129. The answer is C. *(Robbins, ed 3. pp 618-619.)* The abnormal chain in sickle cell hemoglobin is the beta chain and is designated β^s. The alpha chains are normal in both sickle cell disease and trait; an α^s allele does not exist. Individuals with a normal adult hemoglobin would be $\alpha\alpha\beta\beta$; people with sickle cell disease would be $\alpha\alpha\beta^s\beta^s$; therefore, individuals with sickle trait would be $\alpha\alpha\beta\beta^s$. Some individuals may inherit more than one genetic mutation and thus produce not only hemoglobin S but hemoglobin C or D or another abnormal hemoglobin. The genotype for these individuals would be written to reflect such combined defects.

130. The answer is C. *(Williams, ed 3. pp 434-456, 535.)* Chronic alcoholism can cause megaloblastic anemia as a result of folic acid deficiency, which develops from the combined effects of the typically poor dietary habits of persons who are chronic alcoholics and of impaired storage of folic acid by the cirrhotic liver. The other conditions listed are associated with vitamin B_{12} deficiency. In blind-loop syndrome, bacterial overgrowths interfere with normal absorption of vitamin B_{12} by the small intestine. In *Diphyllobothrium latum* infestation, competition between the fish tapeworm and the host tissues for B_{12} usually leads to B_{12} deficiency. Megaloblastic anemia commonly develops 6 years after a total gastrectomy because stored B_{12} is exhausted slowly.

131. The answer is C. *(Williams, ed 3. pp 1222-1223. Wintrobe, ed 8. p 410.)* Vitamin K is not required for the biosynthesis of coagulation factor VIII, which has an uncertain participation as a trace protein in the intrinsic coagulation pathway and is also known as the antihemophilic factor. Vitamin K, although its biochemical mode of action remains unclear, is required for the biosynthesis and maintenance of normal concentrations of coagulation factors II (prothrombin), VII, IX, and X.

132. The answer is A. *(Williams ed 3. pp 1130-1133, 1156-1157, 1178-1180.)* Prostaglandin E_1 inhibits platelet aggregation, probably by increasing cyclic AMP levels within the platelets, whereas all the other agents listed promote it. Other potent inhibitors of platelet aggregation include mercurials and chemicals that react with sulfhydryl groups.

133. The answer is C. *(Williams, ed 3. pp 982, 999-1001, 1009, 1039. Wintrobe, ed 8. pp 1715-1718.)* Since 1966, hairy cell leukemia has been diagnosed with increasing frequency. This specialized form of leukemia should be suspected in patients with splenomegaly; pancytopenia, including thrombocytopenia; bleeding; fatigue; and leukemic lymphocytelike cells in the peripheral blood demonstrating cytoplasmic projections at the cell periphery ("hairy" cells). These cells are unique in that they stain for acid phosphatase within the cell, with the reaction being refractory to treatment with tartaric acid (tartrate-resistant acid phosphatase, or TRAP). The cells demonstrate varying B- and T-cell characteristics and are thought to originate from pluripotent stem cells.

134. The answer is A. *(Robbins, ed 3. pp 146-153, 617-618.)* The photomicrograph in the question shows the presence of lipid ladened macrophages replacing much of the splenic parenchyma. The macrophages have a somewhat vacuolated cytoplasm, which is characteristic of Gaucher's disease. This is an autosomal recessive disease characterized by a reduction or a deficiency of glucocerebrosidase. Thus glucocerebroside accumulates mainly in the mononuclear phagocytic system. Three clinical types occur. The classic is type I, which occurs in adults and generally spares the central nervous system with the glucocoerebrosides limited to the mononuclear phagocyte system of the spleen, liver, and bone marrow. This is mainly found in European Jewish patients and is the most common form of Gaucher's disease. Type II is the infantile form, which involves the brain and presents no detectable glucocerebrosidase activity. Death occurs at an early age. Type III may be thought of as being an intermediate between types I and II; it is found in adolescent patients and mainly involves the mononuclear phagocyte system early but will involve the brain by the third decade of life. Trihexosylceramide alpha-galactosidase deficiency is Fabry's disease, which is characterized by angiokeratomas of the skin resulting in marked ceramide trihexoside accumulations within the endothelial and smooth muscle cells of blood vessels, ganglion cells, heart, renal tubules, and glomeruli. Glucosidase deficiency is type II glycogen storage disease, which is one of the variants of liver phosphorylase deficiency. Glucose-6-phosphate dehydrogenase deficiency results in hemolytic disease in both sexes, with the male more severely affected.

135. The answer is C. *(Williams, ed 3. pp 172-173.)* Complement-dependent erythrocyte lysis in acidified serum is relatively specific for paroxysmal nocturnal hemoglobinuria. Hemolytic-uremic and Goodpasture's syndromes are microangiopathic hemolytic disorders with an immunologic basis. Pyruvate kinase deficiency and acute intermittent porphyria do not show this type of erythrocyte lysis. Activation of complement by acidification of serum is known as the Ham test.

136. The answer is D. *(Anderson, ed 8. pp 1296-1298. Rosai, Arch Pathol 87:63-70, 1969.)* Clinicians and pathologists alike should be familiar with the benign syndrome of lymph node enlargement called "sinus histiocytosis with massive lymphadenopathy." This is a self-limiting, invariably benign disorder found classically in young, black, African and Caribbean patients, but it has been found in others as well. It is characterized clinically by profound enlargement of regional cervical lymph nodes, fever, and leukocytosis. Histologically, the lymph nodes show marked histiocytic proliferation within the sinuses, with engulfment of lymphocytes within the histiocytes. There may be skin involvement, and histiocytes containing phagocytosed lymphocytes may be present in the skin biopsy specimen. The patients predictably revert to normal within a period of months. Histiocytic medullary reticulosis is a disease in which a form of malignant histiocytes is found in lymph node sinuses, with engulfed red cells found within the neoplastic histiocytes (erythrophagocytosis). Primitive, round lymphoblastic tumor cells are found in tissue taken from patients with Burkitt's lymphoma.

137. The answer is E. *(Henry, ed 17. p 679.)* The photomicrograph shown in the question demonstrates the results of the metabisulfite sickling test for detecting the presence of hemoglobin S. The test does not differentiate homozygous from heterozygous states. Red cells that contain large amounts of normal or abnormal hemoglobins other than S rarely exhibit sickling. The test is based on the fact that erythrocytes containing a large proportion of hemoglobin S sickle in solutions of low oxygen content. Metabisulfite is a reducing substance that enhances the process of deoxygenation.

138. The answer is D. *(Robbins, ed 3. pp 630-637.)* The photomicrograph in the question shows the presence of megaloblasts accompanied by unusually large neutrophils and precursors. These abnormalities may be caused by either a deficiency or lack of absorption of vitamin B_{12} or of folic acid. In addition to diets deficient in these two substances, any condition leading to poor absorption of them will also lead to megaloblastic anemia. Thus malabsorption (as in celiac disease), gastrectomy, infiltrative disorders of the bowel (including lymphoma and collagen vascular disease such as scleroderma), infections by the fish tapeworm, and metabolic disorders (such as hyperthyroidism and increased demand for folic acid as in advanced stages of malignancy) all will lead to reduced levels of vitamin B_{12} and folic acid. A deficiency of either vitamin B_{12} or folic acid will lead to maturation arrest of the red cell precursors, which yields large and apparently immature red cell precursors—hence the name megaloblastic. The nuclei of red cell precursors are in an immature stage for the maturation of the cytoplasm, which results in an unusually large nucleus. Deficiency in vitamin B_{12} and folic acid leads to abnormalities or inadequate synthesis of DNA, which results in a delayed or blocked mitotic division. There is no abnormality in the synthesis of RNA or cytoplasmic protein, and that portion of the cell continues to mature.

139. The answer is D. *(Wintrobe, ed 8. pp 1744-1745.)* The cluster of cells shown in the photomicrograph in the question was obtained from the marrow of a patient with multiple myeloma. Various inclusions can be found in a myeloma plasma cell, which typically has an eccentric, round nucleus with a chromatin texture intermediate between the fine pattern of the myeloblast and the coarse pattern of the normal plasma cell. Myeloma cells are sometimes large and contain two or three nuclei. The marrow of a patient who has Waldenström's macroglobulinemia shows abnormal collections of immature lymphocytes. In erythroleukemia, mature erythroid forms are usually found in the marrow and peripheral blood.

140. The answer is C. *(Wintrobe, ed 8. pp 1744-1748.)* The bone marrow aspirate exhibits a proliferation of plasma cells that are characterized by well-defined perinuclear clear zones and by dense cytoplasmic basophilia due to increased RNA accumulations. Weakness, weight loss, recurrent infections, proteinuria, anemia, and abnormal proliferation of plasma cells in the bone marrow are findings that highly suggest the presence of multiple myeloma, a plasma cell dyscrasia. The more definitive diagnostic criteria are findings of M-component in the results of serum electrophoresis and plasma cell levels above 15 percent in the bone marrow. Multiple myeloma, occurring more commonly in males than in females, shows an increasing incidence with increasing age, and most patients are in their seventies.

141. The answer is D. *(Williams, ed 3. pp 1416-1417.)* Hemarthroses do not occur frequently in patients who have von Willebrand's disease and usually are caused by trauma. A prolonged bleeding time affects most of the patients and, together with a moderate deficiency in coagulation factor VIII, is usually acceptable for establishing the diagnosis of von Willebrand's disease. Decreased retention of platelets in glass bead filters, normal numbers of platelets, and menorrhagia are usual findings, but petechiae rarely occur. The most common symptoms include epistaxis and increased susceptibility to bruises.

142. The answer is A. *(Williams, ed 3. pp 543, 625-626.)* Increased amounts of δ-aminolevulinic acid (ALA) and coproporphyrin are found in the urine of patients who have ingested lead. Lead interferes with erythropoiesis by inhibiting the activity of several enzymes, including δ-ALA synthetase and ALA dehydrase. Thus the various degrees of anemia that are usually associated with lead poisoning are more likely to be mediated by interference with erythropoietic-dependent enzymes than to be the result of hemolysis.

Hematology

143. The answer is D. *(Anderson, ed 8. pp 107-108.)* The cell in the photomicrograph in the question is known as Gaucher's cell, the pathognomonic histopathologic finding in Gaucher's disease, and is a histiocyte typically found in the spleen, liver, and bone marrow. The cytoplasm contains glucocerebroside in an increased concentration that is demonstrable by the periodic acid-Schiff reagent staining technique and appears wrinkled or striated in ordinary light microscopy. Histochemical ultrastructure studies have revealed that the unique cytoplasmic wrinkles are due to the presence of many spindle-shaped bodies (Gaucher's bodies) that contain 90 percent glucocerebroside and that show increased acid phosphatase activity. A characteristic histopathologic (but not pathognomonic) finding in Niemann-Pick disease is the foam cell; this cell is found mainly in lymphoid tissues.

144. The answer is B. *(Robbins, ed 3. pp 146-150.)* Gaucher's disease is transmitted through an autosomal **recessive** mechanism. The former view that the disease was transmitted through an autosomal **dominant** mechanism was based on erroneous interpretation of the incidence of the disease in several successive generations. The most commonly occurring of the three types of Gaucher's disease is type I. Patients who have this form can expect to live long lives even though symptoms progressively intensify with advancing age.

145. The answer is C. *(Anderson, ed 8. pp 755-756. Robbins, ed 3. pp 103, 649, 1049.)* A woman who manifests a hemorrhagic diathesis following childbirth should be considered to have intravascular coagulopathy until proof to the contrary is obtained—for instance, the condition may be due to retained products of conception. However, the peripheral blood smear depicted in the question shows, in addition to thrombocytopenia (three to four platelets are normally present in every high-power field), remarkably misshaped red blood cells (poikilocytosis) in the form of schistocytes (fragments of red cells), spherocytes, and, importantly, "helmet" red cells, so named because of their similarity in shape to military or football helmets. Helmet cells imply the presence of microangiopathic hemolytic anemia and are thought to form through hemolytic-mechanical red cell membrane disruption by passing through arteriole-capillary beds that have fibrin thrombin meshes. Disorders that cause microangiopathic hemolytic anemia are childhood and adult hemolytic uremic syndrome and thrombotic thrombocytopenic purpura (TTP). The lack of jaundice and neurologic symptoms in this case rules out TTP. The combination of microangiopathic hemolytic anemia and renal insufficiency strongly suggests hemolytic uremic syndrome.

146. The answer is A. *(Robbins, ed 3. pp 620-621, 699.)* Homozygous expression of hemoglobin S results in nearly all the hemoglobin in the red blood cell being of the S type. Thus, most of the circulating red cells have the abnormal sickling forms that are sequestered by the spleen and produce sludging within the splenic capillaries and consequent multiple and continuing infarctions. Eventually the spleen becomes small as it is replaced by fibrous tissue. This is sometimes referred to as autosplenectomy. Multiple crises contribute to this event. Massive enlargements of the spleen may be found in neoplastic blood disorders. Chronic lymphocytic leukemia (CLL) produces some very large spleens late in the disease, but massive splenomegaly has been seen in many examples of leukemias and lymphomas, including hairy cell leukemia. Even conversion from cutaneous T-cell lymphoma (mycosis fungoides) may result in a transformed immunoblasticlike sarcoma state. The syndrome of myelodyspoiesis also results in splenomegaly.

147. The answer is C. *(Williams, ed 3. pp 1007, 1013-1017.)* The patient described has Hodgkin's disease in two separate lymph node groups in regions on the same side of the diaphragm; therefore, the stage of the disease should be classified as II. Staging can be subdivided into either subclass A or subclass B, depending on the absence (A) or presence (B) of the following systemic symptoms: unexplained weight loss in excess of 10 percent of body weight during the 6 months prior to hospitalization, unexplained fever above 38°C (100.4°F), and night sweats. Stage I is assigned when one lymph node region or one extralymphatic organ or site is involved. Stage III is assigned when Hodgkin's disease affects lymph node regions on both sides of the diaphragm and also may be characterized either by localized involvement of an extralymphatic organ or site, by involvement of the spleen, or by both of these. Stage IV is reserved for diffuse or disseminated involvement of one or more extralymphatic organs or tissues.

148. The answer is B. *(Williams, ed 3. pp 1006, 1039. Wintrobe, ed 8. pp 1708-1709.)* First described by Frizzera in 1974 and subsequently described by Lukes and Tindle, immunoblastic lymphadenopathy (IBL), also called angioimmunoblastic lymphadenopathy with dysproteinemia, is an interesting systemic illness characterized by hepatosplenomegaly, skin rash, hemolytic anemia, polyclonal hypergammaglobulinemia, "B" symptoms (including fever and weight loss, with some spontaneous remissions, but often terminating in death), and/or evolution into immunoblastic sarcoma (rare). The lymph nodes show total effacement of their normal architecture by a diffuse proliferation of plasma cells, lymphoid cells, plasmacytoid cells, and immunoblasts. There is a characteristic proliferation of postcapillary venules, with a type of branching called arborization (see photomicrograph). PAS-positive lakes of proteinaceous fluid may also be present in the lymph node. The ultimate prognosis is grim.

149. The answer is E. *(Henry, ed 17. pp 656, 667-668.)* Seen in the photomicrograph are sideroblasts that are demonstrating distinctive rings of Prussian-blue-positive granules that indicate iron. Approximately 35 percent of normoblasts in normal bone marrow contain ferritin granules under normal conditions of iron metabolism. Heme synthetase mediates the attachments of iron onto protoporphyrin for the synthesis of hemoglobin. In sideroblastic anemia the production of globin or of heme is markedly reduced because of the deficiency of pyridoxine and ferritin, which contains iron accumulations with sideroblasts without progression into hemoglobin. The accumulation of these ferritin granules takes place in the mitochondria, where heme synthetase is located, and then can be seen rimming the nucleus of the normoblast—hence the name ring sideroblasts. This is the opposite abnormality from iron deficiency anemia. This type of anemia is also referred to as refractory anemia and may be seen in patients suffering from alcoholism, selective deficiencies of pyridoxine, and in malignant conditions such as breast carcinoma.

150. The answer is B. *(Isselbacher, ed 10. pp 346, 367. Williams, ed 3. p 1111.)* The finding of μ heavy-chain proteins in the serum is diagnostic generally of macroglobulinemia and specifically of μ heavy-chain disease. The benign form of macroglobulinemia has been detected in asymptomatic persons without findings of lymphadenopathy, hepatosplenomegaly, anemia, or bone marrow infiltrates of lymphocytes and plasma cells. Increasing levels of the abnormal serum component, onset of bleeding, anemia, or serum hyperviscosity may indicate the need for treatment.

151. The answer is C. *(Williams, ed 3. pp 216, 243-244. Wintrobe, ed 8. pp 1615-1630.)* The marrow core pictured in the question shows classic marrow myelofibrosis, one of the myeloproliferative syndromes (also known as myelomegakaryocytic metaplasia), and agnogenic myeloid metaplasia. There has been a progressive replacement of the normal hematopoietic marrow cells by dysplastic giant megakaryocytic cells, bizarre fibroblasts, mononuclear cells, and lymphoid cells enmeshed in a fibroconnective stroma (myelofibrosis), with replacement of the normal fat. Some of these patients develop acute leukemia. There is eventual profound splenomegaly, due largely to compensatory extramedullary hematopoiesis and red cell sequestration. These changes produce an alteration of the red cell membrane into the shape of a tear drop. Acanthocytes have spiny projections and are seen in liver diseases and hyperlipidemia. Target cells have a clear halo around a darker nidus of cytoplasm and are seen in hemoglobin C disease, anemia, and liver disease. Helmet cells are seen in microangiopathic hemolytic anemia. A "fish mouth" slitlike center of the red cell is the abnormality seen in stomatocytes and occurs in the very rare hereditary anemia of high-sodium, low-potassium red cell defect. Alcoholics may also have stomatocytes owing to an acquired intrinsic red cell defect, which is reversible on withdrawal of alcohol.

152. The answer is B. *(Henry, ed 17. pp 738-742.)* T-cell lymphomas occurring in the thoracic cavity in young patients usually arise in the mediastinum and have a particularly aggressive clinical course with rapid growth in the mediastinum impinging upon the trachea or mainstem bronchi and leading to marked respiratory deficiency, which can in turn lead to death in a relatively short period of time if not treated. These unique lymphomas are characterized by rapid cell growth and spread into the circulation, where they produce elevated total white counts reflected by circulating lymphoma cells. As T cells they have characteristics of rosette formation with sheep blood cells. T cells also have subtypes and subsets, which can be delineated by use of monoclonal antibodies: OKT4 helper, OKT8 suppressor, and OKT10 intrathymic T cells. FC receptors occur on B cells as well as macrophages. Ia antigen can also be found on some B cells. FC receptor HLA-DR (Ia) can be found on macrophages, Langerhans cells, and dendritic reticulum cells.

153. The answer is B. *(Williams, ed 3. pp 303-304, 306-307.)* Normal serum iron levels range around 100 μg/100 ml, and normal transferrin levels are approximately 300 μg/100 ml. Therefore, approximately 33 percent iron saturation of transferrin is usually found. Increased saturation occurs in hemochromatosis, whereas decreased saturation is present in iron deficiency anemia.

154. The answer is E. *(Wintrobe, ed 8. pp 1708-1709.)* Immunoblastic sarcoma (IBS) is now being recognized as an important, specialized type of large, noncleaved non-Hodgkin's lymphoma. It carries a grave prognosis, as very few patients are alive 12 months after diagnosis. This tumor is composed of a diffuse proliferation of variably sized and developed plasmacytoid and immunoblastic cells, in many cases including scattered pleomorphic, bizarre giant cells. There may or may not be arborized vessels and proteinaceous fluid pools present, as seen in immunoblastic lymphadenopathy, from which some cases seem to evolve. The cells will usually stain heavily with methyl-green pyronin stain (reacts with cytoplasmic RNA), as do normal plasma cells. IBS can be seen as a retroperitoneal entity, presumably arising from lymph nodes. Both T- and B-cell immunoblastic sarcomas have been described.

155. The answer is D. *(Henry, ed 17. pp 684-685.)* Both thalassemia minor and iron deficiency anemia are microcytic disorders in which the mean corpuscular hemoglobin is usually found to be reduced. Red blood cell indexes may be useful in differentiating the two disorders, for while the mean corpuscular hemoglobin concentration (MCHC) is often normal or only slightly reduced in association with thalassemia minor, the MCHC is often definitely reduced in association with iron deficiency anemia. Both pernicious and folate deficiency anemias lead to megaloblastic changes in erythrocytes.

156. The answer is A. *(Williams, ed 3. pp 145, 196-207.)* In chronic granulocytic leukemia (CGL), the platelet count is often elevated rather than depressed. The other findings listed are typical of CGL. In the one-third or more CGL patients with thrombocytosis, the peripheral blood may even show fragments of megakaryocyte nuclei.

157. The answer is C. *(Anderson, ed 8. pp 453-455.)* While the exact interactions between different cells is not totally understood, there is current evidence that an initiating antigen is first processed by a macrophage. The macrophage interacts with helper T cells and B cells in a conceptual triangular fashion with helper T cells functioning in the recognition of the carrier component of the antigen on the macrophage as well as recognizing the major histocompatibility complex (MHC) marker (Ia) on the macrophage surface. The macrophage appears to concentrate the antigen, thereby orchestrating interactions between itself and the T and B lymphocytes. After stimulation, the B cell may differentiate into antibody-producing plasma cells. Eosinophils and basophils function in type I reactions (anaphylaxis) by degranulation and binding of IgE.

158. The answer is B. *(Williams, ed 3. pp 723-724, 804-805, 808, 962, 1017, 1291.)* The findings given are consistent with Wiskott-Aldrich syndrome. The Pelger-Huët anomaly involves leukocytes that have dumbbell-shaped nuclei but function normally. Some of the listed clinical features occur in the Chédiak-Higashi syndrome, but delayed hypersensitivity reactions are normal. In chronic granulomatous disease, leukocytes are unable to kill phagocytized bacteria, but delayed hypersensitivity reactions and platelet counts are normal. In patients who have Hodgkin's disease, a different constellation of symptoms occurs.

159. The answer is D. *(Robbins, ed 3. pp 614, 628-629.)* The autoimmune hemolytic anemias are important causes of acute anemia in a wide variety of clinical states and can be separated into two main types: those secondary to "warm" antibodies and those reactive at cold temperatures. Warm-antibody autoimmune hemolytic anemias react at 37°C in vitro, are composed of IgG, and do not fix complement. They are found in patients with malignant tumors, especially leukemia-lymphoma; with use of such drugs as alpha methyldopa; and in the autoimmune diseases, especially lupus erythematosus. Cold-antibody autoimmune hemolytic anemia reacts at 4 to 6°C, fixes complement, is of the IgM type, and is classically associated with mycoplasma pneumonitis (pleuropneumonialike organisms). These antibodies are termed cold agglutinins and may reach extremely high titers and cause intravascular red cell agglutination.

160. The answer is B (1, 3). *(Robbins, ed 3. pp 670-674.)* The diagnosis of Hodgkin's disease depends on the total histologic picture and the presence of binucleated or bilobed giant cells with prominent acidophilic "owl-eye" nucleoli known as Reed-Sternberg cells. However, Reed-Sternberg-like cells may also be seen in infectious mononucleosis, mycosis fungoides, and other conditions. Thus, while Reed-Sternberg cells are necessary to histologically confirm the diagnosis of Hodgkin's lymphoma, they must be present in the appropriate histologic setting of lymphocyte predominance, nodular sclerosis, mixed cellularity, or lymphocyte depletion.

161. The answer is B (1, 3). *(Williams, ed 3. pp 435-436.)* Macrocytes and hypersegmented neutrophils result from a defect in nuclear maturation within the marrow and are common features of megaloblastic anemia. Myeloblasts would not be seen, and anemia, not polycythemia, would be present.

162. The answer is A (1, 2, 3). *(Williams, ed 3. pp 434-456.)* The megaloblastic cells shown are larger than normal erythroid precursors and do not show nuclear maturation. They are found in erythroleukemia with myeloblasts, in pernicious anemia, in dietary folate and B_{12} deficiencies, and in patients treated with antimetabolite therapy. Megaloblastic anemias responsive to vitamins B_1, B_6, and C, but not to A, have been reported.

163. The answer is E (all). *(Williams, ed 3. pp 434-440.)* Although frequently more pronounced in the erythroid series, megaloblastic changes and nuclear abnormalities occur in the myeloid series, including megakaryocytes. A drop in the myeloid to erythroid ratio and an increased mitotic rate represent a response to the anemia.

164. The answer is B (1, 3). *(Robbins, ed 3. pp 628-629.)* Erythrocytes that are coated with antierythrocyte antibodies are phagocytized more readily by the reticuloendothelial system than are "normal" erythrocytes. They may also be lysed directly by complement. Autoimmune antibodies may be either warm-acting (IgG) or reactive at 5°C (cold agglutinins at 5°C).

165. The answer is C (2, 4). *(Williams, ed 3. pp 1114-1115.)* The substance shown is amyloid, with characteristic staining and polarized light appearance. In so-called primary amyloidosis, amyloid is found in patients with multiple myeloma and is usually deposited in all the tissues mentioned. Amyloid deposition to this degree is uncommon in the tongues of elderly people. Primary amyloidosis that accompanies multiple myeloma is most often associated with decreased immunoglobulin levels.

166. The answer is C (2, 4). *(Williams, ed 3. pp 1114-1115.)* Serum electrophoresis usually shows only decreased normal immunoglobulins and albumin. Urine electrophoresis followed by immunoelectrophoresis, in contrast, usually reveals a monoclonal spike. Rectal and joint biopsies stained with Congo red and viewed in polarized light are helpful in diagnosis. Dye absorption rates and total dye consumption from the circulation are unreliable.

167. The answer is E (all). *(Williams, ed 3. pp 1112-1116.)* Primary amyloidosis, which is associated with plasma cell dyscrasia, can lead to deposits in all the tissues mentioned and produce the symptoms described. Plasma cell disorders related to primary amyloidosis include classic multiple myeloma, Waldenström's macroglobulinemia, benign monoclonal gammopathy, and nonplasma cell dyscrasias, such as immunodeficiency syndromes and non-Hodgkin's lymphomas. The amyloid found in primary amyloidosis contains immunoglobulin light chain components, whereas the amyloid associated with secondary amyloidosis (chronic disease, such as syphilis, tuberculosis, Whipple's disease, rheumatoid arthritis, Hodgkin's disease, and ulcerative colitis) has no structural similarities to immunoglobulin (AA protein).

168. The answer is B (1, 3). *(Robbins, ed 3. pp 670-674.)* Successful treatment of Hodgkin's disease (HD) continues to be the rule, although a few patients have not had the usual dramatic response to therapy. HD is classified as having lymphocyte predominance, lymphocyte depletion, nodular sclerosis, or mixed cellularity according to the histologic appearance. Reed-Sternberg cells, which are the characteristic large, binucleated cells with prominent nucleoli, are more numerous in the mixed cellularity and nodular sclerosis types and are rare in lymphocyte predominance. Since newer protocols for the treatment of HD even in advanced stages (stages III and IV) are yielding dramatic responses, some workers report their results on overall HD cases without regard to the histologic subtype. The overall prognosis for all HD cases in the United States in 1985 can be said to be relatively very good, and the less common lymphocyte predominance subtype carries an excellent prognosis. The letter "A" attached to the stage number means the patient is asymptomatic and is not anemic, whereas "B" denotes the presence of pruritus, fever, weight loss, and anemia. "Stage I" means that there is lymph node involvement in one region only; "stage II" means that the lymph nodes involved are on the same side of the diaphragm; "stage III" means that both sides of the diaphragm are involved (if the spleen is involved, the letter "s" is affixed); and "stage IV" involves dissemination to extralymphatic tissue, such as bone marrow, liver, and lung.

169. The answer is D (4). *(Robbins, ed 3. pp 670-688.)* Acute lymphoblastic leukemia (ALL) and T-cell lymphoma are known for circulating neoplastic lymphoid cells in the peripheral blood (leukemic phase). Mycosis fungoides is a misnomer for cutaneous T-cell lymphoma, which is characterized by the presence of Sézary cells, which are often T helper cells. Up to 25 percent of patients with this disorder have circulating Sézary cells in the peripheral blood. A marked leukemic phase in mycosis fungoides may occur accompanied by generalized erythroderma, which is referred to as Sézary syndrome. A leukemic phase is not seen as a rule in Hodgkin's disease, although there is a very accelerated form of Hodgkin's disease that disseminates to the spleen much in the manner of an immunoblastic sarcoma. This transformation may be viewed as an accelerated immunoblasticlike state, and it may be accompanied by peripheral circulating tumor cells. Except for this event, however, Hodgkin's disease is not known to involve the peripheral blood by circulating tumor cells either of the mononuclear atypical lymphoid or Reed-Sternberg type.

170-174. The answers are: 170-B, 171-E, 172-E, 173-C, 174-D. *(Williams, ed 3. pp 196, 204, 221-236, 239-250, 970-978, 981-990.)* Auer rods are sharply outlined, reddish rods in Romanowsky-type stains that are occasionally present in the cytoplasm of immature cells in acute myelogenous (granulocytic) or monocytic leukemias. All the acute leukemias are characterized by short clinical courses (less than 6 months) if left untreated and show blast cells in the circulating peripheral blood. Purely monocytic leukemias are uncommon but can be distinguished from acute myelocytic or myelomonocytic leukemia by means of negative peroxidase and naphthyl chloracetate esterase stain reactions.

Approximately 90 percent of patients with chronic myelogenous leukemia have the Philadelphia (Ph^1) chromosome, which is present in the neoplastic cells. In these patients, leukocyte alkaline phosphatase activity is frequently very low. Chronic myelogenous leukemia produces more splenomegaly than the other forms of leukemia, extending into the pelvis in some cases.

Although high peripheral counts are common to all leukemias, none shows the variety of cells seen in chronic myelogenous leukemia. Numerous promyelocytes, myelocytes, metamyelocytes, band forms, polymorphonuclear leukocytes, and eosinophilic and basophilic precursors may be present. However, unless the terminal blast crisis has occurred, myeloblasts may be relatively few.

Acute promyelocytic leukemia is characteristically associated with an especially short course and widespread petechiae and ecchymoses from diffuse intravascular coagulation.

Chronic lymphocytic leukemia occurs most frequently in the geriatric population (90 percent of cases involve patients over the age of 50) and often does not require antimetabolite therapy for prolonged periods of time. Chronic lymphocytic leukemia is associated with the longest survival rate for all forms of leukemia.

Cardiovascular System

DIRECTIONS: Each question below contains five suggested answers. Choose the **one best** response to each question.

175. The blood vessel in the photomicrograph below shows evidence of

(A) thrombotic occlusion
(B) acute polyarteritis nodosa
(C) necrotizing angiitis
(D) syphilitic arteritis
(E) medial calcinosis

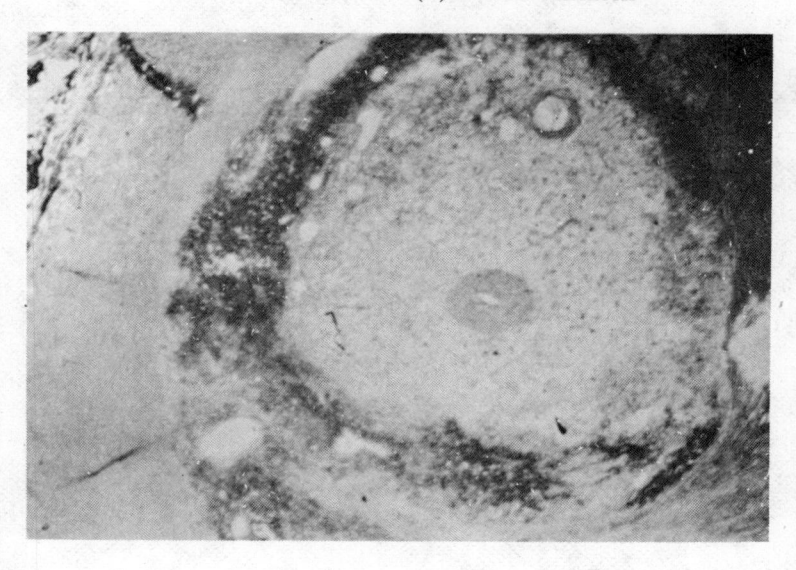

176. Complete obliteration of the aortic lumen by a coarctation proximal to the ductus arteriosus is fatal unless

(A) the foramen ovale is closed
(B) the ductus is ligated
(C) pulmonary stenosis coexists
(D) the ductus remains patent
(E) the tricuspid valve is incompetent

177. Which of the following conditions is most likely to predispose to thrombosis and embolism?

(A) Atrial fibrillation
(B) Pulmonary stenosis
(C) Ventricular septal defect
(D) Aortic stenosis
(E) Atrial septal defect

178. An 82-year-old woman complaining of headaches, visual disturbances, and muscle pain has a biopsy of the temporal artery. The changes revealed by the biopsy specimen are shown in the photomicrograph below. The next course of action is to

(A) administer corticosteroids
(B) verify with a repeat biopsy
(C) administer anticoagulants
(D) perform angiography
(E) order an ESR test

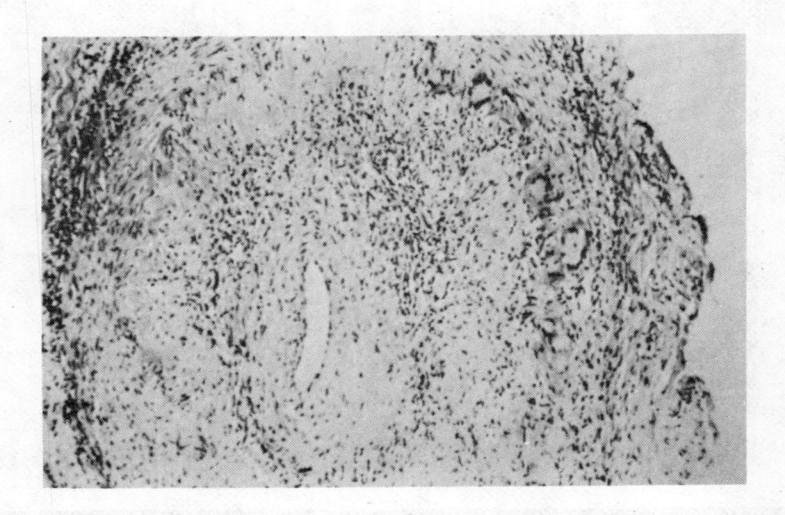

179. Irrespective of the cause of interstitial lung disease the initial pathologic event is generally accepted to be

(A) bronchopneumonia
(B) bronchitis
(C) Alveolitis
(D) bronchiolitis
(E) pleuritis

180. The form of vascular disease responsible for malignant hypertension is

(A) medial calcific sclerosis
(B) arteriosclerosis obliterans
(C) hyperplastic arteriolosclerosis
(D) hyaline arteriolosclerosis
(E) thromboangiitis obliterans

181. A 56-year-old woman dies suddenly and unexpectedly. Postmortem examination discloses a slight bulge in the region of the atrioventricular node. The lesion is seen in the photomicrograph below and is characteristic of

(A) leukemic infiltration of the heart
(B) malignant lymphoma involving the heart
(C) congenital polycystic tumor
(D) metastatic carcinoma to the heart
(E) uremic pericarditis

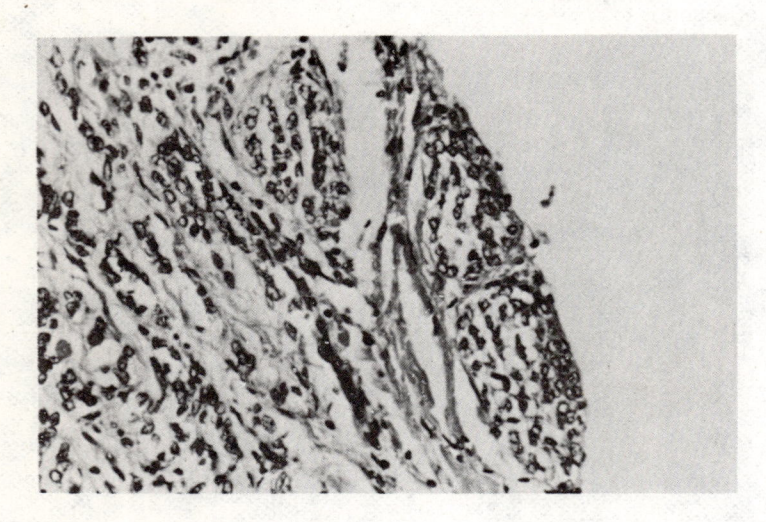

182. The mortality from myocardial infarction is most closely related to the occurrence of

(A) a pericardial effusion
(B) pulmonary edema
(C) coronary artery thrombosis
(D) an arrhythmia
(E) systemic hypotension

183. A synonym for nonbacterial thrombotic endocarditis is

(A) atypical verrucous endocarditis
(B) marantic endocarditis
(C) Libman-Sacks endocarditis
(D) viridans endocarditis
(E) none of the above

184. An elderly man treated for congestive heart failure for years with digitalis and furosemide dies of pulmonary edema. A postmortem examination of the heart would most likely show

(A) severe left ventricular hypertrophy
(B) right and left ventricular hypertrophy
(C) right ventricular infarction
(D) aortic and mitral valve stenosis
(E) a dilated, globular heart with thin walls

185. The pathology evident in the photomicrograph below usually first appears after which of the following lengths of time after a myocardial infarction?

(A) 12 hours
(B) 3 days
(C) 7 days
(D) 14 days
(E) 28 days

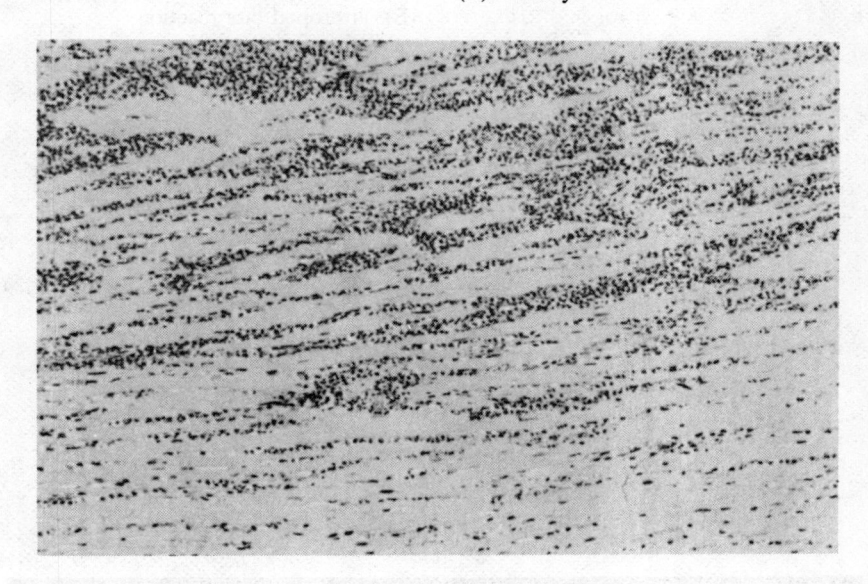

186. The organism that most closely resembles the cultural characteristics of *Streptococcus viridans* is

(A) a staphylococcus
(B) a haemophilus
(C) *Streptococcus pneumoniae*
(D) *Streptococcus pyogenes*
(E) an enterococcus

187. The photomicrograph below depicts the presence of

(A) disseminated candidiasis
(B) pigmented purpuric dermatosis
(C) anaphylactoid purpura (leukocytoclastic angiitis)
(D) erythema multiforme
(E) arthropod bite reaction

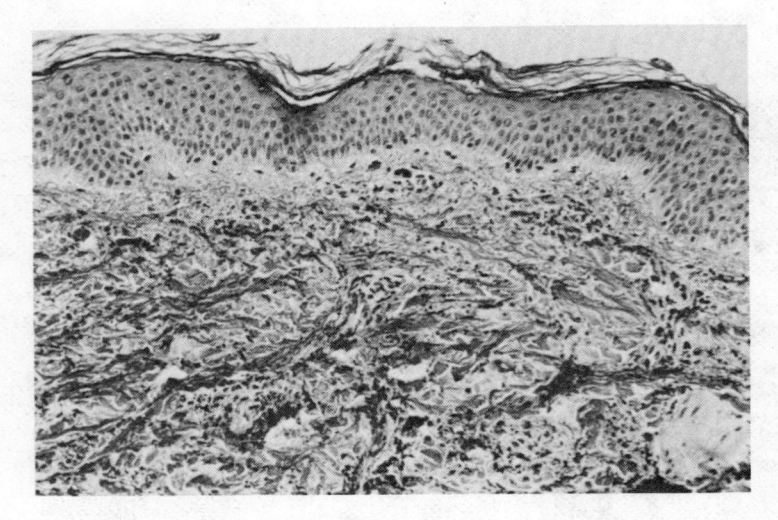

188. A 9-year-old boy is seen in the emergency room with severe, colicky abdominal pain, a purpuric rash, evidence of polyarthralgia, and hematuria. The mother considers these signs and symptoms to be the aftermath of an upper respiratory infection the boy had some time previously. A skin biopsy of the rash would most likely show

(A) no abnormalities
(B) viral vesicles
(C) leukocytoclastic vasculitis (angiitis)
(D) hyaline thrombi
(E) scabies mites

189. Lipofuscin most characteristically accumulates

(A) in glycogen storage disease
(B) in the renal tubular epithelium
(C) in a perinuclear distribution
(D) as a consequence of hemolysis
(E) from extrahepatic obstruction

190. Bacterial endocarditis constitutes the greatest threat to patients who have which of the following forms of congenital heart disease?

(A) Atrial septal defect
(B) Ventricular septal defect
(C) Pulmonic stenosis
(D) Tetralogy of Fallot
(E) Patent ductus arteriosus

191. A 56-year-old woman died in a hospital where she was being evaluated for shortness of breath, ankle edema, and mild hepatomegaly. Because of the gross appearance of the liver at necropsy in the photograph below, one would also expect to find

(A) a pulmonary saddle embolus
(B) right heart dilatation
(C) portal vein thrombosis
(D) biliary cirrhosis
(E) splenic amyloidosis

192. The necrotizing inflammation of the small gastrointestinal artery shown in the photomicrograph below is most likely due to

(A) myasthenia gravis
(B) polyarteritis nodosa
(C) atherosclerosis
(D) dissecting aneurysm
(E) syphilis

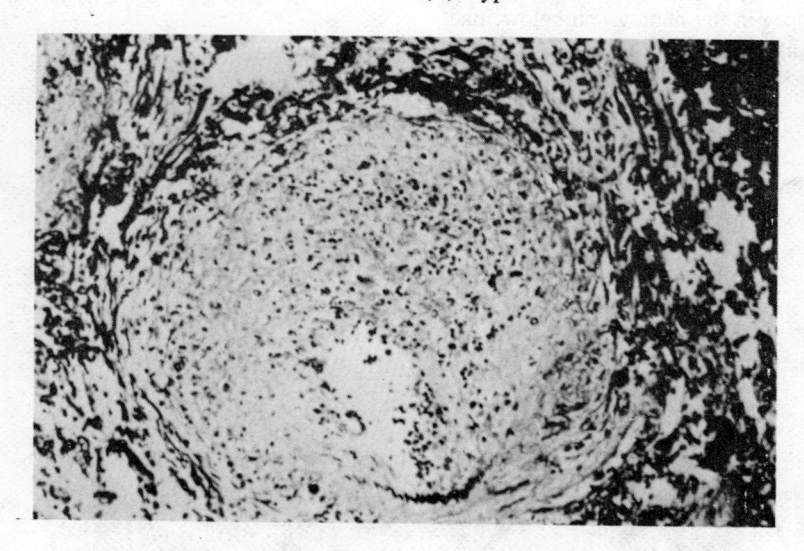

Cardiovascular System

DIRECTIONS: Each question below contains four suggested answers of which **one** or **more** is correct. Choose the answer:

A	if	**1, 2, and 3**	are correct
B	if	**1 and 3**	are correct
C	if	**2 and 4**	are correct
D	if	**4**	is correct
E	if	**1, 2, 3, and 4**	are correct

193. The biopsy specimen shown in the photograph below was taken from one of a number of purple-red nodules on the ankles of an adult male patient. These lesions

(1) may resemble stasis dermatitis
(2) are found mainly in males
(3) may occur in immunosuppressed states
(4) are diagnosed by means of melanin stains

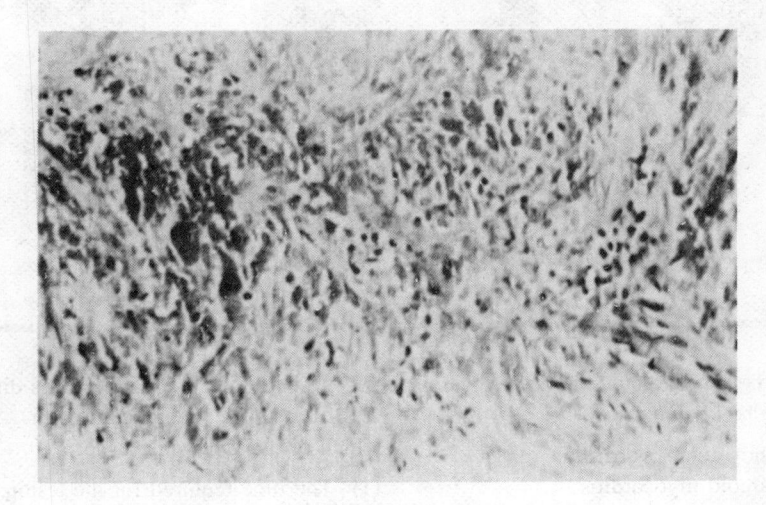

194. Myocardial rupture as a consequence of myocardial infarction

(1) results from long-standing ventricular aneurysm
(2) rarely occurs after the third week
(3) correlates with previous left ventricular hypertrophy
(4) most likely results in tamponade

195. Severe mitral stenosis, as shown in the photograph below, is frequently accompanied by

(1) severe left ventricular hypertrophy
(2) left atrial enlargement with atrial fibrillation
(3) pulmonary valvular stenosis
(4) chronic passive pulmonary congestion

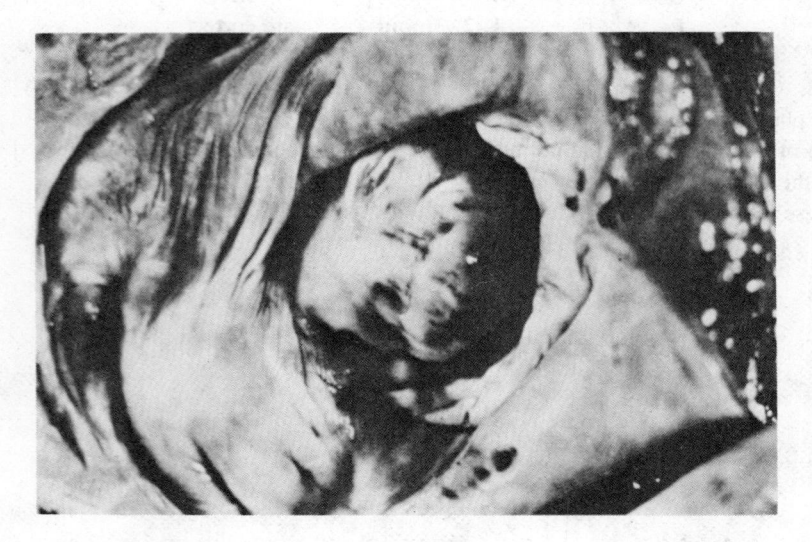

196. Isolated granulomatous myocarditis is also known as

(1) idiopathic myocarditis
(2) sarcoid myocarditis
(3) Fiedler's myocarditis
(4) Friedreich's ataxia myocarditis

197. Acute infective endocarditis differs from subacute endocarditis in which of the following respects?

(1) The time required for the lesion to develop
(2) The nature of the preponderant organism
(3) Embolization and dissemination
(4) The nature of valvular vegetations

198. A 36-year-old man with a long history of cigarette smoking is being evaluated for nausea, sweating, and substernal pressure discomfort. Which of the following determinations would be helpful in excluding an acute myocardial infarction?

(1) Isoenzymes of creatine phosphokinase (CPK)
(2) Serum glutamic oxalacetic transaminase (GOT, AST)
(3) Lactic dehydrogenase isoenzymes (LDH)
(4) Isoenzymes of alkaline phosphatase

199. Tumors known for involvement of the atrium include

(1) metastatic fibrosarcoma
(2) primary myxoma
(3) metastatic colon carcinoma
(4) renal cell carcinoma

200. Types of pericarditis that often lead to a fibrosing, constrictive pericarditis include

(1) staphylococcal
(2) rheumatic
(3) mycobacterial
(4) uremic

201. The heart in the gross photograph below came from a patient who
    (1) may have experienced sudden, unexpected death
    (2) had Libman-Sacks endocarditis
    (3) may have had a family history of similar cardiac involvement
    (4) frequently had obstructive symptoms

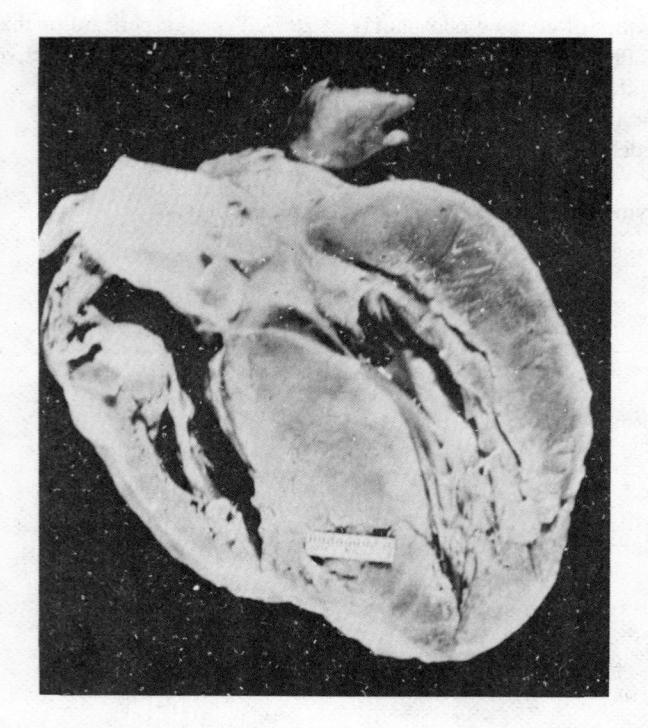

202. The heart can be involved in complications of which of the following conditions?
    (1) Breast carcinoma
    (2) Sarcoidosis
    (3) Chagas' disease
    (4) Trichinosis

203. Cardiac lesions occurring in ankylosing spondylitis closely resemble those of
    (1) rheumatic myocarditis
    (2) rheumatoid heart disease
    (3) syphilitic myocarditis
    (4) syphilitic aortitis

Cardiovascular System

DIRECTIONS: The groups of questions below consist of lettered choices followed by several numbered items. For each numbered item select the **one** lettered choice with which it is **most** closely associated. Each lettered choice may be used once, more than once, or not at all.

Questions 204-207

Match the following descriptive phrases with the appropriate lettered type of cardiomyopathy.

(A) Hypertrophic cardiomyopathy
(B) Dilated (congestive) cardiomyopathy
(C) Constrictive (restrictive) cardiomyopathy
(D) Secondary cardiomyopathy
(E) Endomyocardial fibrosis

204. Thirty percent of patients are prone to sudden cardiac death

205. May develop in patients with multiple myeloma

206. Obstruction of left ventricular blood outflow

207. Usually identified in Southeast Asia and Africa

Questions 208-211

For each cardiac condition choose the infectious agent with which it is most likely to be associated.

(A) Coxsackievirus
(B) *Mycobacterium tuberculosis*
(C) *Streptococcus*
(D) *Treponema*
(E) *Escherichia coli*

208. Primary myocarditis

209. Rheumatic fever

210. Aortic aneurysms

211. Suppurative pericarditis

Questions 212-214

For each aneurysm, choose its usual anatomic location.

(A) Thoracic aorta
(B) Abdominal aorta
(C) Renal arteries
(D) Temporal arteries
(E) Cerebral arteries

212. Berry aneurysm

213. Arteriosclerotic aneurysm

214. Syphilitic aneurysm

Questions 215-217

Match each of the following gross or microscopic cardiac alterations with the most appropriate disease.

(A) Myxedema of the heart
(B) Amyloidosis
(C) Beriberi
(D) Carcinoid syndrome
(E) Fatty degeneration

215. Valvular cusp fibrosis

216. Globose heart

217. "Tabby cat" endocardium

Cardiovascular System Answers

175. The answer is A. *(Robbins, ed 3. pp 556, 559.)* The photomicrograph shows degeneration and calcification of an atherosclerotic coronary artery occluded by a thrombus. For many years it has been thought that ulceration or fracture of an atheromatous plaque, or hemorrhage into a plaque, was responsible for coronary artery thrombosis. Such thrombosis was thought to lead to coronary occlusion and myocardial infarction. Recently, however, it has been suggested that thrombi might be the result of acute myocardial infarction rather than the cause. In support of this contention, recent studies have demonstrated coronary artery thrombosis in less than 50 percent of cases of myocardial infarction. The controversy has not yet been resolved.

176. The answer is D. *(Robbins, ed 3. pp 589-590.)* Coarctation of the aorta occurs in 6 to 14 percent of cases of congenital heart disease. In its infantile form, coarctation takes place in the root of the aorta proximal to the ductus arteriosus, which, if patent, serves as a bypass to allow blood flow to the arterial system. Usually, surgical intervention is necessary for infants who have this anomaly, which may cause death soon after birth or within the first year of life.

177. The answer is A. *(Robbins, ed 3. pp 91, 104-106, 712.)* Stasis of blood in fibrillating atria predisposes to thrombosis and embolism. Systemic embolization from left atrial thrombi may cause infarction in the brain, lower extremities, spleen, and kidneys. Endocardial mural thrombi occur as a consequence of myocardial infarction, bacterial endocarditis, or nonbacterial endocarditis (marantic).

178. The answer is A. *(Robbins, ed 3. pp 524-525.)* Giant cell arteritis (temporal arteritis), although not a major public-health problem, is an important disease to consider in the differential diagnosis of patients of middle to advanced age who present with a constellation of symptoms that may include migratory muscular and back pains (polymyalgia rheumatica), dizziness, visual disturbances, headaches, weight loss, anorexia, and tenderness over one or both of the temporal arteries. The cause of the arteritis (which may include giant cells, neutrophils, and chronic inflammatory cells) is unknown, but the dramatic response to corticosteroids suggests an immunogenic etiology. The disease may involve any artery within the body, but involvement of the ophthalmic artery or arteries may lead to blindness unless steroid therapy is begun. Therefore, if clinically suspected, the workup to document temporal arteritis should be expedited and should include a biopsy of the temporal artery. Frequently, the erythrocyte sedimentation rate (ESR) is markedly elevated to values of 90 or greater. Whereas tenderness, nodularity, or skin reddening over the course of one of the scalp arteries, particularly the temporal, may show the ideal portion for a biopsy, it is important to recognize that temporal arterial segments may be segmentally uninvolved or not involved at all even when the disease is present.

179. The answer is C. *(Robbins, ed 3. pp 742-744.)* Regardless of the etiology of diffuse interstitial lung disease, the earliest recognized event is damage to the alveolar lining cells. The injuring stimulus involves the alveolar lining cell directly, followed by an ingress of polymorphonuclear leukocytes, lymphocytes, and macrophages. If reversal does not take place these changes become chronic, with an increase in cells, including type II pneumocytes as well as inflammatory cells, and eventual scarring and involvement of the septae. The causes of interstitial lung disease include many that begin in an occupational exposure to inorganic dust (e.g., asbestos and silica), gases, aerosols, and organic dust, as well as many drugs (notably bleomycin and nitrofurantoin) and infections, including cytomegalovirus and tuberculosis. Evenually fibrosis replaces the alveolar septal walls and the alveoli become transformed into cystic spaces. Tissue damage also occurs from the release of oxygen free-radicals and proteases following activation of neutrophils by macrophage neutrophil chemotactic factor. Lymphokines and monokines may play a role in the progressive pulmonary fibrosis that occurs.

180. The answer is C. *(Robbins, ed 3. pp 516-519, 526-527.)* Malignant hypertension refers to dramatic elevations in systolic and diastolic blood pressure often resulting in early death from cerebral and brainstem hemorrhages. Pathologically the renal vessels demonstrate a concentric obliteration of arterioles by an increase in smooth muscle cells, and protein deposition in a laminar configuration that includes fibrin material, which leads to total and subtotal occlusion of the vessels. Hyaline arteriolosclerosis as seen in diabetes is presumably caused by leakage of plasma components across the endothelium with or without hypertension. Medial calcific sclerosis (Mönckeberg's arteriosclerosis) is characterized by dystrophic calcification in the tunica media of muscular arteries. Thromboangiitis obliterans (Buerger's disease) is occlusion by a proliferative inflammatory process in arteries of heavy cigarette smokers and is often associated with HLA-A9, B5 genotypes.

181. The answer is C. *(Duray, Arch Path Lab Med 109:302, 1985.)* A rare but interesting primary tumor of cardiac conduction system tissue in the heart is the congenital polycystic tumor, previously called atrioventricular node mesothelioma. The origin of the tumor is controversial and not proven, although some evidence suggests that it is a foregut endoderm derivative. The malformation is constucted of small cystic glandlike structures with intervening packets and nests of cells that resemble urinary bladder, as in the example shown. The lesions are congenital and because of their location in the AV node cause sudden and unexpected death owing to rhythm disturbances. They are more typical in females, although both sexes may have them. Leukemia and lymphoma produce sheets of infiltrative cells that are not in a nestlike configuration. Metastatic carcinoma at times can be difficult to diagnose from the congenital polycystic tumor of the AV node, especially that originating from the GU tract.

182. The answer is D. *(Robbins, ed 3. pp 564-566.)* In myocardial infarction, life-threatening arrhythmias occur in approximately 45 percent of patients without shock and in more than 90 percent of patients with shock. The most common arrhythmias are expressed as ventricular extrasystoles, but atrial extrasystoles, sinus tachycardia, and sinus bradycardia also occur. Even without arrhythmias, nearly two-thirds of patients with acute myocardial infarcts develop heart failure and pulmonary edema. Sudden death (death within 24 hours of onset of symptoms and signs) occurs in about 20 to 25 percent of acute attacks.

183. The answer is B. *(Anderson, ed 8. pp 611-614.)* Nonbacterial thrombotic endocarditis is a form of endocarditis involving the mitral and aortic valves especially, characterized by resemblance to the verrucouslike protuberances of rheumatic valvulitis, which are usually large and friable; smooth and polypoid and shaggy forms are also encountered. These also may resemble the vegetations of bacterial endocarditis, but the lesions are sterile and contain no microorganisms. Both surfaces of the valves are not involved, as they may be in Libman-Sacks or atypical verrucous endocarditis. Viridans endocarditis is a synonym for subacute bacterial endocarditis. Nonbacterial thrombotic endocarditis is also referred to as terminal or marantic endocarditis and is associated in this country with advanced stages of cachexia as is found in advanced stages of malignancy or starvation. It occurs in many other terminal wasting diseases but has recently been described in well-nourished individuals who have died acutely; thus, the older terms of marantic and terminal are probably not appropriate. The pathogenesis is not clear, although there is evidence for increased coagulability in some patients, and the disorder may be associated with disseminated intravascular coagulation.

184. The answer is E. *(Robbins, ed 3. pp 548-550.)* Whereas the morphologic changes of clinical congestive heart failure cannot always be correlated with necropsy findings of the heart because there may be hypertrophy, dilatation, a combination of both, or even an absence of both, many patients with long-standing congestive heart failure after decompensation will have hearts that are maximally dilated, with thinned and unusually soft myocardium rather than hypertrophic ventricular myocardium. This thinning of the myocardium occurs after a long period of compensatory hypertrophy and reflects a state in which the capacity of the myocardium to compensate has been exceeded. The first response of the myocardium to a demand for increased work (load) is to undergo hypertrophy according to Starling's law, leading to an increase in stroke volume. Eventually, this mechanism is exceeded under states of increased oxygen demand or demand for more cardiac output, and cardiac decompensation results, with the worst complication being acute pulmonary edema as a consequence of left ventricular failure.

185. The answer is B. *(Robbins, ed 3. pp 560-562.)* Usually by 3 days after a myocardial infarction, the predominant microscopic features that develop and that can be seen in a stained section of the affected myocardium include coagulation necrosis of fibers and evidence of extensive neutrophilic exudation. Interstitial edema may also be observed in microscopy, and the cross-striations of fibers may appear less recognizable. In gross examination 3 days after the infarction, the infarct has a hyperemic border surrounding a central portion that is yellow-brown and soft as the result of fatty change.

186. The answer is C. *(Henry, ed 17. pp 1082-1088.)* Both *Streptococcus viridans* and *Streptococcus pneumoniae* produce pinpoint colonies as seen in overnight cultures on blood agar plates. Both produce a surrounding rim of partial hemolysis that yields a green appearance and is referred to as alpha-hemolysis. Since both are gram positive and have these similar cultural characteristics, a specialized test is done to distinguish between the two. This is done by bile solubility, wherein bile acids are placed on the blood agar plates by a disk impregnated with the material. Colonies that are bile-soluble belong to *Streptococcus pneumoniae,* while those that are not belong to *Streptococcus viridans.*

187. The answer is C. *(Robbins, ed 3. pp 522-523.)* Anaphylactoid purpura (also known as leukocytoclastic or hypersensitivity angiitis) is characterized clinically by palpable purpura in patients reacting to an antigen derived from drugs (especially the semisynthetic penicillins), from infections (including beta-streptococcal pharyngitis), and possibly from neoplasms. Pathologically, the epidermis is generally intact with vascular damage in the form of fibrinoid necrosis and occlusion of these small capillaries, venules, and arterioles of the dermis by fibrin and proteinaceous deposits, which may include IgA and complement. Hallmarks of the disease histologically are neutrophils that extend out from the damaged vessels and show karyorrhexis (nuclear dust). Extravasated red cells are also seen. Disseminated candidiasis is characterized by varying degrees of severity of epidermal micropustules, folliculitis, or dermal abscesses. Erythema multiforme generally presents with epidermal cell necrosis, an inflammatory cell infiltrate in the dermis, and bullae separating the epidermis from the dermis. Arthropod reactions may have polymorphic inflammatory cells that include neutrophils, eosinophils, macrophages, and lymphocytes, but lymphocytic hyperplasia is frequently the hallmark in the hypersensitivity chronic form.

188. The answer is C. *(Robbins, ed 3. pp 522-523, 643, 1022. Rosai, ed 6. pp 55, 755.)* The development of apparent multiple-system involvement (e.g., of the gastrointestinal tract and the skeletal, renal, and cutaneous systems) by an obscure agent, preceded by an upper respiratory tract infection, should arouse suspicion of hypersensitivity angiitis (Henoch-Schönlein purpura). This syndrome is characterized by a generalized vasculitis distinct from other types of vasculitis, such as Wegener's granulomatosis and polyarteritis nodosa, in that a simple, superficial skin biopsy of the rash demonstrates an acute inflammatory infiltrate of the upper dermal small vessels and capillaries with degenerating neutrophils (karyorrhexis) and extravasated red cells. This form of superficial vasculitis is termed leukocytoclastic vasculitis; its presence in the clinical setting just described enables one to make a diagnosis. Gastrointestinal hemorrhages presumably result from a similar involvement of the vessels in the mucosa. The glomerular mesangium may contain deposits of complement, fibrin, and IgA.

189. The answer is C. *(Anderson, ed 8. pp 86, 102.)* Lipofuscin consists of insoluble lipid pigment. It occurs in the cells of organs and is demonstrated by a brown intracellular pigment deposition that can occur in a wide variety of cell types. It is predominantly seen in the United States in the liver and myocardium of elderly individuals and is characteristically deposited in a perinuclear distribution. Lipofuscin also may result from malnutrition or any disease that causes chronic wasting in other age groups. It represents the accumulation of nondigested material within the cell lysosomes. So much lipofuscin may be deposited in an organ itself (e.g., in the heart) that it may appear grossly brown. Increased bilirubin results from hemolysis of red blood cells as well as obstructive jaundice. The pigmentation appears yellow to yellow-green.

190. The answer is B. *(Robbins, ed 3. pp 580-584.)* Even though children and infants who have small isolated ventricular septal defects are usually asymptomatic, and even though two-thirds of infants who have uncomplicated lesions will have spontaneous closure of their ventricular septal defects by the age of 5, the main risk for these patients is bacterial endocarditis. Protection against bacteremia with antibiotics during routine but potentially infectious procedures is therefore required.

191. The answer is B. *(Robbins, ed 3. pp 550-551.)* The photograph shows the classic pattern of hepatic congestion around central veins, which leads to necrosis and degeneration of the hepatocytes surrounded by pale peripheral residual parenchyma. This is the pattern arising in the liver owing to chronic passive congestion as a result of right heart failure (termed "nutmeg" liver). Mitral stenosis with consequent pulmonary hypertension leads to right heart failure, as does any cause of pulmonary hypertension, such as emphysema (cor pulmonale). Right heart failure also leads to congestion of the spleen and transudation of fluid into the abdomen (ascites) and lower extremity soft tissues (pitting ankle edema) as a result of venous congestion. Portal vein thrombosis is most often seen in association with hepatic cirrhosis.

192. The answer is B. *(Robbins, ed 3. pp 520-522.)* Polyarteritis nodosa, as a necrotizing inflammation that occurs in episodes at random locations within or on the walls of medium-sized and small arteries, has been reported in about 0.1 percent of autopsies and affects, in order of increasing frequency, the arteries associated with peripheral and central nerves, skeletal muscles, pancreas, gastrointestinal tract, liver, heart, and kidneys. Proceeding in stages, the inflammatory reaction features acute necrosis, with fibrinoid deposition and neutrophilic infiltration, and leads to thrombosis of the lumen and destruction of the internal elastic membrane. Polyarteritis nodosa probably could be more accurately called panarteritis nodosa, because *all* vascular coats are subject to inflammation. A remnant of the internal elastic membrane is visible in the photomicrograph.

193. The answer is A (1, 2, 3). *(Gottlieb, N Engl J Med 305:1425, 1981. Robbins, ed 3. pp 543, 1270.)* Kaposi's sarcoma (KS) is a malignant tumor arising mainly in the skin and in the lower extremities, especially the ankles. It is composed of atypical spindle cells arranged around thin, compressed vascular slits and numerous stromal red cells. Lesions may eventually involve the lymph nodes and viscera, either through distant spread or by development of multiple de novo foci. KS was once a rare tumor in the United States, associated primarily with middle-aged men of southern Mediterranean origin and, to a lesser extent, black children. However, KS has been identified increasingly in immunosuppressed organ transplant patients, and in 1981 it was found in young male homosexuals in New York and California, especially those with multiple sexual partners. The mechanisms of development are not clear, but preliminary studies point toward a T-cell dysfunction in male homosexuals.

194. The answer is C (2, 4). *(Anderson, ed 8. pp 592-593.)* Myocardial rupture as a consequence of acute myocardial infarction occurs in 5 to 25 percent of cases of acute infarct, depending on the series reported. Actual rupture of the myocardium is related to the softening of the myocardial wall and occurs usually within the first week of onset of the infarction when there is maximal softening caused by necrosis. It rarely is seen after the third week, at which time fibrosis is taking place. It is seen not uncommonly in females, especially those with preexisting hypertension. More commonly it occurs through the free wall of the left ventricle, in which case cardiac tamponade is produced by massive blood volume displacement into the pericardial sac, which is constrained by its limits of expansibility. This complication occurs in about 70 percent of cases.

195. The answer is C (2, 4) *(Anderson, ed 8. pp 620-622.)* Mitral stenosis is most often associated with aortic valve disease and occasionally with tricuspid valve disease, especially in people with antecedent rheumatic fever. Occasionally, both aortic and mitral disease result from atherosclerosis. Pulmonary valvular stenosis is rarely caused by either aortic or mitral disease. Since severe mitral stenosis prevents significant regurgitation, left ventricular enlargement would not be expected. Left atrial enlargement and chronic pulmonary congestion are common in mitral disease.

196. The answer is B (1, 3). *(Anderson, ed 8. pp 628-631.)* Idiopathic myocarditis is also known as Fiedler's myocarditis and isolated myocarditis because the inflammation is limited to the myocardium and does not involve the endocardial surfaces, valves, or pericardium. This form of myocarditis may take two forms: a diffuse type consisting of nonspecific lymphocytes, macrophages, eosinophils, rare neutrophils, and plasma cells that are distributed throughout the interstitium of the heart; and a type that is characterized by a granulomatous inflammation with multinucleated giant cells of the foreign body and of the Langhans' type. No caseation is seen in the granulomatous form and acid-fast bacilli microorganisms are not present. While sarcoidosis may involve the heart with noncaseating granulomas, at the present time idiopathic myocarditis is not thought to be related to sarcoidosis. Sudden death may occur in Fiedler's myocarditis. Friedreich's ataxia produces myocardial fibrosis and degeneration of myocardial fibers with a few lymphocytes but is not related to Fiedler's myocarditis.

197. The answer is A (1, 2, 3). *(Robbins, ed 3. pp 580-585.)* Infective endocarditis, unlike rheumatic endocarditis, continues to be a clinical problem even in the antibiotic era, with such new factors as intravenous drug abuse and immunosuppression contributing to its persistence. The successful outcome of treatment is directly dependent on early recognition and diagnosis, since with time the infective organisms (such as yeast, bacteria, rickettsiae) tend to be covered with fibrin and platelets, thereby preventing access of antibiotics to the organisms. In addition, delayed treatment allows time for local valvular destruction. Acute endocarditis (AC) tends to develop within days on previously normal valves (60 percent of cases), whereas subacute endocarditis (SEC) takes more time to develop, may be clinically silent, and may be manifested only by the patient complaining of "not being up to par." The organism causing AC tends to be pathogenic (e.g., *Staphylococcus aureus* or gonococcus); the organism causing SEC tends to be relatively inocuous (e.g., microaerophilic streptococci, *Streptococcus viridans*, and even diphtheroids). Bacterial embolization from the valves to other organs occurs mainly in AC and is much less common in SEC. Despite small differences, such as the smaller vegetations occurring in SEC than in AC, it is not usually possible to distinguish SEC vegetations from AC vegetations through only structural criteria.

198. The answer is B (1, 3). *(Henry, ed 17. pp 273, 254. Robbins, ed 3. p 564.)* The isoenzymes of creatine phosphokinase (CPK) and lactic dehydrogenase isoenzymes (LDH) are the most helpful in assessing myocardial necrosis acutely. Total LDH values are not useful unless the isoenzyme levels have been determined, since LDH is notoriously nonspecific and is widespread in mammalian cells. The highest levels of total LDH, for example, are found in hypoxemic shock, megaloblastic anemia, and widespread carcinomatosis. LDH can be separated into five fractions by electrophoresis; if the LD_1 fraction is greater than the LD_2 fraction, "flipped pattern," this is characteristic of myocardial necrosis. CPK can also be separated into its isoenzyme fractions, with an elevated MB fraction indicating myocardial necrosis. Both the LD_1 and CPK-MB fractions are elevated within 10 to 22 hours of necrosis. GOT (aspartate transaminase, or AST) lacks specificity, since it may leak out of the cells that have not undergone necrosis and its levels may be elevated in pulmonary infarction and liver disease. Alkaline phosphatase levels are elevated in liver disease and metabolic bone disease.

199. The answer is C (2, 4). *(Robbins, ed 3. pp 605-606.)* Primary myxomas of the heart may involve all four chambers; however, there is a propensity for involving the left atrium in a ratio of 3:1 to 4:1. They may be small or large, are attached to the endocardial surface, and often produce a ball-valve action. Portions of them can fragment and embolize to skin, brain, and other organs. Renal cell carcinoma has been known to penetrate the renal vein, which drains the kidney harboring the tumor and extends into the inferior vena cava, and thereby gain access to the right atrium. On rare occasions cardiac symptoms caused by the renal vein extension of renal carcinoma may be the first sign of the tumor. Recently it has been shown that cardiac myxomas may be associated with a familial syndrome that combines cardiac myxomas with cutaneous lentigines, pigmented nodular hyperplasia of the adrenal glands, and Leydig cell tumors. Colon carcinoma may manifest widespread dissemination, but the organ of metastatic involvement is usually the liver. When fibrosarcoma disseminates, it does so by the circulatory system with its favorite site being the lungs.

200. The answer is B (1, 3). *(Robbins, ed 3. pp 604-605.)* The two agents that most commonly lead to constrictive pericarditis are staphylococci and the tubercle bacilli. The pericardial space is obliterated and transformed into a dense scar that may even be calcified. Nonsuppurative pericarditis, as seen in rheumatic fever or uremia, rarely leads to constrictive pericarditis.

201. The answer is B (1, 3). *(Robbins, ed 3. pp 597-599.)* The cardiomyopathy shown in the photograph is designated hypertrophic cardiomyopathy with the synonyms of idiopathic hypertrophic subaortic stenosis (IHSS), hypertrophic obstructive cardiomyopathy, and asymmetric septal hypertrophy (ASH). It is characterized by a prominent and hypertrophic interventricular septum that is out of proportion to the thickness of the left ventricle. Histologically the myocardial fibers have disarray caused by wide fibers with unusual orientation, and prominent hyperchromatic nuclei. There is increased incidence within families and there is evidence that it may be an autosomal dominant disorder. Patients may have dyspnea, light headedness, and chest pain, especially upon physical exertion; however, many patients appear to be asymptomatic although a sudden, unexpected death occurs not infrequently, especially following or during physical exertion. There may be abnormalities of the coronary arteries. The mitral valve may be thickened and patients may experience endocarditis on it. Cardiac output can be markedly reduced in some patients because of reduced volume of the left ventricle. As the patient ages, however, cardiac dilatation often improves the reduced left ventricular volume.

202. The answer is A (1, 2, 3). *(Anderson, ed 8. pp 407-409, 626-627.)* The heart can be involved by many outside influences, either directly via an infiltrate (amyloidosis) or indirectly (hypercalcemia), although the most devastating disorder in terms of morbidity and mortality in the United States continues to be atherosclerotic cardiovascular disease. The heart may be involved secondarily by a number of malignant tumors metastasizing to epicardium, ventricular endocardium, or even the conduction system. The most common malignant tumors involving the heart are cancers of the lung and breast, malignant melanoma, and lymphoma. The most common cause of sudden cardiac death in the young in South America is cardiomyopathy owing to Chagas' disease, which is caused by *Trypanosoma cruzi*. Not widely appreciated is the fact that sarcoidosis may involve the heart through the formation of sarcoid granulomas, which may be associated with cardiac arrhythmias and sudden death. Trichinosis of the voluntary skeletal muscle was more common in the past in the United States than it is now, but infestation is still possible if contaminated pork is improperly cooked. Trichinosis organisms (*Trichinella spiralis*) do not, however, encyst in the heart.

203. The answer is D (4). *(Anderson, ed 8. pp 603-610.)* Ankylosing spondylitis, also know as Marie-Strümpell disease, was previously classified under the rheumatoid disorders, especially rheumatoid spondylitis, but evidence shows that it is separate from rheumatoid disease. Ankylosing spondylitis has a high incidence in men, whereas rheumatoid arthritis occurs predominantly in women. It is negative for rheumatoid factor in the sera and, other than involving the vertebrae, usually spares the peripheral joints. Rheumatic myocarditis is characterized by Aschoff cells in interstitial myocardium, which are not seen in the cardiac lesions of ankylosing spondylitis. Ankylosing spondylitis most closely resembles syphilitic aortic valvulitis and aortitis in that the aortic valve ring is dilated, with thickened, rolled aortic valve leaflets and adhesions that cause fusion of the commissure. The tunica media of the aorta frequently shows necrosis and a lymphocytic infiltration as in syphilis. Rheumatoid heart disease, on the other hand, shows granulomatous lesions resembling the rheumatoid nodules seen in the skin and in soft tissues over the joints.

204-207. The answers are: 204-A, 205-C, 206-A, 207-E. *(Robbins, ed 3. pp 596-601.)* The cardiomyopathies (CMP) may be classified into primary and secondary forms. The primary forms are mainly idiopathic (unknown cause). The causes of secondary CMP are many and range from alcoholism (probably the most common cause in the United States) to metabolic disorders to toxins and poisons. Whereas there are not many gross organ and microscopic anatomical features of CMP, a few rather characteristic hallmarks are well recognized in separating the types. However, extensive clinical, historical, and laboratory data contribute as much if not more to classification of the type of CMP present than biopsy or even the postmortem heart examination.

Hypertrophic CMP encompasses those cases in which the major gross abnormality is to be found within the interventricular septum, which is usually thicker than the left ventricle. If there is ventricular outflow tract obstruction, there will be moderate hypertrophy in the left ventricles as well, but the septum usually remains thicker, yielding an appearance of asymmetric hypertrophy. This form of CMP occurs in families (rarely sporadically) and is thought to be autosomal-dominant. Up to one-third of these patients have been known to die sudden cardiac deaths, often under conditions of physical exertion. Histologically, the myofibers interconnect at angles and are hypertrophied.

In dilated (congestive) CMP, the ventricular chambers are markedly dilated, with the walls either of normal thickness or thinner than normal. Whereas many idiopathic cases exist, some patients have a history of heavy alcohol intake. The microscopic appearance is not distinctive. The ventricles may have mural thrombi.

Constrictive (restrictive) CMP is associated in the United States with amyloidosis and endocardial fibroelastosis and is so named because the infiltration and deposition of amyloid in the endomyocardium and the layering of collagen and elastin over the endocardium affect the ability of the ventricles to accommodate blood volume during asystole. The heart is more likely to be so involved if the systemic amyloidosis is associated with primary systemic or plasma cell tumors (myeloma). Endocardial fibroelastosis occurs mainly in infants and in the first 1 to 2 years of life and causes a prominent fibroelastic covering to form over the endocardium of the left ventricle. There may be associated aortic coarctation, ventricular septal defects, mitral valve defects, and other abnormalities.

Endomyocardial fibrosis is a form of restrictive CMP found mainly in young adults and children in Southeast Asia and Africa, where it accounts for a not insignificant number of deaths in these age groups. It differs from endocardial fibroelastosis in the United States in that elastic fibers are not present. Its cause is totally unknown.

208-211. The answers are: 208-A, 209-C, 210-D, 211-B. *(Anderson, ed 8. pp 609-611, 626-628, 706-712. Robbins, ed 3. pp 591-596, 571-576, 603-604.)* Primary myocarditis, an isolated lesion that is not secondary to a generalized disease, is most commonly caused by such agents as type B coxsackievirus, echoviruses, and *Toxoplasma gondii.*

Streptococci are generally considered the causative agents of rheumatic fever; and although group A-beta-hemolytic streptococci are most strongly implicated, viruses continue to be suspected as among the causes of this systemic nonsuppurative inflammatory disease. Abundant evidence supports the view that antibodies generated in the immunologic reaction to A-beta-hemolytic streptococcus infection cross-react with myocardial fibers, smooth muscle cells, and connective tissue glycoproteins. Aschoff bodies, produced in response to this cross reaction, are regarded as pathognomonic for rheumatic fever.

Aortic aneurysms of luetic carditis constitute the tertiary manifestation of syphilis and become evident 15 to 20 years after persons have contracted infection with *Treponema pallidum*. Elastic tissue and smooth muscle cells of the media undergo ischemic destruction as a result of the treponemal infection. As a consequence of ischemia in the media, musculoelastic support is lost, lending to aortic aneurysms, widening of the aortic valve ring, and narrowing of the coronary ostia.

Suppurative pericarditis is a form of acute pericarditis that can be caused by *Mycobacterium tuberculosis* and is considered to invariably denote entry into the pericardium of bacterial, mycotic, or parasitic agents. In the suppurative pericarditis caused by *M. tuberculosis* (tuberculous pericarditis), tuberculosis of the mediastinal nodes has been a finding in the majority of affected adults. Up to 500 ml of thick fluid (typical of caseation necrosis) may be formed in the pericardium, containing granulocytes, erythrocytes, and, in 50 percent of patients who have tuberculous pericarditis, tubercle bacilli.

212-214. The answers are: 212-E, 213-B, 214-A. *(Robbins, ed 3. pp 529-535, 1393-1394.)* Congenital berry aneurysms usually affect the cerebral vessels. Berry aneurysms cause death through subarachnoid hemorrhage, with blood being demonstrated in the cerebrospinal fluid (CSF) by lumbar tap; however, there may be little or no bleeding into the CSF if the berry aneurysm is located in the anterior communicating artery. Saccular ("berry") aneurysms are likely to be congenital, whereas fusiforms are thought to be caused by arteriosclerosis. In any of the major aneurysms, branches of the circle of Willis may be involved, but at least 90 percent of aneurysms occur in the internal carotid artery feeders. There is no correlation between the extent of bleeding and the size of the aneurysm.

Ninety-seven percent of abdominal aneurysms are arteriosclerotic. Arteriosclerotic aneurysms occur in a male to female ratio of 5:1 after the age of 50 and make up the majority of all aneurysms seen in this country. Most are in the abdominal aorta between the iliac bifurcation and the renal arteries. Aneurysms found in atherosclerosis are formed by progressive thinning and destruction of the tunica media.

Syphilitic aneurysms are virtually always confined to the thoracic aorta. Leutic aneurysms may also cause dilatation of the aortic valve or narrowing of the coronary ostia. Other causes of aneurysms include Kawasaki's disease, arteritis (polyarteritis nodosa), and infection (mycotic aneurysm).

215-217. The answers are: 215-D, 216-C, 217-E. *(Anderson, ed 8. pp 565, 568-569, 573-574.)* The carcinoid syndrome produces valve cusp fibrosis, principally of the right side of the heart but including the tricuspid and pulmonary valves. Fibrous plaques form, resulting in pulmonary stenosis and tricuspid insufficiency, probably under the influence of serotonin release from the carcinoid tumor.

Cardiovascular System

Cardiac enlargement is seen in myxedematous heart as well as in cardiac interstitial edema and myocardial basophilic degeneration. The cardiac enlargement seen in thiamine deficiency (vitamin B_1) also produces enlargement of the heart, but this involves a characteristic globose shape produced by concurrent chamber dilatation and ventricular hypertrophy. Beriberi heart is usually a result of chronic alcoholism in the United States.

Primary or secondary amyloidosis may involve the heart but is seen more prominently in primary amyloidosis, along with amyloid deposits in the tongue, lungs, skin, voluntary muscles, and GI tract. The atrial walls are strikingly thick and rigid and do not collapse after blood volume is removed.

Fatty degeneration of the heart is to be separated from fatty infiltration of the heart (usually in the right ventricle), which occurs in obesity. Fatty degeneration produces lipid vacuolar change in the myocardial fibers. Irregular, yellowish streaks or lines of involved muscle alternate with lines of unaffected muscle, giving the "tabby cat" appearance. Fatty degeneration is seen in anoxia, toxins, sepsis, and neonatal deaths.

Respiratory System

DIRECTIONS: Each question below contains five suggested answers. Choose the **one best** response to each question.

218. Allergic bronchopulmonary aspergillosis is related to sarcoidosis involving the lung by which cell type?

(A) Macrophage
(B) Type II pneumocyte
(C) Plasma cell
(D) Eosinophil
(E) Neutrophil

219. Alpha-1-antitrypsin deficiency is associated with

(A) thalassemia
(B) nephrotic syndrome
(C) panlobular emphysema
(D) anthracosis
(E) renal cell carcinoma

220. A chest x-ray that shows a shaggy cavity with a thick, irregular border and satellite densities in the right-lower lobe is most compatible with a diagnosis of

(A) histoplasmosis
(B) bronchogenic carcinoma
(C) tuberculosis
(D) *Nocardia asteroides* infection
(E) abscess

221. A young woman succumbed after an 8-month course of severe dyspnea, fatigue, and cyanosis that followed an uneventful delivery of a healthy infant. At necropsy, small atheromas were present in the large and small branches of the pulmonary arteries. Which of the following findings can be predicted in the histologic slides of the lungs?

(A) Diffuse hemorrhage and infarctions
(B) Diffuse alveolar hyaline membranes
(C) Severe atelectasis and edema
(D) Marked medial hypertrophy of pulmonary arterioles
(E) Multiple pulmonary emboli

222. Which of the following bronchogenic carcinomas is associated with hematoxyphilia of blood vessels?

(A) Bronchioalveolar adenocarcinoma
(B) Papillary adenocarcinoma
(C) Acinar adenocarcinoma
(D) Oat-cell carcinoma
(E) Squamous cell carcinoma

223. An adult male dies after a protracted clinical course characterized by dyspnea, cough, weight loss, fatigue, and right heart failure. Chest roentgenograms obtained before death were not strikingly abnormal. At autopsy, each lung weighed more than 1100 g. The photomicrograph below shows a section of lung. This condition is also associated with

(A) pulmonary edema
(B) cholesterol crystal plates
(C) interstitial inflammation
(D) bronchocentric granulomatosis
(E) mineral oil aspiration

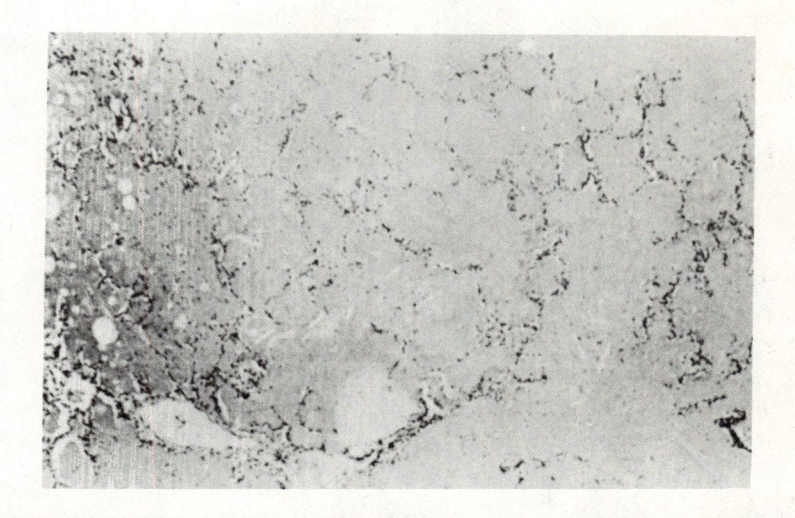

224. A patient hospitalized for fractures of the long bones who develops mental dysfunction, increasing respiratory insufficiency, and renal failure should be suspected to have

(A) fat embolism syndrome
(B) disseminated intravascular coagulopathy
(C) myocardial infarction
(D) aortic valve disease
(E) respiratory distress syndrome

225. Which of the following statements concerning thymomas is most appropriate?

(A) Most commonly occur in the anterosuperior mediastinum
(B) The lymphocytes present are neoplastic
(C) Epithelial cells are not required for the diagnosis
(D) Most are malignant in nature
(E) They occur predominantly in adolescents

226. A 48-year-old woman with a 26 pack-year history of cigarette smoking was noted to have abnormal cells suspicious for malignancy in sputum cytology. The chest x-ray is presented below. What is the most likely diagnosis?

(A) Sarcoidosis
(B) Adenocarcinoma
(C) Breast carcinoma
(D) Small-cell carcinoma
(E) Squamous cell carcinoma

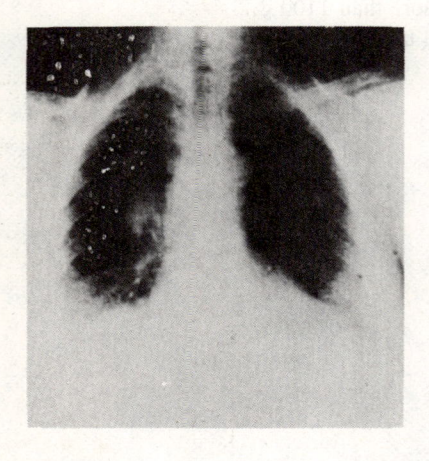

227. The organism that is most likely to cause the necrotizing pulmonary lesion shown in the photomicrograph below is

(A) *Pseudomonas aeruginosa*
(B) *Mycobacterium tuberculosis*
(C) *Pneumocystis carinii*
(D) *Trichinella spiralis*
(E) *Candida albicans*

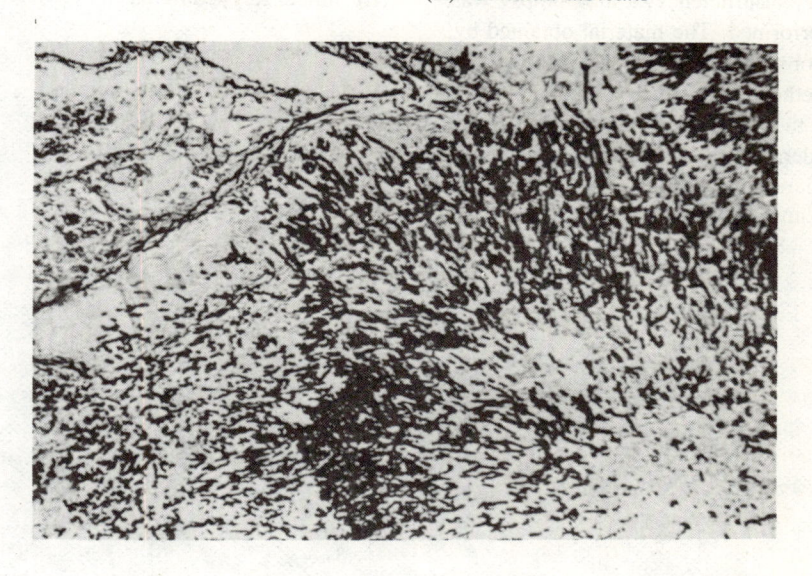

228. Acute lymphoblastic leukemia was diagnosed in a 10-year-old child. When this child later developed a patchy pulmonary infiltrate and respiratory insufficiency, a lung biopsy was performed. The material obtained by biopsy was then stained with Gomori's methenamine-silver stain and is shown in the photomicrograph below. In consideration of the patient's signs and microscopic evaluations, the prognosis is now complicated by

(A) *Pseudomonas* pneumonia
(B) *Aspergillus* pneumonia
(C) *Pneumocystis carinii* pneumonia
(D) pneumococcal pneumonia
(E) influenza pneumonia

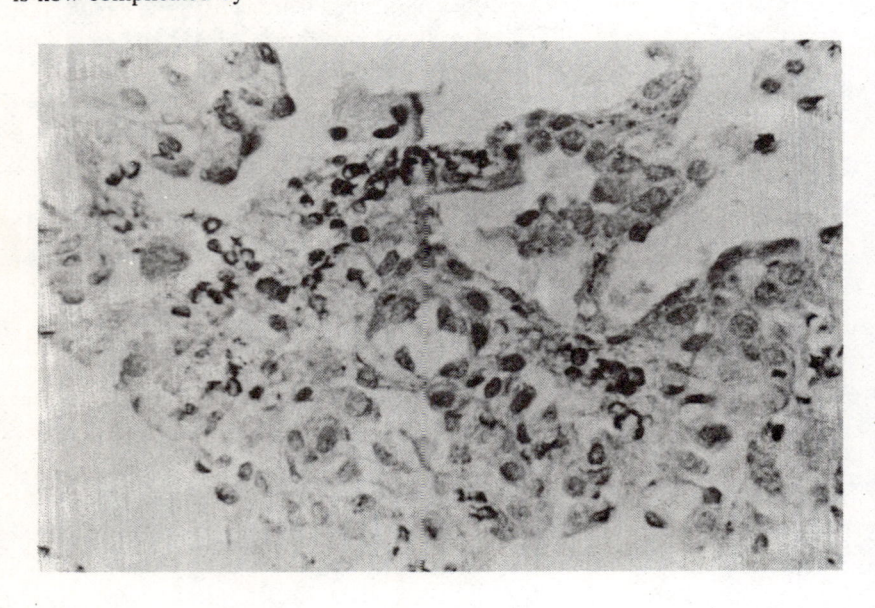

DIRECTIONS: Each question below contains four suggested answers of which **one** or **more** is correct. Choose the answer:

A	if	**1, 2, 3**	are correct
B	if	**1 and 3**	are correct
C	if	**2 and 4**	are correct
D	if	**4**	is correct
E	if	**1, 2, 3, and 4**	are correct

229. Legionnaire's disease is suspected in an adult hospital maintenance worker who became ill with headaches, malaise, and a dry cough. The diagnosis can be confirmed rapidly and reliably by

(1) open lung biopsy
(2) chest roentgenography
(3) checking serum agglutinin levels
(4) immunofluorescence testing

230. Conditions that predispose to the development of bronchiectasis include

(1) asthma
(2) chronic sinusitis
(3) avitaminosis A
(4) fibrocystic disease

231. Tumors that are considered unique to the nasal cavities and paranasal sinuses include

(1) angiofibroma
(2) esthesioneuroblastoma
(3) isolated plasmacytoma
(4) transitional-cell carcinoma

232. In AIDS patients evidence that hypoimmunity exists comes from the

(1) lack of intracellular antimicrobial activity of macrophages
(2) absence or abnormality of macrophage activation
(3) absence of B cells, especially plasma cells
(4) impaired production of lymphokines

233. The condition seen below in the gross photograph of a sagittal section of the lung may occur in which of the following?

(1) Adenocarcinoma
(2) Oat-cell carcinoma
(3) Malignant mesothelioma
(4) Benign spindle-cell mesothelioma

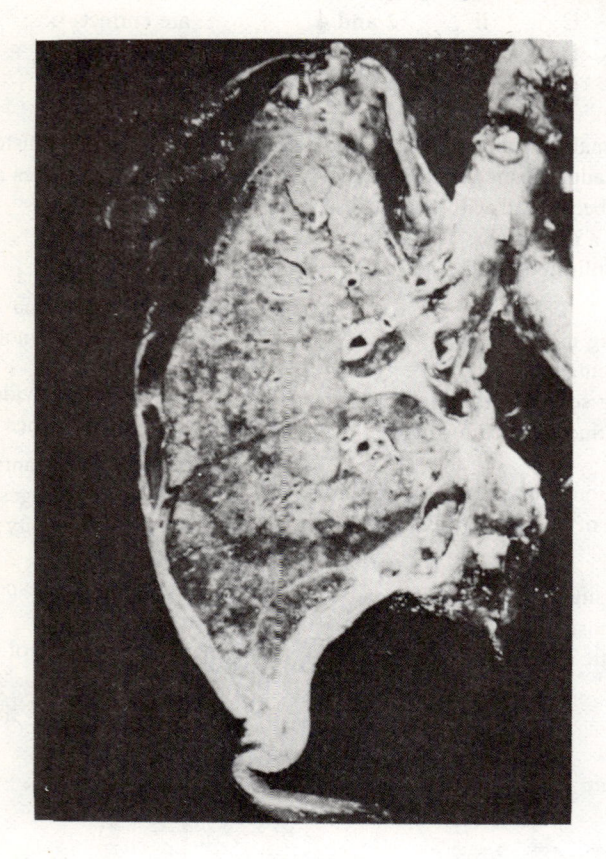

234. "Usual interstitial pneumonia" (fibrosing alveolitis) is characterized by
(1) pulmonary insufficiency and death occurring within a year of the onset of symptoms
(2) cellular thickening of alveolar walls with fibrosis and chronic inflammatory infiltrates
(3) an increased incidence of primary pulmonary malignancy
(4) alveolar-capillary block

235. Pulmonary interstitial fibrosis is reported to result from the use of
(1) busulfan
(2) nitrofurantoin
(3) methysergide
(4) oxygen

Questions 236-237

Shown in the photomicrograph below is a section of alveolar tissue that was taken at autopsy of a 4-day-old premature infant.

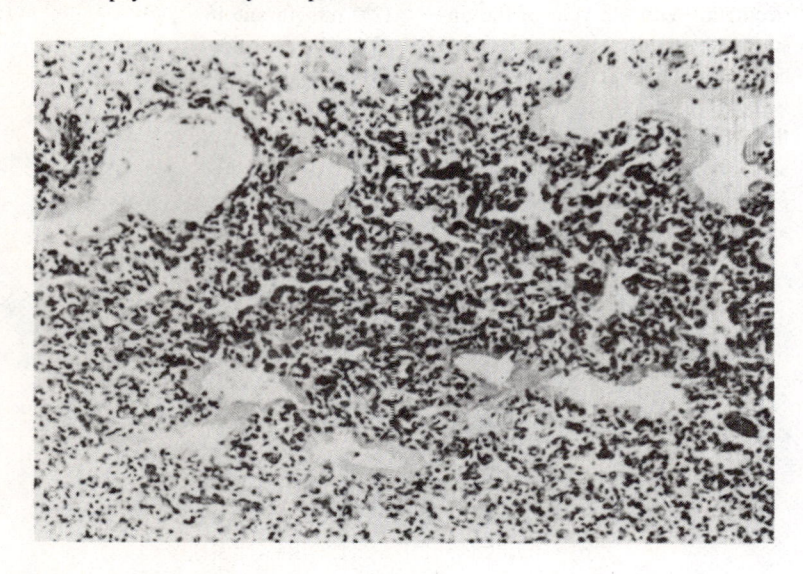

236. The pathologic process that is evident is consistent with

(1) congenital pulmonary cystic malformation
(2) extralobar pulmonary sequestration
(3) primary fungal pneumonitis
(4) respiratory distress syndrome (hyaline membrane disease)

237. A similar histopathologic condition can be seen in lungs of adults who have

(1) viral pneumonia
(2) uremia
(3) pulmonary irradiation
(4) severe bacterial infection

238. A 40-year-old woman undergoes excision of a well-circumscribed lesion in the subpleural upper lung after a shadow was seen on a preemployment chest x-ray. The lesion is demonstrated in the photomicrograph below. Which of the following statements applies to this disease process?

(1) Metastasis can be expected
(2) This is a relatively rare tumor
(3) The tumor is radiosensitive
(4) The tumor is diagnosed predominantly in adults

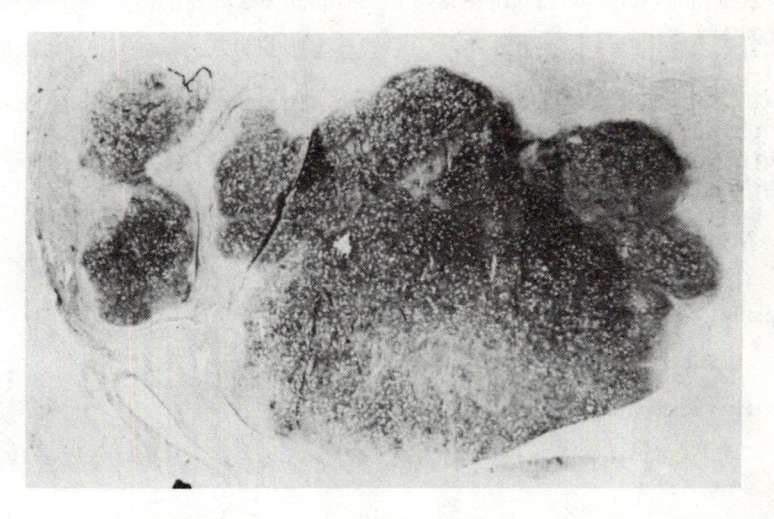

239. Extrapulmonary manifestations of bronchogenic carcinoma

(1) include Cushing's syndrome
(2) include inappropriate antidiuretic hormone activity
(3) include peripheral neuropathy and myopathy
(4) occur in patients who have normal bone scans

240. A 2-year-old infant seen in the emergency room with respiratory distress, fever, dyspnea, wheezing, and sternal retractions would probably have which of the following in terminal episodes?

(1) Apparently normal gross examination
(2) Marked pleural effusions
(3) Bronchiolar inflammatory infiltrates
(4) Hyaline membranes

DIRECTIONS: The groups of questions below consist of lettered choices followed by several numbered items. For each numbered item select the **one** lettered choice with which it is **most** closely associated. Each lettered choice may be used once, more than once, or not at all.

Questions 241-244

Match the following clinicopathologic conditions with the appropriate lung tumors.

(A) Oat-cell carcinoma
(B) Squamous cell carcinoma
(C) Adenocarcinoma
(D) Giant-cell carcinoma
(E) No specific tumor type

241. Myasthenic syndrome

242. Hypertrophic pulmonary osteoarthropathy

243. Hopeless prognosis

244. Hypercalcemia

Questions 245-248

For each tumor, choose its most common site of origin.

(A) Pleura
(B) Bronchial lining
(C) Submucosal bronchial glands
(D) Alveolar lining cells
(E) Bronchial lymphatics

245. Squamous cell carcinoma

246. Alveolar cell carcinoma

247. Adenoid cystic carcinoma

248. Mesothelioma

Respiratory System Answers

218. The answer is D. *(Anderson, ed 8. pp 879-881.)* Peripheral blood eosinophilia associated with infiltration of the lungs by eosinophils constitutes a clinical syndrome referred to as pulmonary infiltration and eosinophilia (PIE syndrome). While not a primary disease in and of itself, it is a central and peripheral manifestation of underlying conditions that include aspergillosis of the lungs; chronic penumonia; reactions to drugs; parasitic infections, especially by *Ascaris, Strongyloides,* or *Toxocara;* vasculitis, especially Churg-Strauss type; other bacterial and fungal infections of the lungs; certain neoplasms; and sarcoidosis. If caused by parasites, it is usually a result of migration of larva through the lungs before they reach their destination in the intestines. Hence, stool examination at this time will not show ova.

219. The answer is C. *(Robbins, ed 3. pp 56, 721, 930.)* Patients who are homozygous for alpha-1-antitrypsin deficiency develop severe panlobular emphysema, often before the age of 40. This genetic disorder accounts for about 10 percent of cases of emphysema. Other factors in the pathogenesis of emphysema include air pollution and smoking. The disorder results from any variant of the numerous alleles on the chromosomal locus of Pi (proteinase inhibitor). Cigarette smoking greatly accelerates the emphysema in the homozygous (Pi ZZ) state.

220. The answer is B. *(Robbins, ed 3. pp 750-754.)* Bronchogenic carcinoma, the most common visceral malignancy in men, accounts for 40 percent of all male cancer deaths. Lung cancer is at least 10 times as common in smokers as in nonsmokers. Bronchogenic carcinomas arise most often near the hilus of the lung, in the lower trachea, and in first, second, or third order bronchi.

221. The answer is D. *(Robbins, ed 3. pp 750-754.)* Many pathologic pulmonary changes can be found in the lungs of patients who expire under conditions of progressive, unexplained dyspnea, fatigue, and cyanosis. These changes range from pulmonary fibrosis to hypersensitivity pneumonitis and to recurrent, multiple pulmonary emboli. Furthermore, traditional hospital treatment modalities for progressive pulmonary deterioration (including high oxygen delivery, overhydration, lack of pulmonary ventilation, irregular ventilation by mechanical respiratory assist [PEEP], and superimposed nosocomially acquired pneumonitis) can complicate pulmonary pathologic findings. However, unremitting, progressive dyspnea, cyanosis, and fatigue in a young woman should suggest the diagnosis of primary pulmonary hypertension. Pulmonary vascular sclerosis is always associated with pulmonary hypertension primary or secondary to other states, such as emphysema and mitral stenosis.

222. The answer is D. *(Anderson, ed 8. pp 922-924.)* By common clinical convention squamous cell carcinoma, small-cell carcinoma, adenocarcinoma, and large-cell carcinoma are considered to be a group of pulmonary tumors referred to as bronchogenic carcinoma. Each has a different histopathologic appearance and unique clinical behavior. Small-cell carcinoma can be divided into three histologic subtypes: oat-cell carcinoma, intermediate cell-type, and oat-cell carcinoma combined with squamous features. The small-cell carcinoma has a characteristic sign first described by Azzopardi, wherein blood vessels near the necrotic areas of the tumor have deposits of DNA, presumably from the tumor necrosis, which stain with hematoxylin and produce a bluish color. When present this histologic sign is a clue that the tumor has at least a component of small-cell carcinoma.

223. The answer is B. *(Rosen, N Engl J Med 258:1123, 1958.)* The alveolar spaces are filled with proteinaceous, eosinophilic, amorphic fluid with relatively intact alveolar septal walls and very little inflammation, all of which are characteristic of pulmonary alveolar proteinosis (PAP), a disorder first described in 1958. Occurring in a male to female ratio of 3:1, it is characterized by weight loss, chest pain, fatigue, and coughing of yellow to gray sputum containing gelatinous particles and diagnostic lamellar bodies. If abnormal at all, x-rays show a central, hazy butterfly pattern. In addition to surfactant polmitoyl lecithin and phospholipids, polarizable cholesterol crystals called aciculate spaces are found. On electron microscopy, the type II pneumocytes show many osmiophilic lamellated bodies. Experimentally, rat alveolar macrophages have produced the lesion on exposure to aluminum and silica dust. There is no associated inflammation in PAP, but 10 percent of cases involve complicating nocardiosis.

224. The answer is A. *(Robbins, ed 3. pp 107-110.)* Fat embolism syndrome can supervene as a complication within 3 days following severe trauma to the long bones. However, the pathogenesis must be regarded as unknown because simple entrance of microglobular fat into the circulation as a result of damage to small vessels in marrow tissue occurs in over 90 percent of patients with trauma and bone fracture, yet the syndrome occurs in only a minority of such patients. Laboratory and clinical findings can simulate those of intravascular coagulopathy, which may be a component of fat embolism syndrome, with a major difference of split products of fibrin seen mainly in intravascular coagulopathy. Plasma levels of free fatty acids are elevated in fat embolism and may contribute to pulmonary vascular alterations. At autopsy fat material can be demonstrated in fat stains of frozen sections of lung, brain, and kidney in patients who had the syndrome.

225. The answer is A. *(Robbins, ed 3. pp 1250-1252.)* Thymomas are tumors of epithelial cells containing variable amounts of lymphocytes with the lymphocytic component either a major or minor contributor to the bulk. Despite the degree of lymphocytic participation in thymomas, the tumor is defined as one arising from thymic epithelial cells with the lymphocyte component considered mainly to be incidental. The lymphocytes per se in thymomas are not neoplastic and are merely secondary participants. About 90 percent of thymomas are benign and occur at a mean age of 50 years. They are very rare in children. Most thymomas arise from the anterosuperior portion of the mediastinum, but if they attain large size they may occupy most of the mediastinum. Malignant thymomas are diagnosed histologically by a finding of nuclear atypicality, accompanied by capsular invasion, with or without lymphatic or vascular invasion. If lymphatic or vascular invasion can be unequivocally demonstrated, the tumor is probably malignant. Thymomas have been noted in association with myasthenia gravis, red cell aplasia, collagen vascular diseases such as lupus, and states of reduced gamma globulin. The differential diagnosis of thymomas includes Hodgkin's disease and large-cell lymphomas.

226. The answer is D. *(Anderson, ed 8. pp 922-924.)* The chest x-ray in this clinical example demonstrates a central mass in the region of the hilum of the right lung. The differential diagnosis of a radiographic central mass includes consideration of undifferentiated small-cell carcinoma, sarcoidosis, lymphoma, and, less commonly, other forms of bronchogenic carcinoma. In sputum cytology, small-cell carcinomas demonstrate clusters of lymphocytelike tumor cells in strands, with adjacent tumor nuclei indentation (nuclear molding). The incidence of carcinoma of the lung in males is dropping somewhat, but the overall incidence continues because of greater numbers of women taking up the cigarette habit in recent years, with many of these women starting in their teens. As a consequence, oat-cell carcinoma is being seen with greater frequency in women.

227. The answer is E. *(Anderson, ed 8. pp 431-432, 860-861.)* Gomori's methenamine-silver staining technique emphasizes the pseudohyphae and yeast forms of *Candida* species. The pattern of vessel invasion is characteristic of many pathogenic fungi, including *Candida*. Such infections tend to occur in immunologically suppressed patients with other severe, usually neoplastic, diseases.

228. The answer is C. *(Anderson, ed 8. pp 860-861. Rosai, ed 6. pp 245-246.)* Infection by the protozoan *Pneumocystis carinii* is characterized by the presence of oval and helmet-shaped organisms whose capsules are made more visible by use of Gomori's methenamine-silver staining technique. This organism, although having low virulence, is opportunistic, for it is often seen to attack severely ill, immunologically depressed patients.

229. The answer is D (4). *(International Symposium on Legionnaire's Disease, Ann Intern Med 90:491, 1979. Stout, N Engl J Med 306: 466, 1982.)* Since the widely publicized outbreak of Legionnaire's disease at an American Legion convention in Philadelphia in 1976, Legionnaire's bacillus (*Legionella pneumophila*) has been isolated in various buildings and institutions, especially in air ventilation systems, air conditioners, and even in tap water, faucets, and shower heads in a large hospital. The organism responsible is a gram-negative bacillus that is difficult to isolate and stain in tissues and that causes a patchy alveolar space infiltration of polymorphonuclear leukocytes, scattered round cells, and histiocytes. Silver stains may be used to identify the bacilli within inflammatory cells. It is possible but not expeditious to gain supporting clinical evidence that the organism is responsible for pneumonitis by such means as lung biopsy and serum agglutination, but tracheal aspirates may contain this rare organism, which can be identified relatively rapidly via direct immunofluorescence in large hospital laboratories. Successful termination of the infection has been achieved with erythromycin and tetracycline.

230. The answer is E (all). *(Robbins, ed 3. pp 729-732.)* Bronchiectasis is a chronic necrotizing infection of the bronchi and bronchioles associated with abnormal dilatation of these airways. It is not clear whether obstruction leads to the dilatation and infection, or whether the infection is the primary lesion. Evidence for both hypotheses is provided by the associations of bronchiectasis with asthma, chronic sinusitis, avitaminosis A, and fibrocystic disease.

231. The answer is E (all). *(Robbins, ed 3. pp 763-764.)* A handful of tumors are noted to arise in the nasal cavity and the paranasal sinuses with sufficient propensity to be considered unique to those regions. Among these are the squamous papilloma (Schneiderian), lymphoepithelioma, esthesioneuroblastoma (also called olfactory neuroblastoma), nasopharyngeal angiofibroma, isolated plasmacytoma, and carcinomas arising from the respiratory lining but which have an epidermoid differentiation and even transitional cells as seen in the bladder. Nasopharyngeal angiofibroma is a vascular tumor which can lead to heavy bleeding and occurs almost exclusively in young males. The Schneiderian or inverted squamous papilloma of the nasal cavity has a high rate of recurrence and rarely may behave aggressively.

232. The answer is C (2, 4). *(Murray, N Engl J Med 310:883, 1984.)* Recent work has shown that a markedly reduced and even absent production of lymphokines occurs in AIDS patients. T lymphocytes from AIDS patients have a reduced capacity to produce gamma interferon even in response to microbial antigen. In in vitro experiments, if normal lymphokines or gamma interferon is added to monocytes from AIDS patients, there is effective activity against intracellular microorganisms. B cells, including plasma cells, are not ordinarily decreased in AIDS patients, especially during the early phases of the disease, and may even be seen in increased numbers within the lymph nodes, as the helper T cells are reduced. Opportunistic infections in AIDS patients may result from reduced gamma interferon and other lymphokine production.

233. The answer is B (1, 3). *(Robbins, ed 3. pp 750-761.)* Malignant mesothelioma and adenocarcinoma are two neoplasms that may involve the pleural surfaces as seen in the gross photograph. Malignant mesothelioma arises from the pleural surfaces and is thus a pleural neoplasm developing in association with significant and chronic exposure to asbestos, usually occupationally incurred. As the malignant mesothelioma spreads, it lines the pleural surfaces including the fissures through the lobes of the lungs and results in a tight and constricting encasement. This restricts the excursions of the lungs during ventilation. Adenocarcinoma of the lung also may invade the pleural surfaces and spread in an advancing manner throughout the pleural lining surfaces. The differential diagnosis histologically between an epithelial type of malignant mesothelioma and an adenocarcinoma may be difficult and sometimes impossible without special techniques. Oat-cell carcinoma usually arises in the central portions of the lungs near the hilum and does not invade the pleura in a spreading fashion. Benign spindle (fibrous) mesothelioma of the lung arises as a discrete mass that is spherical to ovoid in shape in a subpleural configuration and expands as this localized mass without spread over the surfaces.

234. The answer is C (2, 4). *(Anderson, ed 8. pp 880-882.)* The morphologic features of usual interstitial pneumonia (UIP) include interstitial edema and edema with hyaline membrane formation within the small air spaces in early lesions. An infiltrate of monocytes and lymphocytes then occurs. Regenerating alveolar epithelium relines damaged alveoli by "growing over" the alveolar exudate and thus incorporates this material into the interstitium. Fibrosis follows and may produce a pattern of randomly communicating air spaces lined by fibrous walls and metaplastic epithelium referred to as "honeycomb lung." Many people with UIP survive for many years. No increase in the incidence of primary malignancy has been described.

235. The answer is E (all). *(Anderson, ed 8. pp 880-882.)* All the agents mentioned produce interstitial fibrosis if given in sufficient quantity over an extended period of time. Investigators have shown that the interstitial fibrosis associated with bisulfan may be the result of organization of intraalveolar fibrin and edematous fluid, with subsequent incorporation into the interalveolar septa. Reported oxygen damage is related to the concentration of oxygen and the duration of exposure. The response of the lung to these agents may represent a reaction that can follow pulmonary injury caused by several different agents.

236. The answer is D (4). *(Anderson, ed 8. pp 833-839.)* The photomicrograph shows classic hyaline membranes coating alveolar sacs and ducts and is diagnostic of the respiratory distress syndrome of the newborn. The eosinophilic, fibrinlike material is related to the alveolar surfactants. Atelectasis is usually also present, especially in premature infants. The deposited material appears not to form in utero, as it is found in infants who have breathed and is not found in stillborns. There is a direct correlation, however, between severity and the degree of prematurity.

237. The answer is E (all). *(Anderson, ed 8. pp 873-874.)* The presence of hyaline membranes indicates a diagnosis of acute alveolar injury, which can occur in all the conditions mentioned. Indeed, the alveoli-lining, fibrinlike material may be found in multiple conditions of circulatory compromise and in poor perfusion states, such as hypovolemia; it may also be seen where 100 percent oxygen has been utilized for longer than 32 hours (e.g., "shock lung" of Vietnam casualties). At autopsy, the lungs are relatively airless and heavy, and this finding is frequently accompanied by pulmonary edema and hemorrhage.

238. The answer is C (2, 4). *(Rosai, ed 6. p 256.)* Pulmonary hamartomas are not common tumors, but it is very important to recognize them radiologically as well as pathologically, because simple, conservative excision is curative. The lesion is composed of components of tissue normally found in the region where it develops, but in abnormal amounts and configurations. This is the definition of hamartomas in general. In the lung, they are composed of hyaline cartilage, variable smooth muscle, and respiratory epithelium-lined clefts. Minimal growth has been recorded with chest x-rays, but rapid growth (as seen in lung carcinoma) would be an unusual event for pulmonary hamartomas. They are never necrotic with cavity or air-fluid level formation.

239. The answer is E (all). *(Anderson, ed 8. pp 924-925.)* All the systemic symptoms and syndromes mentioned occur in conjunction with bronchogenic carcinomas of various histologic types. The most common endocrine manifestation is probably Cushing's syndrome, but the number and variety of tumor-associated endocrine syndromes have increased dramatically in recent years. Additional neuromuscular abnormalities associated with lung tumors include mental status changes ranging from impaired acuity to dementia, degenerative myopathy, and a myasthenia gravis-like syndrome. Hypercalcemia may be seen in patients with squamous carcinoma and large-cell carcinoma who have no evidence of bony metastases, but it is not seen in patients with oat-cell carcinoma.

240. The answer is B (1, 3). *(Anderson, ed 8. pp 843-845.)* The age of an infant of 2 years or less with acute respiratory distress syndrome manifested clinically by sternal retractions, fever, and rapid breathing suggests bronchiolitis. Infants who die of upper respiratory infections usually have pneumonia or bronchiolitis, and the causes most often involve respiratory syncytial virus, followed by parainfluenza virus, adenovirus, and *Mycoplasma pneumoniae*. These organisms can cause bronchiolitis, which is manifested pathologically by infiltration of inflammatory cells of the peribronchial tissues as well as the lumens and walls of the small airways. This will produce pinpoint narrowing of the small airways, which may or may not be seen at autopsy. Often the lungs will appear normal at autopsy unless close examination is done of the small airways.

241-244. The answers are: 241-A, 242-E, 243-D, 244-B. *(Rosai, ed 6. pp 257-277.)* Pulmonary tumors may be associated with characteristic clinical paraneoplastic syndromes, some of which are specific for a single tumor type. Ectopic hormonal production by the tumor itself accounts for some of the endocrine manifestations.

Other distant, systemic effects are obscure in etiology but may be secondary to as-yet-unidentified biogenic amines.

Oat-cell carcinomas are responsible for a great variety of syndromes, some caused by direct synthesis of such hormones as ACTH and serotonin. Other effects on the neuromuscular system are not well understood, such as central encephalopathy (toxic psychosis, dementia) and myasthenia gravis-like syndrome (Eaton-Lambert syndrome). While they do carry a poor prognosis, oat-cell carcinomas have responded to multiagent chemotherapy.

Lung tumors that involve the region of the pleura may produce peripheral effects referred to as hypertrophic pulmonary osteoarthropathy, with or without clubbing of the distal phalanges. There is no specific tumor cell type involved; any lung tumor may produce this effect as long as it involves the pleura or subpleura. The mechanism is unknown.

Many tumors throughout the body are capable of inducing hypercalcemia through ectopic parathormone production, prostaglandin effect, osteoblastic-osteolytic bone metastases, or a combination of all these. Examples outside the lung include parathyroid carcinoma, pancreatic carcinoma, renal cell carcinoma, hepatocellular carcinoma, and some ovarian tumors in young women. When hypercalcemia is present in lung cancer, the tumor is most often a squamous carcinoma, and the hypercalcemia is thought to be brought about by a parathormonelike substance.

Giant-cell carcinoma of the lung is one of the most lethal lung carcinomas, with practically no cures; fortunately, it is relatively rare.

245-248. The answers are: 245-B, 246-D, 247-C, 248-A. *(Robbins, ed 3. pp 753-756, 760-761.)* Squamous cell carcinoma, the most prevalent type of bronchogenic carcinoma (50 to 60 percent of cases), arises from bronchial lining cells. Squamous metaplasia and dysplasia precede the development of squamous carcinoma in many cases. Squamous metaplasia of the normal ciliated pseudostratified columnar respiratory epithelium is reversible, but dysplasia probably persists prior to the onset of in situ carcinoma.

Alveolar cell (bronchioalveolar) carcinoma, which arises from alveolar or bronchiolar lining cells, tends to be diffusely infiltrative and may be peripheral and subpleural. It often looks like pneumonitis on chest x-rays and even in the gross organ state.

Adenoid cystic carcinoma arises from the subbronchiole seromucous glands and has the same histopathologic appearance as carcinoma arising in the salivary glands. Uniform, dark-staining neoplastic duct and myoepithelial cells are seen peripheral to large pools of pale, basophilic mucosubstance, yielding a "sieve" or netlike tubular pattern.

Mesothelioma arises from the pleural lining mesothelial cells and may be predominantly glandular (epithelial) or spindle-cell (fibrous) in type. When malignant, it characteristically encases one or both whole lungs in a fashion like "cake frosting," thus restricting lung compliance.

Gastrointestinal System

DIRECTIONS: Each question below contains five suggested answers. Choose the **one best** response to each question.

249. The photomicrograph below is of a biopsy of a rectal lesion in a 50-year-old male with recent weight loss, bloody diarrhea, and night sweats. The arrow is pointing to

(A) a macrophage
(B) a tumor cell
(C) a lipodystrophy cell
(D) an ischemic glandular cell
(E) an ameba

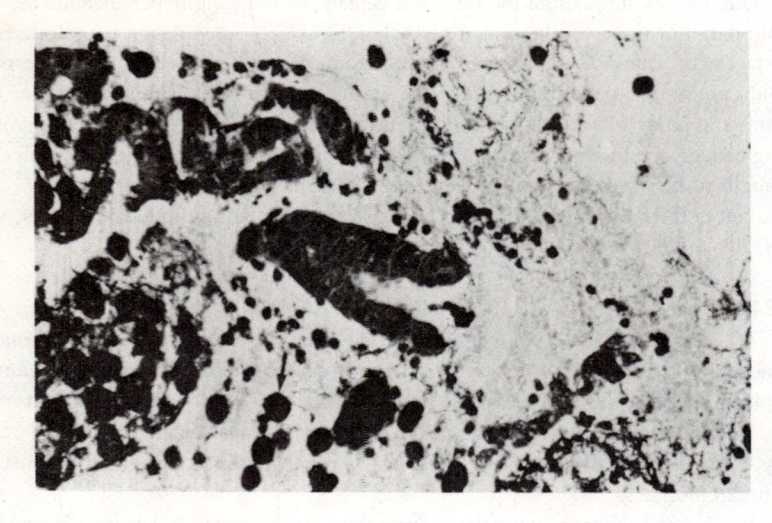

250. A 25-year-old schoolteacher was well until she attended a church bazaar where she partook copiously of barbecued turkey. The following day she developed bloody diarrhea, crampy pain, and tenesmus. A gastroenterologist who did not take a history took a colon biopsy specimen that showed mucosal edema, congestion, and numerous lymphoid cells in the lamina propria. Which of the following differential diagnoses would apply?

(A) Staphylococcal gastroenteritis vs. Crohn's disease
(B) Viral gastroenteritis vs. acute diverticulitis
(C) Colonic endometriosis vs. amebic dysentery
(D) Early ulcerative colitis vs. *Salmonella* colitis
(E) Bleeding hemorrhoids vs. Meckel's diverticulitis

251. A 32-year-old woman sees her physician because of "stiffness" and intolerance to cold temperatures in her fingers. Her face has a "masklike" quality. It would be appropriate in the systems review to ask about

(A) headaches and dizziness
(B) swallowing difficulties
(C) sun hypersensitivity
(D) thyroid trouble
(E) family history

252. The lesion seen in the photomicrograph below is referred to as

(A) adenoid cystic carcinoma
(B) lymphoepithelioma
(C) thyroglossal duct neoplasm
(D) Warthin's tumor
(E) sebaceous lymphadenoma

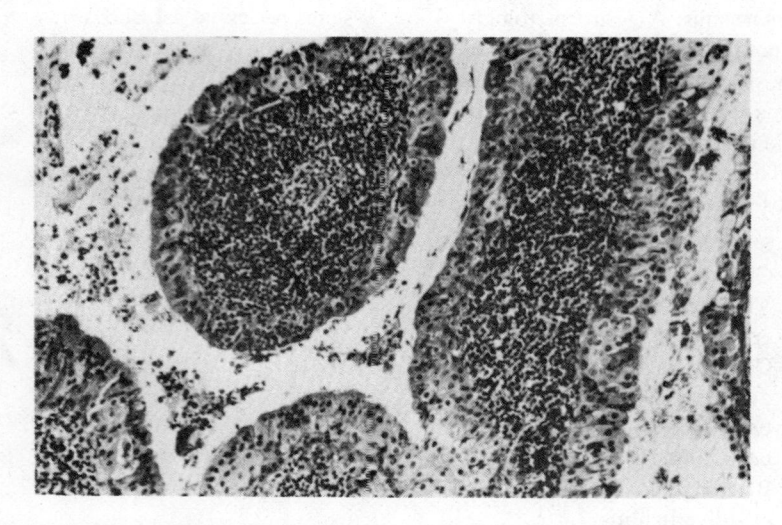

253. The most common malignant tumor of minor salivary glands is the

(A) pleomorphic adenoma
(B) adenoid cystic carcinoma
(C) acinic cell carcinoma
(D) mucoepidermoid carcinoma
(E) squamous cell carcinoma

254. The photomicrograph below is of a biopsy specimen obtained from the head of the pancreas in a middle-aged man with gastric outlet syndrome. The diagnosis is

(A) adenocarcinoma
(B) pseudocyst
(C) nesidioblastosis
(D) islet-cell carcinoma
(E) chronic pancreatitis

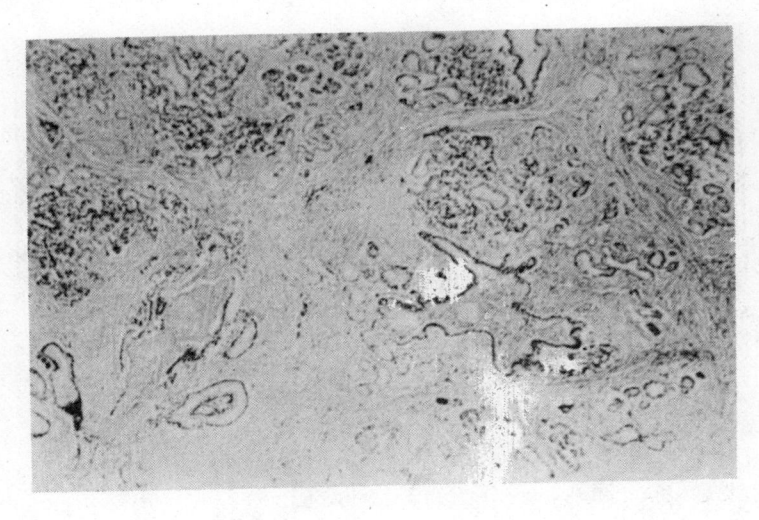

255. Adenocarcinoma of the colon, pictured below arising in a villous adenoma, also occurs with increased frequency in association with

(A) polypoid adenoma
(B) hemorrhoids
(C) chronic ulcerative colitis
(D) diverticulosis
(E) Meckel's diverticulum

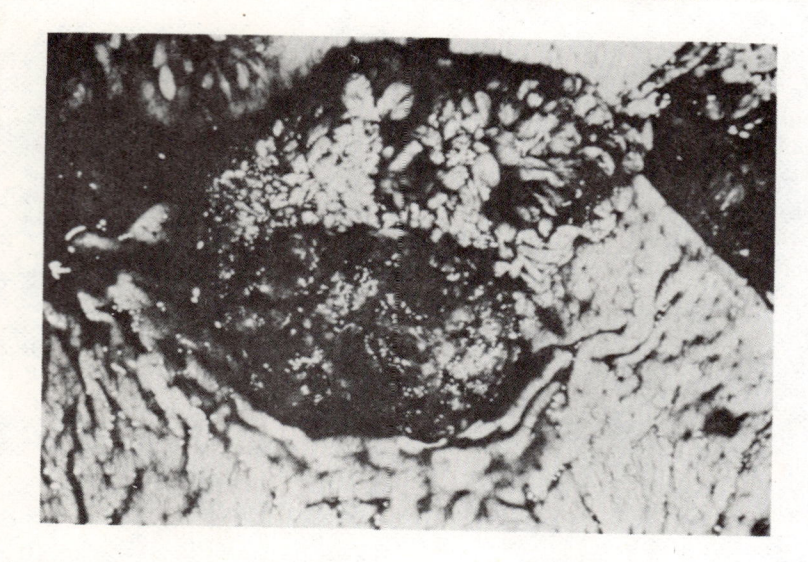

256. The photomicrograph below was prepared after a distal colonic biopsy was performed. The most likely diagnosis is

(A) clonorchiasis
(B) enterobiasis
(C) filariasis
(D) strongyloidiasis
(E) schistosomiasis

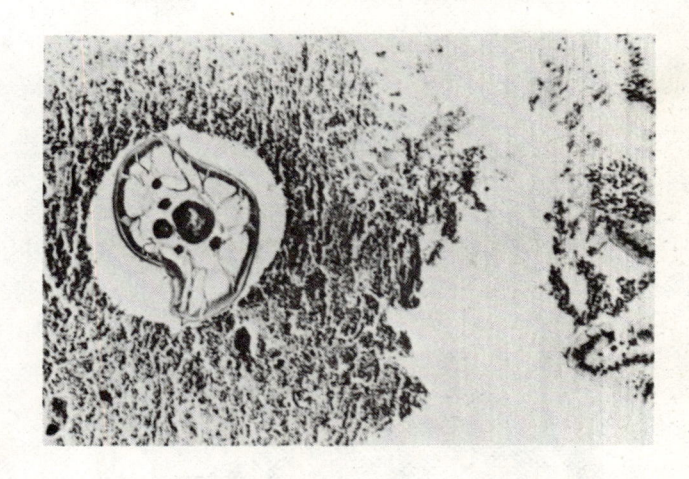

257. In the photograph below, an ulcerated mucosal lesion is shown at the anorectal junction. This lesion is probably

(A) a villous adenoma
(B) an epidermoid carcinoma
(C) a hemorrhoid
(D) a polypoid adenoma
(E) a mesenteric thrombus

258. A mononuclear portal inflammatory infiltrate that disrupts the limiting plate and surrounds individual hepatocytes (piecemeal necrosis), as shown in the photomicrograph below, is characteristic of

(A) ascending cholangitis
(B) chronic active hepatitis
(C) acute alcoholic hepatitis
(D) cholestatic jaundice
(E) nutritional cirrhosis

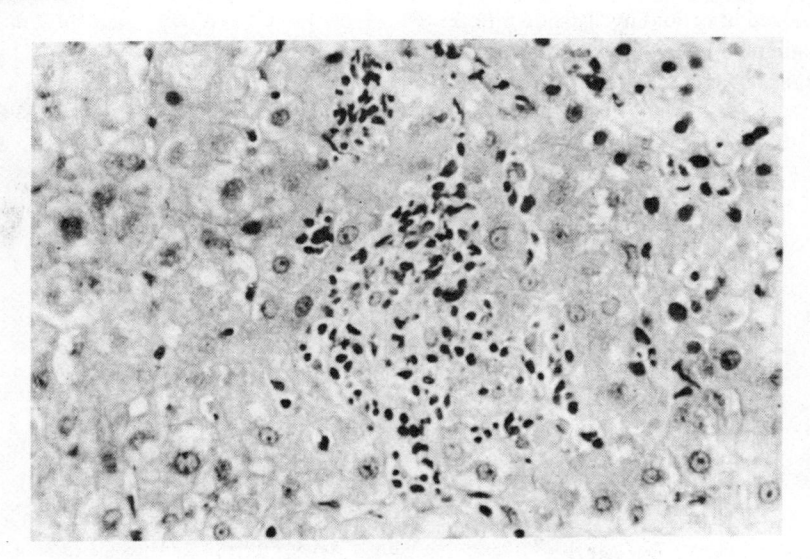

259. A middle-aged patient is undergoing surgical exploration for a tumor in the pancreatic fundus. No clinical history is given to the pathologist, who notes that the tumor has an "endocrine" appearance in frozen section. An appropriate step in the subsequent evaluation would be to consider

(A) immunoperoxidase
(B) brain scans
(C) computerized tomography
(D) celiac angiography
(E) immunofluorescence testing

260. A middle-aged male alcoholic has had repeated bouts of pancreatitis following periods of binge drinking. In recent months he has had a low-grade fever, and on examination a mass is palpated in the epigastrium. This mass, removed at celiotomy, is shown in the photograph below. What is the diagnosis?

(A) Pancreatic carcinoma
(B) Mucinous cystadenoma
(C) Perforated ulcer
(D) Pancreatic pseudocyst
(E) Cystic hepatoma

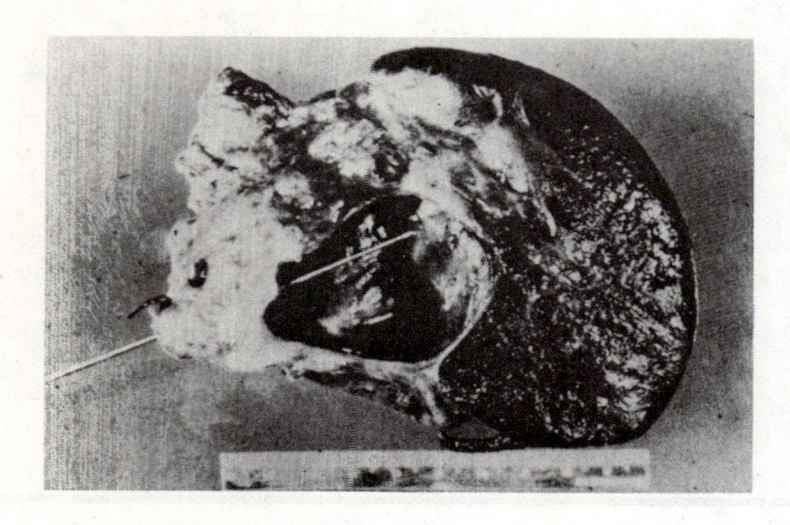

DIRECTIONS: Each question below contains four suggested answers of which **one** or **more** is correct. Choose the answer:

A	if	**1, 2, and 3**	are correct
B	if	**1 and 3**	are correct
C	if	**2 and 4**	are correct
D	if	**4**	is correct
E	if	**1, 2, 3, and 4**	are correct

261. Congenital pyloric stenosis
  (1) occurs predominantly in male infants
  (2) is manifested during the first few days of life
  (3) is manifested by vomiting, dehydration, and malnutrition
  (4) resolves spontaneously if symptomatic medical management is promptly instituted

262. Associative factors or indicators for a greater risk of gastric carcinoma include
  (1) large gastric ulcers
  (2) intestinal metaplasia
  (3) acute gastritis
  (4) gastric adenomatous polyps

263. Two subtotal colectomy specimens are sent to the laboratory with both showing a hemorrhagic cobblestone appearance of the mucosa. One, however, shows longitudinal grooving of the surface, which suggests
  (1) ischemic bowel disease
  (2) multiple polyposis syndrome
  (3) ulcerative colitis
  (4) Crohn's disease

264. An increased incidence of carcinoma of the esophagus is seen in
  (1) black men and women
  (2) residents of northern China
  (3) persons with Barrett's esophagus
  (4) persons who consume large amounts of alcohol

265. A 51-year-old male who is well known to the house staff of a metropolitan hospital for his chronic alcoholism is seen in the middle of the night in a toxic, stuporous state with massive hematemesis. Which of the following conditions should be considered as causative?
  (1) Esophageal varices
  (2) Mallory-Weiss syndrome
  (3) Gastric ulcers
  (4) Barrett's esophagus

266. Hormones found within the islets of Langerhans include
  (1) somatostatin
  (2) pancreatic polypeptide
  (3) glucagon
  (4) gastrin

267. A 67-year-old woman with a history of aortic stenosis (compensated) suffers from recurrent lower intestinal bleeding and anemia. Radiologic studies fail to disclose the bleeding site. Colonoscopy of the cecum and the terminal ileum finally shows multiple mucosal vascular "blushes," one of which is seen to be oozing blood. This lesion is shown in the photomicrograph below (taken from the terminal ileum, which was resected). These findings are compatible with

(1) arteriovenous malformations
(2) angiodysplasia
(3) vascular malformation
(4) Rendu-Osler-Weber syndrome

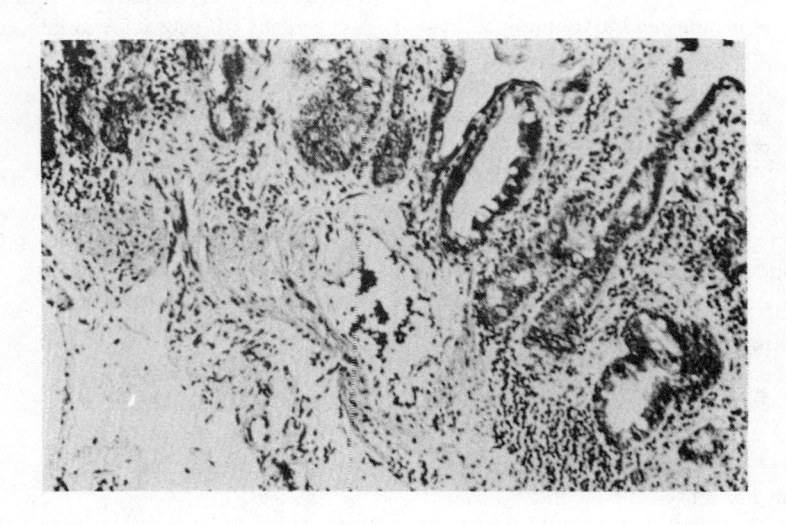

268. Which of the following statements would correctly characterize the colonic lesion shown in the photograph below?

(1) The prevalence is highest in people under 50 years of age
(2) The lesions are more common in women than in men
(3) Lesions occur most frequently in the ascending and transverse segments of the colon
(4) The lesions occur more commonly in the colon than in other portions of the gastrointestinal tract

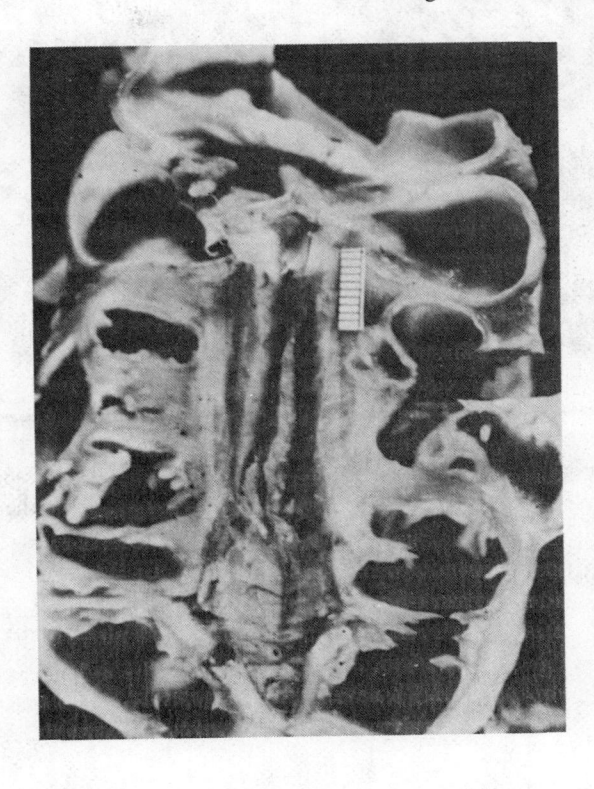

269. A patient who has ascending cholangitis, as illustrated in the photomicrograph below, probably also has

(1) common duct obstruction
(2) cholelithiasis
(3) gram-negative bacteremia
(4) cholestasis

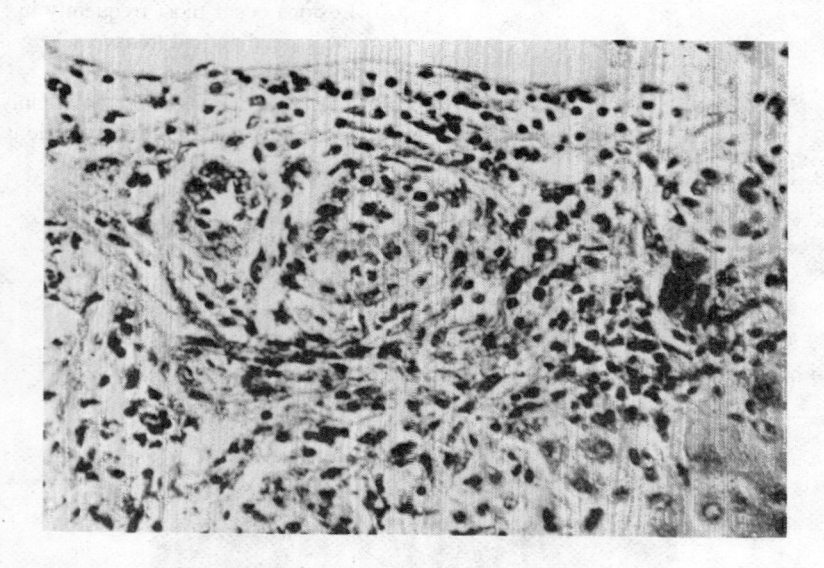

270. Hepatic granulomas may be seen in

(1) sarcoidosis
(2) tuberculosis
(3) histoplasmosis
(4) Hodgkin's disease

271. Anemia may be associated with gastric malignancies as the result of

(1) tumor ulceration of vascular structures
(2) achlorhydria with decreased intrinsic factor
(3) marrow myelophthisis secondary to bone marrow metastases
(4) iron malabsorption

272. Finely nodular (micronodular) cirrhosis, as evident in the photomicrograph below, is usually associated with

(1) massive hepatic necrosis
(2) increased fat within hepatocytes
(3) viral hepatitis
(4) alcohol abuse

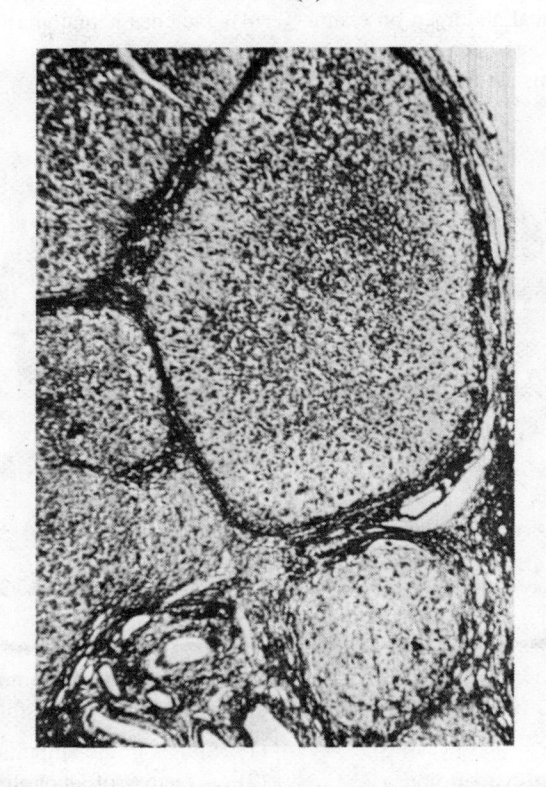

273. When gastric epithelial cells undergo malignant transformation, which of the following morphologic types of cancer can occur?

(1) Superficial spreading
(2) Polypoid
(3) Ulcerating
(4) Diffusely spreading

274. In primary biliary cirrhosis abnormal results are found in which of the following?

(1) Serum IgM
(2) Alkaline phosphatase
(3) Serum copper level
(4) Mitochondrial antibody test

275. The gross photograph below shows a portion of a liver removed during emergency surgery from a 26-year-old woman who had abdominal pain and a surgical abdomen on examination and who had been taking birth control pills. This disorder

(1) also occurs in infants and men
(2) was rare before birth control pills were introduced
(3) shows an absence of bile ducts
(4) includes hematoma formation

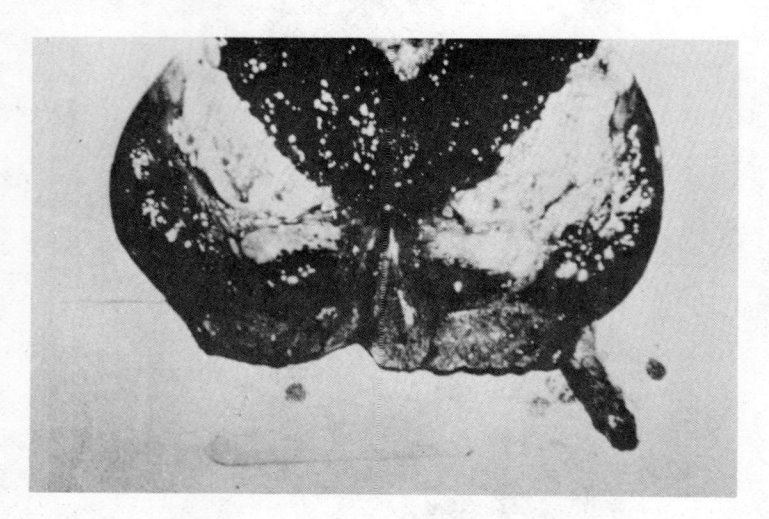

276. In a needle biopsy of the liver, diseases likely to be confused with cirrhosis include

(1) mesenchymal hamartoma
(2) infantile hemangioendothelioma
(3) liver cell adenoma
(4) focal nodular hyperplasia

277. The types of ulcers that develop in tuberculosis of the bowel classically include

(1) undermined ulcers
(2) transmural ulcers
(3) ulcers parallel to the long axis of the bowel
(4) ulcers perpendicular to the long axis of the bowel

278. Pancreatitis is commonly associated with which of the following?

(1) Stones in the ampulla of Vater
(2) A history of alcoholism
(3) Cholecystitis
(4) Hypertension

279. Intestinal lipodystrophy is an uncommon disorder that is associated with

(1) steatorrhea
(2) emaciation
(3) enlarged mucosal and mesenteric lymph nodes
(4) atrophic intestinal mucosa

Gastrointestinal System

DIRECTIONS: The groups of questions below consist of lettered choices followed by several numbered items. For each numbered item select the **one** lettered choice with which it is **most** closely associated. Each lettered choice may be used once, more than once, or not at all.

Questions 280-282

Match each of the following clinicopathologic descriptions with the appropriate bowel disorder.

(A) Ischemic colitis
(B) Granulomatous colitis (Crohn's colitis)
(C) Ulcerative colitis
(D) Pseudomembranous colitis
(E) Amebic colitis

280. Anal fistula

281. Normal mucosa

282. Flask-shaped ulcers

Questions 283-286

Match the following.

(A) Primary biliary cirrhosis
(B) Laennec's cirrhosis
(C) Both
(D) Neither

283. Associated with alcohol abuse

284. Bile duct proliferation

285. Xanthomas of skin and ulcerative colitis

286. Equal sex incidence

Questions 287-290

Match each of the following clinicopathologic syndromes with the appropriate disorder.

(A) Cronkhite-Canada syndrome
(B) Gardner's syndrome
(C) Turcot's syndrome
(D) Peutz-Jeghers syndrome
(E) Whipple's syndrome

287. Neoplasms of bone and soft tissues, and mandibular osteomas

288. Atrophy of the nails, alopecia, and hyperpigmentation

289. Lentigines of the buccal mucosa, lips, and fingers

290. Colonic polyps and brain tumors

Gastrointestinal System Answers

249. The answer is E. *(Robbins, ed 3. pp 362, 848-850, 858, 862.)* Numerous trophozoites of *Entamoeba histolytica* are seen in the photomicrograph. They resemble macrophages, but careful examination shows a somewhat larger size than ordinary macrophages. Other differences include multiple nuclei, which can be seen in some trophozoites, but the characteristic features are portions of ingested red cells and debris and material that have been internalized. A trichrome stain would stain the nuclei red while other elements would be other colors. The macrophages of Whipple's disease would have paler cytoplasm and when stained with PAS stain would demonstrate the multiple bacilliform structures. Ischemic damage to colonic and rectal mucosa can lead to atypical cell features, especially if regeneration is taking place at the same time; however, these cells do not resemble the trophozoites of amebas nor do the usual adenocarcinoma cells.

250. The answer is D. *(Robbins, ed 3. pp 319-321, 836-837, 859-862. Rosai, ed 6. p 516.)* Early stages of ulcerative colitis (UC) may be indistinguishable from gastroenteritis caused by *Salmonella choleraesuis* and *S. typhimurium*. In early stages, both diseases may show histologically a dense mononuclear inflammatory infiltrate in the lamina propria, occasional crypt abscesses, and mucosal edema and congestion. Even the respective clinical symptomatologies and colon x-ray changes may be similar, although marked vomiting should point to food poisoning. Salmonellae have been the cause of outbreaks and epidemics of acute gastroenteritis, and the cause has often been found to be contaminated fowl that has been insufficiently cooked to inactivate endotoxins.

251. The answer is B. *(Robbins ed 3. pp 190-193, 529.)* The constellation of Raynaud's phenomenon, acral sclerosis, and fibrotic tightening of the muscles of facial expression should raise the spector of progressive systemic sclerosis (scleroderma), a multisystem disease that involves the cardiovascular, gastrointestinal, cutaneous, musculoskeletal, pulmonary, and renal systems through progressive interstitial fibrosis. Small arterioles in the forenamed systems show obliteration caused by intimal hyperplasia accompanied by progressive interstitial fibrosis. Evidence implicates a lymphocyte overdrive of fibroblasts to produce an excess of rather normal collagen. Eventually, myocardial fibrosis, pulmonary fibrosis, and terminal renal failure ensue. Over half of all patients have dysphagia with solid food caused by the distal esophageal narrowing in the disease.

252. The answer is D. *(Robbins, ed 3. pp 791-792.)* Warthin's tumors occur mainly in the lower regions of the parotid gland, especially near the angle of the mandible, and on rare occasion may be bilateral. They are completely benign neoplasms although they carry some undesirable synonyms: adenolymphoma, which is a misnomer, and papillary cystadenoma lymphomatosum, a term undesirable both for the *lymphomatosum* part as well as its length. For these reasons most workers prefer the term Warthin's tumor. The pattern is highly characteristic of an epithelial surface lining of acidophilic cells that overlay benign lymphoid tissue elements, including germinal centers. The epithelial portion probably arises from early duct cells that become entrapped within developing parotid lymph nodes during embryogenesis. Sebaceous lymphadenoma would have sebaceous cells within the lymphoid tissue. Thyroglossal duct cyst is located in the midline of the neck but may be found extending up to the base of the tongue, and there is a similarity between the lymphoid islands seen in thyroglossal duct cysts and in Warthin's tumor; however, thyroid follicles may lead to the correct diagnosis in the former. Lymphoepithelioma is a tumor that is recognized by hyperplastic duct epithelium surrounded by lymphoid tissue. Myoepithelial islands embedded in lymphoid tissue may be seen in the minor and major salivary glands in Sjögren's syndrome.

253. The answer is B. *(Anderson, ed 8. pp 1040-1044.)* The adenoid cystic carcinoma is the most common malignant tumor of minor salivary glands, often arising in the minor salivary glands of the palate. They have a propensity for extending into perineural spaces and may metastasize by the lymphatic route. Pleomorphic adenoma is a benign neoplasm of major and minor salivary tissue but may be malignant in a minority. The mucoepidermoid carcinoma accounts for about 7 percent of all salivary gland tumors and occurs mainly in the parotids. Acinic cell carcinoma also occurs more commonly in the parotids than in the minor salivary glands.

254. The answer is E. *(Robbins, ed 3. pp 966-967.)* Gastric outlet syndrome with components of hypoalbuminemia, cholelithiasis, steatorrhea, and varying jaundice may occur in a "benign" form secondary to chronic fibrosing pancreatitis (CFP) or caused by carcinoma of the head of the pancreas (CAP). CFP has two forms: a calcifying type, as found in alcoholics, and an obstructive type that is associated with disease at the sphincter of Oddi (stenosis or calculus). In the obstructive type, duodenal obstruction may ensue. Histologically, there is loss of the acini (exocrine pancreas) in both types, with duct dilatation, chronic inflammation and fibrosis, and preservation of islet-cell nests (endocrine pancreas). It may be difficult to exclude adenocarcinoma in 100 percent of cases.

255. The answer is C. *(Robbins, ed 3. pp 869-873.)* Up to 33 percent of patients with chronic ulcerative colitis develop carcinoma. The cancers develop, on average, 16 years after onset of colitis. Cancer is found in a high percentage of villous adenomas. Many bowel adenocarcinomas probably arise from antecedent adenomatous polyps, as well as those in Gardner's and Turcot's syndromes.

256. The answer is B. *(Anderson, ed 8. pp 429-431.)* In the photomicrograph, a cross section of an *Enterobius* adult worm is shown. Apparent morphologic features of this nematode include the bilateral crests, the meromyarial type of musculature, and the noncellular cuticle with spines. *Enterobius vermicularis*, the agent responsible for the helminthic infection most common in the United States, usually produces pruritus ani as the outstanding and most disturbing symptom of enterobiasis (pinworm infection). *Enterobius* worms often attach themselves to the cecal mucosa and contiguous regions, but the usual host sites for schistosomiasis, clonorchiasis, and filariasis are the veins of the large intestine, the bile ducts, and the lymphatics, respectively. Elephantiasis is a characteristic feature in filariasis, and infection by *Strongyloides stercoralis* usually produces hyperemia and edema of the small intestinal mucosa.

257. The answer is B. *(Rosai, ed 6. pp 564-566.)* The lesion pictured is a basaloid or cloacogenic carcinoma that has the same gross appearance as the more common epidermoid carcinoma, although the lesion histologically resembles the basal cell carcinoma of the skin. The tumor arises from the anal canal within the transitional zone epithelium (anal columns). Some of these tumors resemble transitional epithelium, whereas others vary in their patterns, including one pattern similar to that of small-cell (oat-cell) carcinoma of the lung and other patterns that are totally undifferentiated. The prognosis for cloacogenic carcinoma is directly proportional to the degree of differentiation.

258. The answer is B. *(Rosai, ed 6. pp 602-614.)* Chronic hepatitis has been defined as an inflammatory process of the liver that lasts longer than 1 year and lacks the nodular regeneration and architectural distortion of cirrhosis. In chronic active hepatitis, an intense inflammatory reaction with numerous plasma cells spreads from portal tracts into periportal areas. The reaction destroys the limiting plate and results in formation of periportal hepatocytic islets. Prognosis is poor, and the majority of patients develop cirrhosis. Chronic persistent hepatitis is usually a sequela of acute viral hepatitis and has a benign course, without progression to chronic active hepatitis or cirrhosis. The portal inflammation does not extend into the periportal areas, thus differentiating it from chronic active hepatitis.

259. The answer is A. *(Robbins, ed 3. pp 986-987, 989. Schwarz, N Engl J Med 305:917, 1981.)* Any tumor of the pancreas seen to have an organoid (endocrine-like) pattern histologically, even in frozen section, should arouse suspicion of an islet-cell tumor, a carcinoid, or a component tumor of multiple endocrine neoplasia. The pathologist may be alert to this possibility if appropriate clinical information relating the patient's symptoms accompanies the biopsy specimen. Electron microscopy will show specialized types of electron-dense core granules ("neurosecretory" granules) in the cytoplasm in the presence of tumors of the amine precursor uptake decarboxylation class (APUDomas). Islet-cell tumors may contain alpha (glucagon), beta (insulin), delta (somatostatin), and pp (pancreatic polypeptide) dense-core granules. Direct staining of the hormones can be accomplished with immunoperoxidase, which contains the specific antibody to the hormone being sought and forms rust-brown granules that can be seen with the ordinary light microscope.

260. The answer is D. *(Robbins, ed 3. pp 968-969.)* Pseudocysts of the pancreas are so named because the cystic structure is essentially unlined by any type of epithelium. True cysts, wherever they are found in the body, are always lined by some type of epithelium, whether columnar cell, glandular, squamous, or flattened cuboidal cell. The pancreatic pseudocyst is most commonly found in a background of repeated episodes of pancreatitis. Eventual mechanical large duct obstruction by either an inflammatory process per se, periductal fibrosis, or an abscess along with inspissated duct fluid from secretions and enzymes leads to the expanding mass. The mass lesion may be located between the stomach and liver, between the stomach and colon or transverse mesocolon, or in the lesser sac. Drainage or excision is necessary for adequate treatment. Acute bacterial infection may complicate the course.

261. The answer is B (1, 3). *(Anderson, ed 8. p 1056.)* Congenital pyloric stenosis is seen predominantly in male infants at the age of approximately 3 weeks. The outlet pyloric lumen is narrowed by pronounced smooth muscle hypertrophy of the pylorus. Vomiting is seen following feedings and is remarkably projectile in view of the infant's age. In some cases, the pyloric area is palpable on abdominal examination. There is a classic "double-bubble" radiologic sign. The only cure is surgery.

262. The answer is C (2, 4). *(Robbins, ed 3. pp 821-825.)* There are many predisposing factors associated with the development of gastric carcinoma. Older knowledge has had to be altered, however, as significant exceptions to prior observations have come to light. One is the size of the gastric ulcer. While benign gastric peptic ulcers are generally small, being less than 2 cm in diameter, some 10 percent of benign gastric ulcers are greater than 4 cm in diameter. Chronic and long-standing atrophic gastritis predisposes to gastric cancer, but acute gastritis has no such risk. Intestinal metaplasia is a conversion of gastric epithelium into goblet cells in villous formation just as in the small bowel; this will occur in the background of inflammatory changes, including gastritis, and is a marker for the development of carcinoma but is not a precursor itself. Gastric polyps of an adenomatous type correlate highly with the development of carcinoma, especially if multiple.

263. The answer is D (4). *(Anderson, ed 8. pp 1064-1066.)* Hemorrhagic cobblestone appearance of the colon and small bowel may be seen in multiple states including inflammatory bowel disease, a term that can apply both to ulcerative colitis and regional enteritis (Crohn's disease). Other conditions that resemble cobblestoning of the mucosa of the bowel include multiple polyps such as occurs in Gardner's syndrome, Turcot's syndrome, familial polyposis, and multiple acquired polyps. Crohn's disease, however, differs from the others in that longitudinal ulcers may be present, yielding a long axis grooving, parallel to the long axis of the bowel. Such ulcers may also be seen in tuberculous enteritis; however, when inflammatory bowel disease is in the differential diagnosis, longitudinal ulcers are indicative of Crohn's disease.

264. The answer is E (all). *(Robbins, ed 3. pp 804-806.)* Carcinoma of the esophagus is not as prevalent in the United States as it is in Iran, portions of South Africa, and northern China where the incidence is almost 25 times greater than that of North America. Persons ingesting large amounts of alcohol have a 20- to 25-fold increase in risk, while tobacco use in the form of cigarettes, cigars, and pipes causes a 6- to 8-fold increase in risk. Black men and women have a 4-fold increase in the incidence of carcinoma of the esophagus over whites in the United States. Barrett's esophagus is defined as a metaplasia or transformation of the normal squamous mucosa into a glandular mucosa, usually in response to regurgitation of the gastric contents into the lower portions of esophagus as a result of a hiatal hernia. Glandular mucosa in the esophagus, if long standing, carries an increased risk of developing carcinoma and is preceded by forms of dysplasia.

265. The answer is A (1, 2, 3). *(Robbins, ed 3. pp 800-804.)* Chronic alcoholism predisposes to critical upper gastrointestinal (UGI) hemorrhaging, with the source of bleeding found in esophageal varices in many patients with portal hypertension secondary to Laennec's cirrhosis. The varices are mural esophageal veins that connect to high-pressure left gastric veins. Tearing of the lateral esophageal wall in the distal third (cardia) of the esophagus occurs in many alcoholics after protracted vomiting (Mallory-Weiss syndrome). Often overlooked in the alcoholic with severe UGI bleeding are multiple or single superficial mucosal ulcers in the setting of gastritis. Bleeding from these may be as severe as bleeding from esophageal varices. Barrett's esophagus involves gastric glandular mucosalike transformation of the esophageal squamous mucosa and nearly always results from reflux peptic esophagitis.

266. The answer is E (all). *(Robbins, ed 3. pp 986-989.)* The endocrine portion of the pancreas (islets of Langerhans) comprises approximately one million endocrine units containing multiple cell types, with the preponderance made up of beta cells that produce insulin, alpha cells that produce glucagon, and delta cells that produce somatostatin. Pancreatic polypeptide (PP) cells produce a vasoactive polypeptide. While gastrin secreting cells have not been identified in the normal human pancreas, it is well known that neoplasms, especially adenomas, of islet cells do produce gastrin (Zollinger-Ellison syndrome) and have cells with ultrastructural similarities to gastric G cells. Islet-cell adenomas and even carcinomas may produce insulin (insulinoma), glucagon (glucagonoma), and somatostatin (somatostatinoma). A rare islet-cell tumor known as a vipoma is associated with a syndrome that consists of achlorhydria, hypokalemia, and watery diarrhea (WDHA syndrome). These rare lesions are associated with the release of vasoactive intestinal peptide. Adrenocorticotropic hormone (ACTH), melanocyte-stimulating hormone (MSH), norepinephrine, serotonin, and vasopressin have all been identified in some secreting islet-cell tumors.

267. The answer is E (all). *(Moore, Arch Surg 111:381-388, 1976.)* Gastrointestinal angiodysplasia has received justifiable attention since 1960, when Margolis showed the feasibility of detecting the otherwise radiographically occult vascular lesions by means of selective mesenteric angiography. Numerous articles have clarified the nature of the disorder, which has been given numerous names, such as arteriovenous malformation, vascular malformation, vascular ectasia, cecal hemangioma, and angiodysplasia. Some researchers even doubted the existence of the entity, but most authors now agree that it exists, although it appears to have several types. These types include larger lesions occurring in the small and large intestine that tend to occur in young patients; smaller, occult lesions occurring in the right colon in elderly patients; and multiple telangiectatic types, as seen in hereditary hemorrhagic telangiectasia and the Rendu-Osler-Weber syndrome. The pathogenesis is still being debated, but chronic cecal mural pressure on muscular veins is thought to play a role in the type of angiodysplasia found in the right colon in older patients. Segmental bowel resection, electrocautery, and laser therapy are currently being compared for treatment efficacy. There appears to be a minor association with von Willebrand's disease and valvular heart disease.

268. The answer is D (4). *(Anderson, ed 8. p 1057.)* Diverticula occur most frequently in men over the age of 50 in the descending and sigmoid colon. The colon is the most commonly involved segment of the gastrointestinal tract. A majority of these lesions are not "true" diverticula, since the mucosa and muscularis mucosa herniate through defects in the muscular wall.

269. The answer is E (all). *(Anderson, ed 8. pp 1149-1150.)* Extrahepatic biliary obstruction caused by stones in the common duct may lead to jaundice, ascending cholangitis, and gram-negative sepsis. Prompt surgical intervention is indicated in order to remove the obstruction and prevent further sepsis. Liver biopsy may be helpful in chronic obstruction; in acute obstruction it may not serve to differentiate extrahepatic obstruction from intrahepatic cholestasis caused by viral hepatitis, drug reactions, or other diseases.

270. The answer is E (all). *(Rosai, ed 6. p 614.)* Hepatic granulomas may be part of numerous pathologic processes, including sarcoidosis, histoplasmosis, and tuberculosis. Granuloma formation is a feature of primary biliary cirrhosis, and some patients with Hodgkin's disease have noncaseating hepatic granulomas even in the absence of involvement of the liver by neoplastic cells. Unfortunately, in many cases, the etiology of hepatic granulomas cannot be determined with certainty.

271. The answer is A (1, 2, 3). *(Anderson, ed 8. p 1898.)* Atrophic gastritis is commonly associated with gastric carcinoma and regularly occurs concomitantly with pernicious anemia. Decreased HCl secretion (or achlorhydria) results from the decrease in number (or absence of) parietal cells that is typical in gastric atrophy. Pernicious anemia is also associated with achlorhydria. Blood loss from ulcerating tumor masses is common throughout the gastrointestinal tract. Since most iron is absorbed in the small intestine, iron malabsorption would not be directly associated with gastric tumors.

272. The answer is C (2, 4). *(Robbins, ed 3. pp 917-923.)* Chronic alcohol abuse may lead to Laennec's (micronodular) cirrhosis and is usually accompanied by fat accumulation. In massive hepatic necrosis from viral hepatitis or drug or chemical toxicity, the pattern of scarring and regeneration is random, scars are broad, and nodules form that are 3 to 4 cm in diameter. In alcoholic cirrhosis the lobules are regenerated liver parenchyma lacking central veins (pseudolobules).

273. The answer is E (all). *(Anderson, ed 8. pp 1084-1086.)* A number of classifications of gastric carcinoma have been proposed, because the tumor may assume different morphologies. Stout's classification is based on the direction of growth of the malignant cells and the characteristic gross configuration of the tumor. The superficial spreading type grows in the mucosa or submucosa and has a more favorable prognosis than the linitis plastica—a diffusely spreading type in which tumor infiltration involves all layers, with extensive lymphatic penetration.

274. The answer is E (all). *(Anderson, ed 8. pp 1150-1153.)* Laboratory findings in mitochondrial antibody tests, alkaline phosphatase, serum gamma globulins including IgM, and serum copper are all abnormal in primary biliary cirrhosis. This disorder in the United States and in Europe predominantly involves middle-aged women (a mean age of 52). It is characterized clinically by an insidious clinical course starting with pruritus, which gives way eventually to jaundice and hyperlipemia manifested by xanthomas of the palms of the hands, the arms, and the eyelids. The laboratory findings include a positive antimitochondrial antibody, elevated IgM, elevated alkaline phosphatase, hyperglobulinemia, elevated serum copper levels, and circulating immune complexes. Sjögren's syndrome is increased in this disorder as are some of the other collagen vascular diseases including scleroderma, lupus erythematosus, and thyroiditis. Histopathologic changes of the liver include portal triaditis with destruction of the limiting plate and of the bile ducts with eventual replacement of the portal triads by cirrhosis and a loss of bile ducts. Granulomas and xanthomatous giant cells are frequently seen.

275. The answer is E (all). *(Anderson, ed 8. pp 1188-1189.)* Hepatic adenomas (HAs) did occur before the introduction of oral contraceptive pills in the 1960s. Furthermore, these adenomas of liver cells do occur in women not taking birth control pills, infants, children, and even men, but they are exceedingly rare in these patients, and accompanying hemorrhage with hematoma formation appears not to occur unless the patient has been using birth control pills. Women taking oral contraceptives (mestranol) who develop liver cell adenomas are at risk of hemorrhage with rupture into the abdominal cavity and exsanguination. Microscopically, bile duct branches are not present in HAs, which helps to distinguish them from focal nodular hyperplasia of the liver, which is seem primarily in adult women.

276. The answer is D (4). *(Robbins, ed 3. pp 917-935.)* Focal nodular hyperplasia is likely to be confused with nutritional or alcoholic cirrhosis and on occasion, depending on the stage, with primary biliary cirrhosis also. Focal nodular hyperplasia is most likely a hamartoma and is recognized by a stellate scar formation grossly, which microscopically demonstrates increased fibrous connective tissue with scattered bile ductules and regenerative nodules of liver cells. Liver cell adenoma does not contain an increase in bile ducts and most often they are even absent. Hemangioendotheliomas in the liver in childhood show fibrosis and an increase in bile ducts, which are found at the periphery mainly with small capillaries throughout the lesion mixed with prominent endothelial cells. The mesenchymal hamartoma of the liver also has a fibrous stromal bed but has alternating clusters of proliferative bile ducts with epithelial cells distributed in an islandlike fashion throughout the lesion. There have been questions raised concerning the relationship of focal nodular hyperplasia to oral contraceptives, but the evidence is less than clear. Of interest is the fact that Felty's syndrome has been reported in association with focal nodular hyperplasia.

277. The answer is C (2, 4). *(Robbins, ed 3. pp 834-835.)* Primary intestinal tuberculosis denotes infection with ingested bovine tuberculosis bacilli. The secondary form occurs when a patient with pulmonary tuberculosis coughs up bacilli from the lung lesions and then swallows the infectious material. These bacteria, resistant to destruction by gastric acid, pass into the small intestine, where they enter the lymphatics of the ileum. Formation of tubercles in the encircling lymphatics of the intestine may lead to mucosal necrosis and subsequent ulceration. Classically, tuberculous ulcers are transversely oriented and have shaggy overhanging margins. The ulcers may penetrate deeply and occasionally perforate.

278. The answer is A (1, 2, 3). *(Anderson, ed 8. pp 1237-1239.)* Most of the postulated etiologic factors for pancreatitis invoke mechanisms of partial or complete obstruction of the pancreatic duct and increased pancreatic secretion. Malignant hypertension may cause vascular necroses in the pancreas, but only focal necrosis of pancreatic tissue occurs, not general pancreatitis.

279. The answer is A (1, 2, 3). *(Robbins, ed 3. pp 848-851.)* Whipple's disease (intestinal lipodystrophy) is characterized by steatorrhea, accumulation of lipids in lacteals and in mucosal and mesenteric lymph nodes, and deposition of PAS-positive carbohydrate-protein complexes in histiocytes within the lamina propria of the intestinal villi and in other tissues. Although the villi of the small intestine become blunted and distended by masses of histiocytes, the mucosa is not atrophic. Patients who have Whipple's disease are emaciated and often have gray-brown melanin pigmentation of the skin. Evaluation of an intestinal biopsy to detect glycoprotein-laden histiocytes in the villi may be necessary to confirm a diagnosis, because patients often have many nonspecific systemic symptoms.

280-282. The answers are: 280-B, 281-D, 282-E. *(Philips, N Engl J Med 305:603, 1981. Robbins, ed 3. pp 836-840, 858-862. Rosai, ed 6. pp 460-464, 506-517, 915.)* The inflammatory bowel diseases, which include classic ulcerative colitis, granulomatous bowel (Crohn's) disease, bacterial colitis, and pseudomembranous colitis, have some similar histologic and clinical features. For instance, features of both ulcerative colitis and Crohn's disease sometimes appear in a single patient, which does not always allow a definitive diagnosis. Clinical follow-up with appropriate observation of the natural course will usually clarify the dilemma. Useful criteria for diagnosing Crohn's disease include transmural lymphoid aggregates, submucosal lymphectasia, granulomas, uninvolved bowel segments (skip areas), and a propensity for forming fissures and cutaneous fistulas in the perineum and occasionally in the vulva. Classic ulcerative colitis (UC) usually is nontransmural, is confined to the superficial bowel, and shows diffuse involvement, gland crypt abscesses, and dense mononuclear lamina propria inflammation. There are, however, unclassifiable types with symptoms that may overlap with those of Crohn's colitis (CC). Pyoderma gangrenosum of the lower extremities may be present, but enterocutaneous fistulae are not features of UC. UC carries a greater risk of developing adenocarcinoma of the bowel, but it is clear that CC may also be associated with development of carcinoma, albeit to a lesser degree than UC.

Pseudomembranous colitis is a distinct condition tending to arise in older patients postoperatively or when antibiotics such as clindamycin and lincomycin have been given. The colonic mucosa is strangely normal microscopically, but there is a superficial "clot" of mucin overlying the surface mucosa that contains numerous neutrophils. Some researchers believe ischemia may play a role in pathogenesis.

Amebic colitis is characterized clinically by bloody diarrhea, cramping, and tenesmus. In these findings it is similar to UC, but it is unique in that large mucosal ulcers have undermining peripheral edges resembling the shape of an Erlenmeyer flask. The organisms resemble large macrophages but stain intensely with periodic acid Schiff reagant (PAS). Amebic colitis has recently been described in male homosexuals.

283-286. The answers are: 283-B, 284-C, 285-A, 286-D. *(Anderson, ed 8. pp 1110-1111, 1141-1143, 1150-1153.)* Alcohol abuse, alcoholic hepatitis, and Laennec's (micronodular) cirrhosis are closely related. Cirrhosis of alcoholic liver disease is characterized by micronodules of regenerated hepatocytes surrounded by peripheral fibrosis. Central veins are only rarely seen within the pseudonodules. The fibrotic network contains varying bile duct proliferation and chronic inflammatory cells.

Atypical bile duct proliferation is a diagnostic feature of primary biliary cirrhosis, although it also occurs in Laennec's cirrhosis. High levels of serum cholesterol result in dermal xanthomas and ulcerative colitis and are associated with primary biliary cirrhosis. Primary biliary cirrhosis (PBC) presents in middle-aged women, who experience pruritus, jaundice, and nontender hepatomegaly. Alkaline phosphatase levels in the serum are elevated, and antimitochondrial antibodies can be demonstrated. There is evidence that PBC is autoimmune, with sensitized T cells involved in the granulomatous and bile duct inflammatory lesions. There is a gradual loss of intrahepatic bile ducts after an initial stage of lymphocytic and granulomatous inflammation. This is followed by a stage of bile duct proliferation. The third stage is active fibrosis.

Laennec's cirrhosis occurs more frequently in men. Primary biliary cirrhosis occurs much more frequently in women (9:1 ratio).

287-290. The answers are: 287-B, 288-A, 289-D, 290-C. *(Anderson, ed 8. pp 1077-1082, 1075-1076.)* Multiple polyps of the colon and small intestine may be acquired in middle age, or they may be familial and transmitted as mendelian dominant traits. These polyposis syndromes can be associated with a number of abnormalities in sites seemingly unrelated to the development of the gastrointestinal tract.

In Turcot's syndrome, for instance, central nervous system tumors can be found associated with colonic polyposis. The central nervous system tumors are generally malignant and may have astrocytic components.

In the Cronkhite-Canada syndrome, in addition to multiple polyposis of the colon, there are changes of the skin including alopecia, nail atrophy, and hyperpigmentation. In addition, polyps are found in the stomach and small intestine. These have histopathology of retention or juvenile polyps.

In Gardner's syndrome, in addition to polyps of the colon there are lesions of the bone and soft tissues in the form of fibromas, osteomas, and keratocytes. Fibromatosis may also be seen in the abdominal mesentery, especially if colectomy is done in therapy for the colonic polyposis. In Puetz-Jeghers syndrome there are lentingines or melanin spots occurring in the mouth, lips, and over the fingers, in addition to the small intestinal polyps occurring in the upper small intestine. However, polyps may also be found in the colon and the stomach in some cases. These polyps are of a hamartomatous nature. Whipple's disease is an intestinal lipidystrophy and is not ordinarily associated with polyposis.

Endocrine System

DIRECTIONS: Each question below contains five suggested answers. Choose the **one best** response to each question.

291. The most common etiologic factor in Cushing's syndrome is

(A) adrenal adenoma
(B) bilateral adrenal hyperplasia
(C) adrenal carcinoma
(D) ectopic adrenal tissue
(E) hypercorticism secondary to non-endocrine malignant tumors

292. An adult patient with seizure disorder controlled by phenytoin (Dilantin) is noted to have enlarged gingivae. Select the proper course of action below.

(A) No action necessary because this is a drug effect
(B) No action necessary because this is a physiologic response
(C) Schilling differential
(D) Roentgenograms of the maxillae and mandible
(E) Biopsy with histologic examination

293. The combination of cystic bone lesions, precocious puberty, and patchy skin pigmentations is known as

(A) Albright's syndrome
(B) Letterer-Siwe disease
(C) Asherman's syndrome
(D) Morquio's disease
(E) Schaumann's disease

294. Which of the following histologic types of thyroid carcinoma carries the best prognosis?

(A) Follicular carcinoma
(B) Medullary carcinoma
(C) Anaplastic carcinoma
(D) Papillary carcinoma
(E) Malignant lymphoma

295. The degree of hyperfunction in parathyroid glands affected by parathyroid adenoma depends on

(A) the type of cell involved
(B) the location of the adenomas in the neck or mediastinum
(C) the rate of growth of the adenoma
(D) the weight of parathyroid tissue
(E) serum calcium levels

296. A 42-year-old man complains of recently having to change his shoe size from 9 to 10½, and he also says that his hands and jaw are now larger. The disorder is most likely mediated through

(A) prolactin
(B) ACTH
(C) somatomedin
(D) pitressin
(E) thyrotropin

297. The section of tissue shown in the photomicrograph below (taken under low power) was probably removed from a patient who has

(A) a normal thyroid gland
(B) colloid storage goiter
(C) Graves' disease
(D) Riedel's struma
(E) Hashimoto's thyroiditis

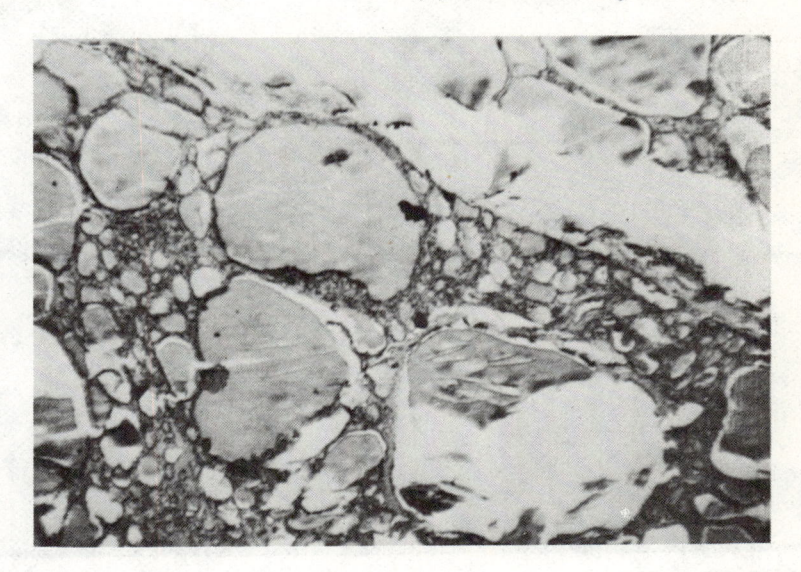

298. Select the one tumor among the following that will have the longest, most indolent clinical course if metabolic tumor effects are controlled.

(A) Parathyroid carcinoma
(B) Adrenal corticol carcinoma
(C) Thyroid medullary carcinoma
(D) Thyroid anaplastic carcinoma
(E) Neuroblastoma after 1 year of age

299. Secondary hyperparathyroidism may be caused by

(A) chronic renal insufficiency
(B) Hashimoto's thyroiditis
(C) pituitary hyperplasia
(D) alcoholic hepatitis
(E) acute pancreatitis

300. A perimenopausal woman complains of slight swallowing difficulty, fatigue, and a change in bowel habits. The photomicrograph below is of her thyroid gland. This disorder is

(A) subacute thyroiditis
(B) thyrotoxicosis
(C) autoimmune thyroiditis
(D) Riedel's thyroiditis
(E) conversion hysteria

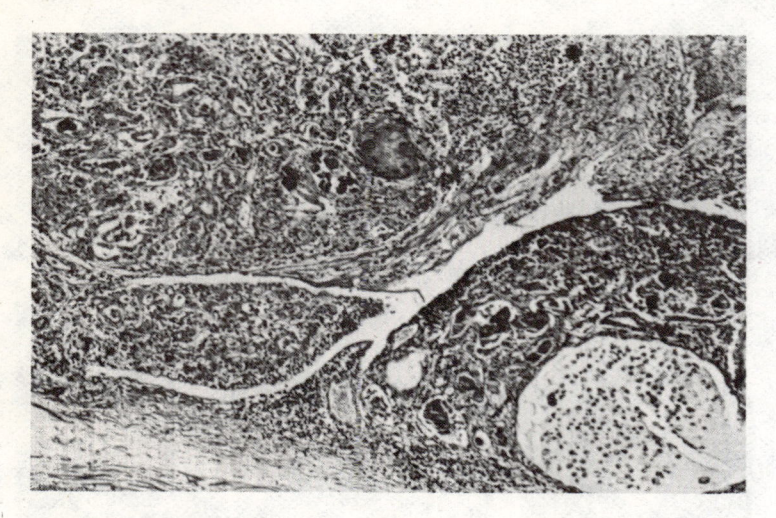

301. Which of the following neoplastic conditions has been identified in patients with Hashimoto's thyroiditis?

(A) Malignant lymphoma
(B) Multiple endocrine neoplasia type IIa
(C) Parathyroid carcinoma
(D) Thyroid sarcoma
(E) Squamous carcinoma

302. Primary hyperaldosteronism is associated with all the following features EXCEPT

(A) carcinoma
(B) adenoma
(C) muscle weakness
(D) expansion of intravascular volume
(E) edema

Questions 303-304

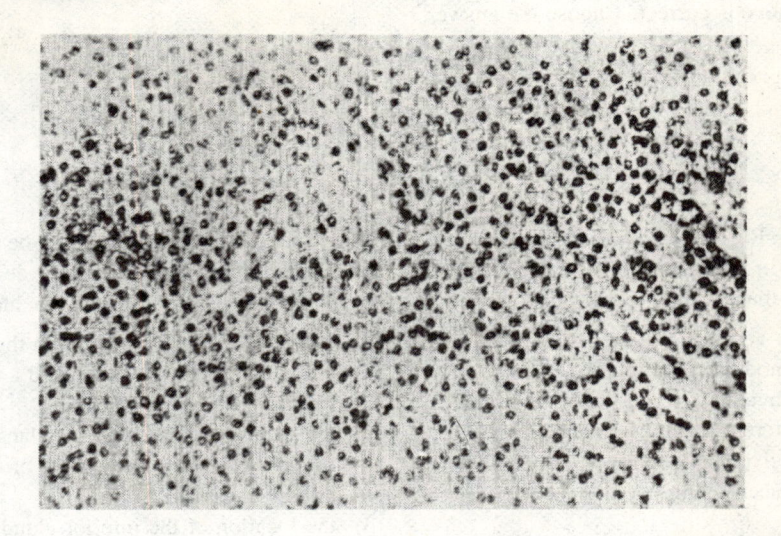

303. A young patient with renal insufficiency and bone lesions undergoes surgical neck exploration for investigation of a metabolic defect. The photomicrograph above indicates that the patient has

(A) malignant lymphoma
(B) chronic thyroiditis
(C) thyroid hyperplasia
(D) parathyroid hyperplasia
(E) Castelman's disease

304. These bone lesions represent

(A) lymphomatous dissemination
(B) osteomyelitis
(C) osteomalacia
(D) osteopetrosis
(E) osteochondrosis

305. A 49-year-old man who smokes two packs of cigarettes a day presents with a lung mass on x-ray and recent weight gain. Laboratory examination shows hyponatremia with hyperosmolar urine. The patient probably has

(A) renal failure
(B) pituitary failure
(C) Conn's syndrome
(D) cardiac failure
(E) inappropriate ADH

DIRECTIONS: Each question below contains four suggested answers of which **one** or **more** is correct. Choose the answer:

A	if	**1, 2, and 3**	are correct
B	if	**1 and 3**	are correct
C	if	**2 and 4**	are correct
D	if	**4**	is correct
E	if	**1, 2, 3, and 4**	are correct

306. Renal lesions that are more common in patients who have diabetes mellitus than in the general population include

(1) nodular glomerulosclerosis
(2) hyaline arteriolosclerosis of the efferent renal arterioles
(3) glycogen nephrosis
(4) necrotizing papillitis

307. Pheochromocytomas have been demonstrated in which of the following conditions?

(1) Multiple endocrine neoplasia, type IIb
(2) Von Hippel-Lindau syndrome
(3) Multiple endocrine neoplasia, type IIa
(4) Sturge-Weber syndrome

308. The parathyroid glands can be described in terms of anatomic or developmental characteristics that include

(1) embryonic development from the endodermal tissue of the third and fourth pharyngeal pouches
(2) the location of the superior glands normally at the lower border of the cricoid cartilage
(3) the location of the inferior glands sometimes in the superior mediastinum of the thorax
(4) a spatial relationship with the thyroid and a temporal developmental relationship with the thymus

Endocrine System

DIRECTIONS: The groups of questions below consist of lettered choices followed by several numbered items. For each numbered item select the **one** lettered choice with which it is **most** closely associated. Each lettered choice may be used once, more than once, or not at all.

Questions 309-312

For each of the conditions possibly related to carcinomas of the thyroid, select the appropriate diagnosis.

- (A) Papillary carcinoma of the thyroid gland
- (B) Medullary carcinoma of the thyroid gland
- (C) Both
- (D) Neither

309. Metastases occur most frequently in adjacent lymph nodes of the neck

310. Associated with psammoma bodies

311. Associated with other endocrine tumors

312. Rapidly growing, focally infiltrative growth with a poor prognosis

Questions 313-317

For each of the disorders listed, select the most appropriate feature or description.

- (A) Panhypopituitarism in adults
- (B) Isolated growth hormone deficiency in children
- (C) Acute hemorrhage into a pituitary tumor
- (D) Postpartum pituitary necrosis
- (E) A common cause of diabetes insipidus in children

313. Hand-Schüller-Christian disease

314. Sheehan's syndrome

315. Simmonds' disease

316. Pituitary apoplexy

317. Ateliotic dwarfism

Endocrine System

Answers

291. The answer is B. *(Isselbacher, ed 10. pp 641-646.)* Cushing's syndrome may be the result of bilateral adrenal hyperplasia, adrenal neoplasia, or excessive use of adrenocorticotropic hormone or glucocorticoids. However, bilateral adrenal hyperplasia is the most common etiologic factor. The clinical manifestations of the syndrome whether induced by ectopic ACTH (small-cell carcinoma of the lung), exogenously, or endogenously by the adrenal are similar in all. Plasma and urine cortisols and urinary 17-hydroxycorticoid levels are usually elevated.

292. The answer is C. *(Robbins, ed 3. pp 773-774.)* There are multiple causes for enlarged gingivae, some of which are physiologic and transient and require no investigative or necessary therapeutic measures. Among these is pregnancy, which under the stimulation of hormones produces a vascular proliferation that presents histology similar to that of pyogenic granuloma. Another physiologic response is that seen at puberty. Nutritional disorders such as vitamin C deficiency can also lead to enlarged gums. Phenytoin (Dilantin) has been known to cause enlargement of the gums in some patients. If the setting does not suggest a physiologic response, consideration should be given to leukemia, especially monocytic leukemia, which can present enlarged gums as the initial manifestation. Thus, a complete blood count, including a Schilling differential to enumerate the white cells, is indicated.

293. The answer is A. *(Anderson, ed 8. pp 1021, 1263-1265, 1759.)* The triad of cystic bone lesions, precocious puberty, and patchy brownish skin pigmentation is known as Albright's syndrome. The bone lesions are those of fibrous dysplasia and apparently result from abnormal activity by the bone-forming mesenchyma. Packing of the medullary cavity by fibrous tissue that contains trabeculae of poorly mineralized fibrous bone is seen in the lesions. Recent reports have described cases of fibrous dysplasia in both males and females who also have had a wide variety of endocrine abnormalities, including hyperthyroidism, acromegaly, and Cushing's syndrome.

294. The answer is D. *(Anderson, ed 8. pp 1410-1417.)* Carcinoma of the thyroid is more common than primary malignant lymphoma and is divided into four histologic subtypes: papillary, follicular, medullary, and anaplastic or undifferentiated. Rare tumors include squamous carcinoma, mucinous carcinoma, and mucoepidermoid carcinoma. The 10-year survival rate for patients with papillary carcinoma is

80 to 95 percent, and that for those with follicular carcinoma is 50 to 70 percent. Papillary carcinomas may have local invasion and distant metastases, but patients with papillary carcinoma may live for long periods of time even with bony metastasis. Papillary carcinoma of the thyroid is the type seen in postradiation, but papillary carcinoma may arise without an antecedent history of radiation. The prognosis at 10 years for patients with medullary carcinomas is 65 percent, while that for those with anaplastic carcinomas is markedly reduced to 5 to 10 percent with a median survival of about 2 months following diagnosis.

295. The answer is D. *(Rosai, ed 6. pp 382-392.)* Primary hyperparathyroidism can be caused by adenomas, chief cell hyperplasia, water-clear cell hyperplasia, or carcinoma. In the large majority of reported cases, single adenomas constitute the cause. Whether the histologic abnormality is hyperplasia or adenoma, a distinct correlation between the degree of hyperfunction and the weight of the parathyroid tissue has been demonstrated.

296. The answer is C. *(Henry, ed 17. pp 301-303. Robbins, ed 3. pp 1194-1196.)* The constellation of cartilaginous-periosteal soft tissue growth of the distal extremities (acromegaly) and growth of the skull and face bones is characteristic of hypersecretion of growth hormone (GH) from an anterior pituitary adenoma. GH modulates the production of hepatic somatomedin (sulfation factor). Somatomedins are small peptides that act on the target organs after being synthesized under the influence of growth hormone. They have insulinlike properties but are immunologically distinct from insulin. In addition to acral-skeletal expansion, patients with hyperpituitarism of the adult-onset variety (occurring after epiphyseal plate closure) have organomegaly, including increased size of the heart, kidneys, liver, and spleen. Cardiac failure is usually the mechanism of death.

297. The answer is B. *(Anderson, ed 8. pp 1402-1404.)* The histologic appearance of colloid storage goiter generally includes abnormally large, colloid-filled follicles compressing the intervening small or normal-sized follicles that contain very little colloid. The epithelium of the follicles is predominantly flat cuboidal, with occasional epithelial papillary structures protruding into the follicles. In primary hyperplasia with Graves' disease, the follicular epithelium is tall, with papillary infoldings and peripheral vacuolation of the colloid. Riedel's struma appears as a marked fibrous tissue replacement of the normal thyroid histology. In Hashimoto's thyroiditis, only remnants of thyroid follicles and epithelial cells are found in sheets of lymphocytes with germinal centers.

298. The answer is A. *(Robbins, ed 3. pp 1222-1224, 1228-1229, 1243, 1247-1248.)* Malignant tumors of the endocrine system are protean and varied in their manifestations; the prognosis depends a great deal on their clinical stage at presentation and whether metabolic derangements are present. Parathyroid carcinomas may be small and clinically nonapparent, with the effects of hypercalcemia causing the patient to seek medical care. Parathyroid carcinoma rarely kills through massive tumor dissemination, inanition, or superimposed infections; fatalities are due to renal damage secondary to hypercalcemia. Long-term survival of 12 to 14 years is not unusual with parathyroid carcinoma. Adrenal cortical carcinoma and anaplastic carcinoma have very short, rather stormy clinical courses, with few survivors at 2 to 3 years. Approximately 50 percent of patients are alive at 5 years with medullary carcinoma. If the patient with neuroblastoma is over 1 year of age, the outlook is grim, with less than 20 percent survival at the end of 2 years.

299. The answer is A. *(Robbins, ed 3. pp 1229-1230.)* Chronic hypocalcemia, whatever its origin, leads eventually to secondary hyperparathyroidism. Chronic renal failure is the most important cause, but secondary hyperparathyroidism also occurs in malabsorption syndromes, rickets, disseminated metastatic carcinoma, and multiple myeloma.

300. The answer is C. *(Robbins, ed 3. pp 1206-1208.)* Hashimoto's (autoimmune) thyroiditis is one of the conditions of chronic thyroiditis. It is not that uncommon in the United States. The stroma is permeated by a dense lymphoplasmacytic infiltrate with lymphoid follicles (germinal centers) that distorts and transforms thyroid follicles into collections of acidophilic cells (oncocytes, Hürthle-like cells). Not uncommonly, patients develop hypothyroidism as a result of follicle disruption, consisting of fatigue, myxedema, cold intolerance, hair coarsening, and constipation. Whereas subacute (DeQuervain's) thyroiditis, Riedel's thyroiditis, and psychosomatic complaints may cause common symptoms, biopsy findings of these disorders are distinctly different from those of Hashimoto's disease.

301. The answer is A. *(Robbins, ed 3. pp 1206-1208.)* Although there are conflicting reports in the literature, there appears to be a small risk of developing malignant lymphoma in a small percentage of cases of Hashimoto's thyroiditis. Some authors have claimed an increased incidence of thyroid carcinoma in Hashimoto's thyroiditis, but the known incidence of carcinoma in this form of thyroiditis has not been shown to be clinically significant. Since the lymphoid infiltrate in autoimmune thyroiditis may be histologically provocative, care must be taken by both the attending physician and the diagnosing pathologist in making a diagnosis of lymphoma in these patients.

302. The answer is E. *(Robbins, ed 3. pp 1237-1242.)* Edema is not a feature of primary hyperaldosteronism (Conn's syndrome), which is characterized by weakness, hypertension, polydipsia, and polyuria. The underlying physiologic abnormalities include alkaline urine, an elevated level of serum sodium, hypokalemic alkalosis, and excessive potassium loss by the kidneys. The level of serum aldosterone is elevated; that of plasma renin is suppressed. The elevated level of serum sodium causes expansion of the intravascular volume. A single adenoma has been described as the etiologic factor of primary hyperaldosteronism in the majority of patients, and carcinoma, multiple adenomas, and cortical hyperplasia have been cited occasionally as causes of this syndrome.

303. The answer is D. *(Robbins, ed 3. pp 1226-1230.)* Hypocalcemia resulting from any chronic cause may lead to hyperparathyroidism. The mechanism of hypocalcemia in chronic renal failure is thought to be related to phosphate retention. Sustained parathormone release results from the chronic hypocalcemia. The parathyroid hyperplasia under these circumstances may involve one, two, three, or all four parathyroid glands in the form of chief cell hyperplasia, frequently with scattered nests of eosinophilic, oxyphilic cells (oncocytes). There is an accompanying replacement of the intraglandular fat by the hyperplasia. Surgical extirpation is the treatment of choice.

304. The answer is C. *(Robbins, ed 3. pp 1226-1229.)* Primary hyperparathyroidism (HPT), as in parathyroid adenoma, leads to more extensive bone disease than is found in secondary hyperparathyroidism, as in chronic renal failure. Calcium levels are generally higher in the primary form of the disease than in the secondary form, in which calcium levels are low or low-normal; accordingly, the bone lesions are more severe in primary HPT, and through a process of bone resorption and fibrous replacement, cystic spaces result (osteitis fibrosa cystica). Repeated hemorrhages may occur in these focal lesions, with the formation of reactive granulomas (brown tumors). This is a rare event, since hypercalcemia is actively sought out and is treated early in most medical centers. The bone lesions in secondary hyperparathyroidism are of a milder degree and consist basically of a demineralization process (osteomalacia); this can be recognized as too much osteoid without appropriate mineralization. Osteoporosis involves a loss of bone, with osteoid-mineralization reduction being proportionately reduced. Osteopetrosis (Albers-Schönberg disease, or marble bone disease) is an inherited bone disease characterized by bony sclerosis and excess bone growths with loss of marrow spaces.

305. The answer is E. *(Robbins, ed 3. p 754.)* The syndrome of inappropriate antidiuretic hormone release (SIADH) is an important cause of dilutional hyponatremia that, whereas it has been identified in tumors of the thymus gland, malignant lymphoma, and pancreatic neoplasms, occurs predominantly as a result of ectopic secretion of ADH by oat-cell carcinomas of the lung. Since the tumor cells per se are autonomously producing ADH, there is no feedback inhibition from the hypothalamic osmoreceptors, and the persistent ADH effect on the renal tubules causes water retention even with concentrated urine. Hence the term "inappropriate ADH" arises. Laboratory findings of the syndrome include low plasma sodium levels (dilutional hyponatremia), low plasma osmolality, and high urine osmolality caused by disproportionate solute excretion without water.

306. The answer is E (all). *(Robbins, ed 3. pp 984, 1022-1025.)* Nodular glomerulosclerosis (Kimmelstiel-Wilson disease) and glycogen nephrosis (Armanni-Ebstein lesion) are virtually pathognomonic for diabetes mellitus. Hyaline arteriolosclerosis and diffuse glomerulosclerosis may be seen in nondiabetics but are more common in diabetics. Necrotizing papillitis tends to occur in nondiabetic individuals only in the presence of urinary obstruction or analgesic abuse.

307. The answer is A (1, 2, 3). *(Robbins, ed 3. pp 1244-1247, 1269.)* Multiple endocrine neoplasia (MEN, or adenomatosis) syndromes are an interesting collection of predominantly benign tumors of the endocrine system that are inheritable in an incompletely penetrating autosomal dominant manner. MEN type I consists of functioning adenomas of the pituitary, pancreas, parathyroid, and adrenal glands with peptic ulcers. Type II (medullary thyroid carcinoma) disorders include pheochromocytomas and parathyroid adenomas and are subclassified as type "a" (no neuromas) and type "b" (lip and oral neuromas). Patients with von Hippel-Lindau syndrome may also have pheochromocytomas, in addition to adrenal myelolipomas, epididymal cystadenomas, and cerebellar hemangioblastomas. Patients with Sturge-Weber syndrome (oculomeningeal nevus flammens) have not been noted to have pheochromocytomas.

308. The answer is E (all). *(Anderson, ed 8. pp 1420-1421.)* The parathyroid glands develop from the endodermal tissue of the dorsal diverticula of the third and fourth pharyngeal pouches and usually consist of four flattened, encapsulated, oval bodies that lie against the dorsum of the thyroid gland. The superior glands, derived from the fourth pharyngeal pouches, have an anatomic position that is more constant than that of the inferior pair. The inferior parathyroids, because they develop and move caudally with the thymus, sometimes become located below the thyroid level, and the inconstant location of these parathyroids is an important factor to consider in the search for pathologic parathyroid tissue during autopsy or surgery.

309-312. The answers are: 309-C, 310-A, 311-B, 312-D. *(Rosai, ed 6. pp 356-364.)* Papillary, medullary, and other carcinomas of the thyroid commonly metastasize, often to lymph nodes. Thyroid carcinoma among young people is usually papillary, but papillary carcinomas may be found in individuals of various ages. Papillary carcinoma is the type that develops in patients who have had prior neck irradiation. About 50 percent of all papillary thyroid carcinomas contain a follicular component, but this component does not alter their biologic behavior. They tend to behave as if they were pure papillary carcinomas. Psammoma bodies, or calcospherules, occur in approximately 40 percent of tumors of the papillary type. The prognosis for papillary carcinoma patients is good; some survive 10 to 15 years following the development of metastasis.

The medullary carcinoma metastasizes more frequently than the papillary carcinoma. Medullary carcinoma of the thyroid is derived from the parafollicular C cells of the APUD neurosecretory system. The tumor nearly always has an amyloid stroma. The tumor produces mainly calcitonin, but reports have documented the production of ACTH, prostaglandin, serotonin, and histaminase. Psammoma bodies are virtually never seen in medullary carcinoma. Medullary carcinoma associated with hormone-forming tumors is also known as Sipple's syndrome, a type of multiple endocrine neoplasia in which pheochromocytoma is a dominant feature. There have been only sporadic reports of associations between thyroid lesions other than medullary carcinoma and hormone-forming tumors. Although medullary carcinomas are more aggressive than papillary carcinomas, the medullary type is not a high-grade malignancy with poor prognosis.

313-317. The answers are: 313-E, 314-D, 315-A, 316-C, 317-B. *(Anderson, ed 8. pp 1379, 1381-1382, 1385.)* Panhypopituitarism results from destruction of at least 75 percent of the anterior pituitary. This destruction usually is caused by tumors (metastatic carcinoma, e.g., breast melanoma) and infarction, but destruction can also be caused by inflammatory disorders, abscesses, granulomas (giant-cell granulomas of older women), and histiocytic infiltrates.

Simmonds' disease—the eponym for the classic clinical syndrome caused by panhypopituitarism in the adult—involves insufficiency of the gonads, thyroid, and adrenals and is secondary to the absence of stimulation by the respective trophic hormones.

Sheehan's syndrome is composed of symptoms of pituitary failure that occur as the result of an infarction of the pituitary because of postpartum hemorrhage or other types of massive hemorrhage. In Sheehan's syndrome the infarction of the pituitary frequently occurs in the presence of intravascular coagulopathy of pregnancy. The pituitary's great enlargement during pregnancy may play a role in predisposition to infarction.

Hand-Schüller-Christian disease (HSC) and Hurler's syndrome both feature histiocytic infiltrates in the pituitary. HSC also involves xanthomatous deposits in the skull and dura. Because the infundibular portion of the pituitary may be involved in HSC, that disease may cause diabetes insipidus to ensue in children as the pituitary is subjected to bony encasement with destruction of the nerve tracts in the neurohypophysis. In Hurler's syndrome there is an accumulation of mucopolysaccharide in the cells of the anterior pituitary.

If a tumor is present, acute hemorrhage can cause pituitary apoplexy—massive degeneration and hemorrhagic necrosis of the gland. The onset of this pituitary failure may be heralded clinically by ophthalmoplegia, headache, and signs and symptoms of meningeal irritation.

Ateliotic dwarfism is the result of pituitary insufficiency during formative growth periods in children.

Genitourinary System

DIRECTIONS: Each question below contains five suggested answers. Choose the **one best** response to each question.

318. A large abdominal mass arising from the kidney of a child is most likely to be a

(A) neuroblastoma
(B) renal cortical adenoma
(C) Wilms' tumor
(D) histiocytic lymphoma
(E) medullary sponge kidney

319. Primary hyperoxaluria frequently leads to renal failure and death caused by

(A) calcium oxalate deposits
(B) oxalic acid deficiency
(C) impairment of the degradation of oxalic acid
(D) severe acidosis by oxalic acid
(E) blockage of the conversion of glycolic acid to glyoxylic acid

320. The photomicrograph below depicts a biopsy of the uterine cervix performed on a patient who had an abnormal Pap smear report. What would be the most appropriate Pap smear class designation for the biopsy findings?

(A) Class I
(B) Class II
(C) Class III
(D) Class IV
(E) Class V

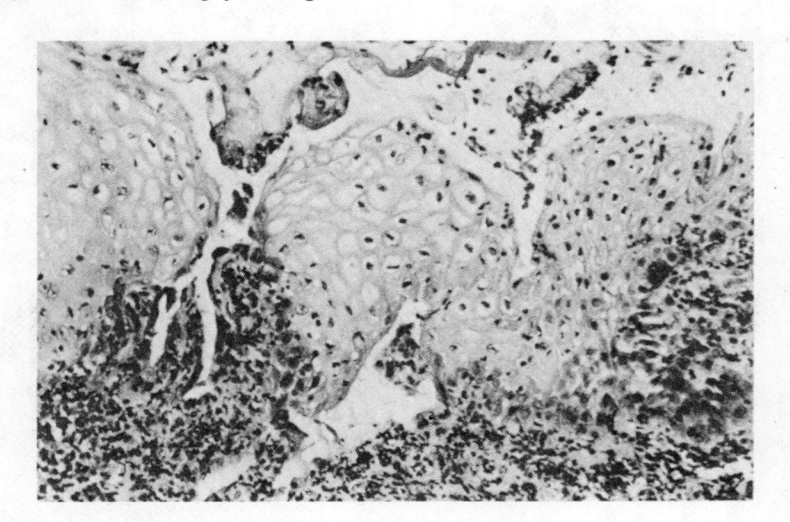

321. A linear pattern of immunoglobulin deposition along the glomerular basement membrane that can be demonstrated by immunofluorescence is typical of

(A) lupus nephritis
(B) diabetic glomerulopathy
(C) Goodpasture's syndrome
(D) Goldblatt's kidney
(E) renal vein thrombosis

322. What is the correct treatment for a patient who has hypertension secondary to unilateral renal artery stenosis when the contralateral kidney shows severe arteriolonephrosclerosis?

(A) Ureteral reimplantation
(B) Removal of the kidney supplied by the stenotic artery
(C) Repair of the renal artery stenosis and ipsilateral nephrectomy
(D) Repair of the renal artery stenosis and contralateral nephrectomy
(E) Nonsurgical management

323. Marked glomerular basement membrane thickening, as shown in the photomicrograph below, may be seen in all the following conditions EXCEPT

(A) lupus nephritis
(B) membranous glomerulonephritis
(C) diabetes mellitus
(D) acute pyelonephritis
(E) renal vein thrombosis

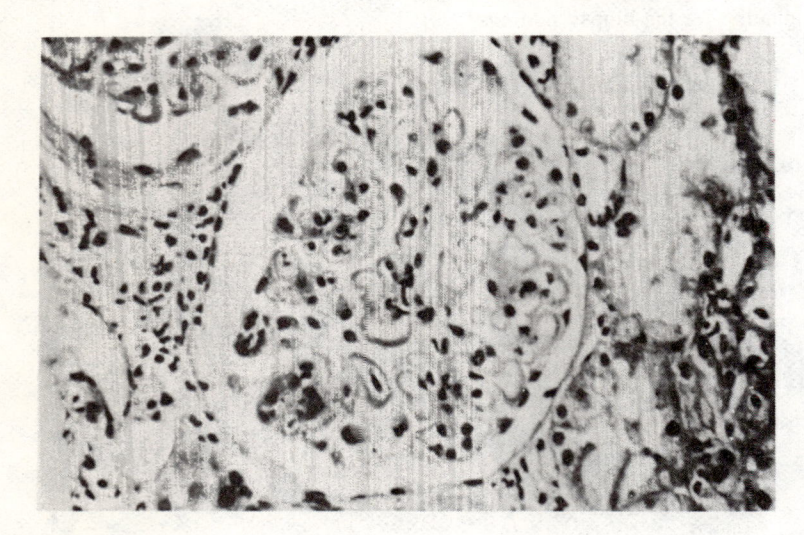

324. The presence of one normal kidney and one shrunken kidney with coarse cortical scars and deformity of the pelvis and calyces is most compatible with a diagnosis of

(A) chronic glomerulonephritis
(B) chronic pyelonephritis
(C) amyloidosis
(D) renal artery stenosis
(E) necrotizing papillitis

325. An adult medical laboratory technician recovering from hepatitis B develops hematuria, proteinuria, and red cell casts in the urine. Which of the following would best describe the changes occurring within the kidney in this patient?

(A) Plasma cell interstitial nephritis
(B) IgG linear fluorescence along the glomerular basement membrane
(C) Granular deposits of antibodies in the glomerular basement membrane
(D) Diffuse glomerular basement membrane thickening by subepithelial immune deposits
(E) Nodular hyaline glomerulosclerosis

326. All the following descriptions are associated with the disorder depicted in the photograph below EXCEPT

(A) massive unilateral enlargement
(B) autosomal dominance in adults
(C) autosomal recessive in childhood
(D) hepatic cysts in childhood form
(E) possible association with berry aneurysms

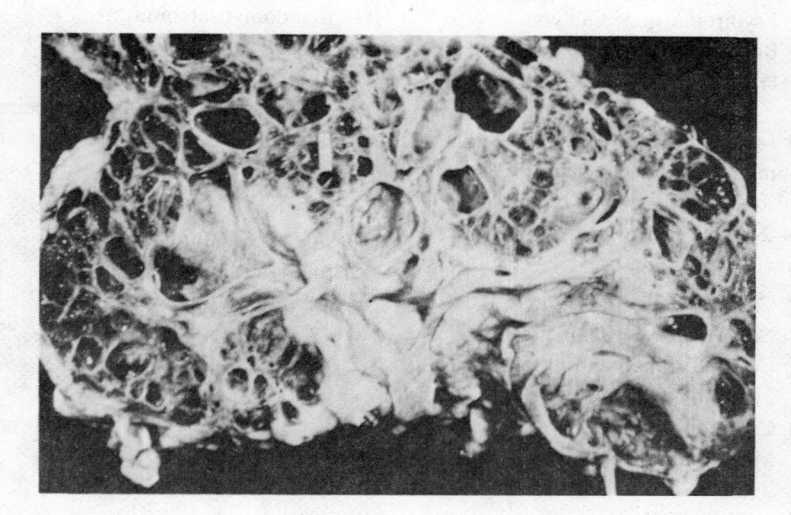

327. A sexually active adult male who has had a negative evaluation for gonococcus infection and who complains of persistent dysuria should be considered to have

(A) prostatic hypertrophy
(B) epididymitis
(C) orchitis
(D) nonspecific urethritis
(E) renal stones

328. A 46-year-old woman undergoes an abdominal hysterectomy for a "fibroid" uterus. The surgeon requests a frozen section on the tumor, which is deferred because of the lesion's degree of cellularity. Which of the following criteria will be used by the pathologist in determining benignancy versus malignancy in permanent sections?

(A) Mitotic rate
(B) Cell pleomorphism
(C) Cell necrosis
(D) NC ratio
(E) Tumor size

329. Which of the following is sufficiently different from the others to be discriminated by histologic examination only?

(A) Bowen's disease
(B) Squamous cell carcinoma in situ
(C) Erythroplasia of Queyrat
(D) Bowenoid papulosis
(E) HPV condyloma

330. A 23-year-old woman with an abdominal Pap smear undergoes a cervical biopsy. The results are read as CIN-2. What is the meaning of this report?

(A) Cervical carcinoma, grade II
(B) Cervical carcinoma, stage II
(C) Cervical inflammation; repeat in 2 months
(D) Carcinoma-in-situ
(E) Moderate dysplasia

331. All the following statements about cryptorchidism are true EXCEPT that

(A) it is related to an increased incidence of malignant germ cell tumors
(B) it carries a 60-fold increase in risk of malignancy
(C) malignancy risk in inguinally placed testes is less than in abdominal placement
(D) there is an increased incidence of malignancy in the contralateral testis
(E) cryptorchidism-related malignancy occurs less frequently in blacks than in whites

332. The malacoplakia that occasionally occurs in the prostate is often associated with

(A) benign nodular hyperplasia
(B) intraacinar papillary hyperplasia
(C) prostatic carcinoma
(D) rhabdomyosarcoma
(E) *Escherichia coli* infections

333. A woman harboring endometrial adenocarcinoma nearly always has antecedent

(A) obesity
(B) diabetes mellitus
(C) endometrial polyps
(D) endometrial hyperplasia
(E) systemic hypertension

334. The ovarian lesion in the photomicrograph below is

(A) chronic salpingitis
(B) an ectopic pregnancy
(C) a granulosa cell tumor
(D) a cystic teratoma
(E) metastatic squamous cell carcinoma

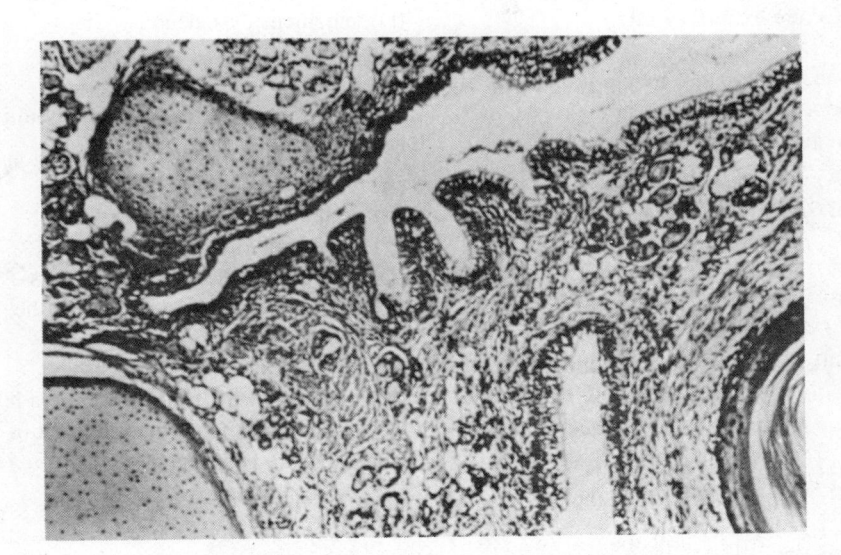

335. A 10-year-old boy has a bout of ordinary upper respiratory infection followed within 36 hours by an episode of hematuria. There are no joint symptoms, gastrointestinal symptoms, petechiae, or rashes. To confirm the suspicion of Berger's disease, which of the following is indicated?

(A) Urine sediment examination
(B) Renal scan
(C) Renal biopsy immunofluorescence
(D) Creatinine clearance
(E) Intravenous pyelogram

336. Vaginal adenosis precedes the development of which of the following?

(A) Cervical carcinoma
(B) Condyloma accuminatum
(C) Clear cell carcinoma
(D) Carcinoma of the endometrium
(E) Squamous carcinoma of the vagina

337. The majority of malignant tumors of the ovary take their origin from

(A) surface epithelium
(B) urogenital stem cell
(C) ovarian germ cells
(D) stromal cells
(E) hilar cells

338. Ovarian cystadenomas or cystadenocarcinomas (serous or mucinous)

(A) always produce androgens
(B) seldom are bilateral
(C) can be papillary
(D) usually occur during pregnancy
(E) are extremely rare

339. Metastatic, mucin-producing, signet-ring cancer cells in the ovary most frequently come from

(A) intestinal carcinoma
(B) endometrial carcinoma
(C) malignant melanoma
(D) astrocytoma
(E) histiocytic lymphoma

340. Primary germ cell tumors of the testis occur predominantly in the younger male with the exception of

(A) embryonal carcinoma
(B) spermatocytic seminoma
(C) polyembryoma
(D) choriocarcinoma
(E) teratocarcinoma

341. The ovarian tumor with the highest degree of bilateral involvement in the list below is the

(A) endometrioid carcinoma
(B) serous cystadenoma
(C) mucinous cystadenocarcinoma
(D) mucinous cystadenoma
(E) serous cystadenocarcinoma

342. Carcinoma of the prostate usually arises

(A) in the median lobe
(B) in the posterior lobe
(C) in the anterior lobe
(D) in either of the two lateral lobes
(E) with equal distribution among the lobes

343. Which of the following genera is most responsible for veneral disease in women in the United States?

(A) *Calymmatobacterium*
(B) *Campylobacter*
(C) *Chlamydia*
(D) *Neisseria*
(E) *Haemophilus*

Genitourinary System

DIRECTIONS: Each question below contains four suggested answers of which **one** or **more** is correct. Choose the answer:

A	if	**1, 2, and 3**	are correct
B	if	**1 and 3**	are correct
C	if	**2 and 4**	are correct
D	if	4	is correct
E	if	**1, 2, 3, and 4**	are correct

344. A patient who has developed hematuria shows on urinary sediment examination clumps of necrotic epithelial cells. The gross photograph below shows the diseased organ removed from the patient. These findings may be associated with

(1) sickle cell anemia
(2) diabetes mellitus
(3) analgesic abuse
(4) benign prostatic hypertrophy

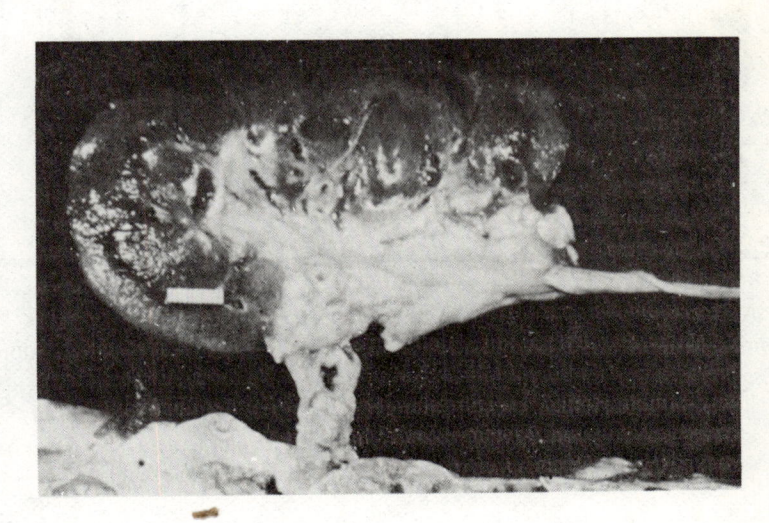

345. A patient being investigated for hematuria and proteinuria has a renal biopsy that shows changes in the glomeruli as depicted below. Which of the following diseases can be associated with changes seen in this biopsy?

(1) Bacterial endocarditis
(2) Anaphylactoid purpura
(3) Systemic lupus erythematosus
(4) Hereditary nephritis (Alport's syndrome)

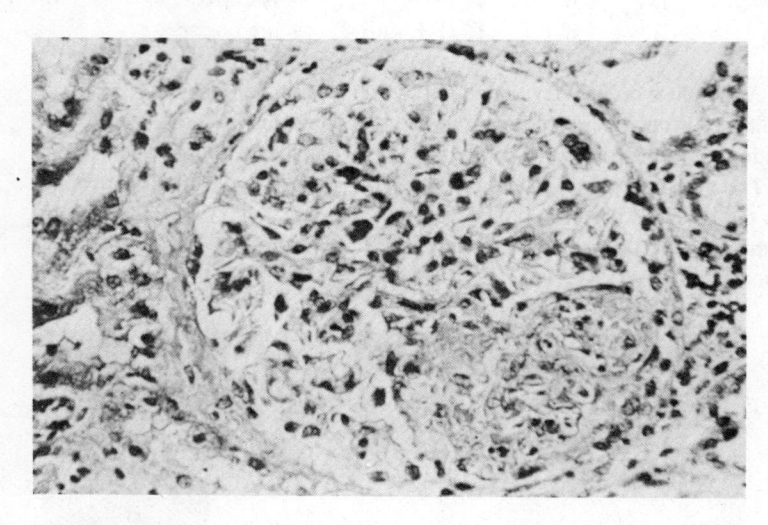

---

346. Acute poststreptococcal glomerulonephritis usually

(1) affects children
(2) follows a streptococcal infection by more than 6 months
(3) is accompanied by decreased serum complement
(4) leads to chronic renal failure

Questions 347-348

The photomicrograph below shows evidence of glomerular fibrin deposition.

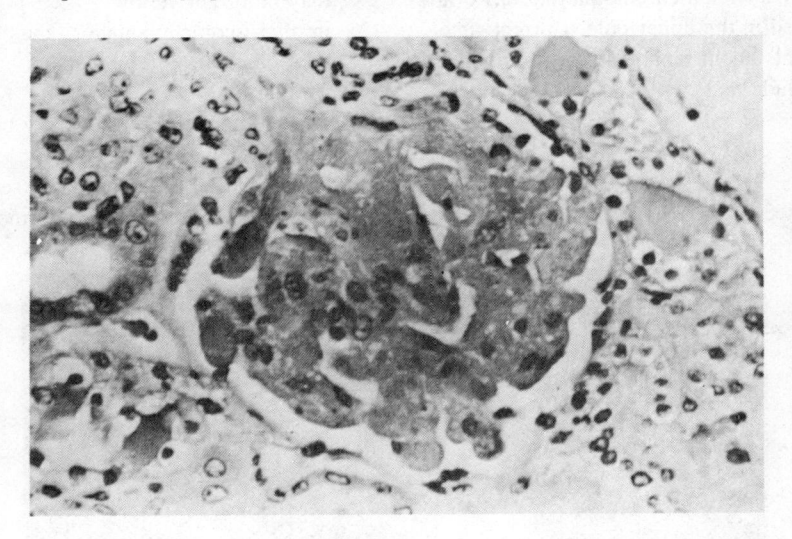

347. If histopathology that is evident in the photomicrograph is a supplemental finding in a 2-year-old child who has a history of acute gastroenteritis followed by acute glomerulonephritis, severe Coombs'-negative hemolytic anemia, and renal failure, then likely diagnoses might include

(1) lupus erythematosus
(2) acute poststreptococcal glomerulonephritis
(3) lipoid nephrosis
(4) hemolytic-uremic syndrome

348. True statements concerning the pathologic process described in the previous question in young children include that

(1) patients with severe, acute disease with long periods of oliguria often die or sustain permanent renal damage
(2) there is evidence to sugggest an infecticus etiology
(3) the disease includes a spectrum ranging from focal or partial glomerular necrosis to cortical necrosis
(4) steroids and anticoagulation therapy have been successful in treating a majority of cases

349. The kidney shown in the photomicrograph below is affected by a primary renal carcinoma that has originated in the upper pole. Correct statements about renal primary carcinoma include that

(1) in gross examination, the lesions are spherical masses of tissue that may be bright yellow
(2) in microscopic evaluation, the cellular character is squamous or papillary
(3) these tumors characteristically invade the renal veins
(4) the neoplastic tissue probably secretes adrenocorticotropic hormone

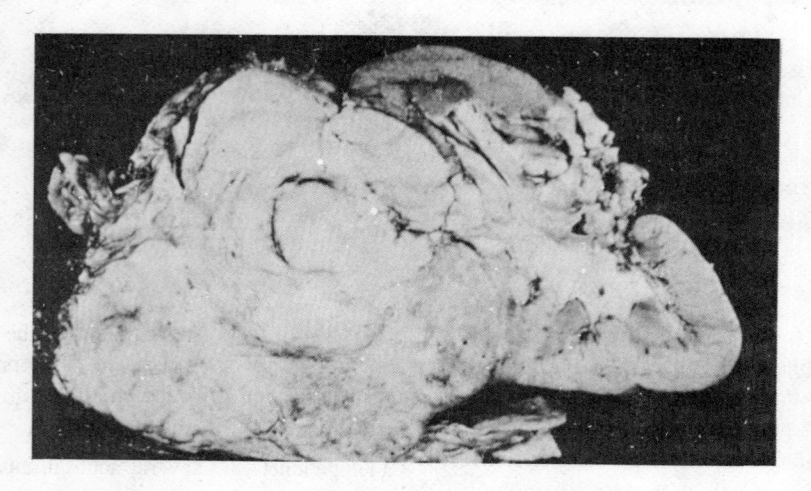

350. Components of diabetic glomerulopathy include

(1) diffuse glomerulosclerosis
(2) nodular glomerulosclerosis
(3) thickening of capillary basement membranes
(4) mesangial proliferation

351. The nephrotic syndrome is associated with which of the following renal disorders?

(1) Membranous glomerulonephritis
(2) Lipoid nephrosis
(3) Membranoproliferative glomerulonephritis
(4) Acute tubular necrosis

352. Which of the following renal diseases may cause hypertension?

(1) Renal artery arteriosclerosis
(2) Fibromuscular dysplasia of the renal artery
(3) Hydronephrosis
(4) Pyelonephritis

353. Neoplasms that occur in the ovary and may yield a yellow color grossly on cut surfaces include

(1) carcinoid
(2) thecoma
(3) lipid cell tumor
(4) hilus cell tumor

354. Renal diseases in which fibrin thrombi play a prominent role include

(1) lipoid nephrosis
(2) membranous glomerulopathy
(3) diabetes mellitus
(4) anaphylactoid purpura (Henoch-Schönlein purpura)

355. True statements regarding carcinoma of the uterine cervix include that

(1) the overall incidence of invasive cervical carcinoma is increasing
(2) estrogens increase the risk of cervical carcinoma
(3) certain races are predisposed to cervical carcinoma
(4) there is an increased incidence with early parity

356. Carcinoma of the prostrate tends to

(1) occur most often in the lateral lobes of the gland
(2) exhibit perineural invasion
(3) be estrogen-dependent
(4) cause elevation of serum acid phosphatase levels

357. An elderly man experiences nocturnal dysuria, polyuria, and frequency. As a result of the process most likely to cause these symptoms at an advanced age, which of the following effects can be predicted?

(1) Hemorrhagic cystitis
(2) Septicemia
(3) Bladder trabeculation
(4) Bladder dilatation

358. A young woman with lower pelvic pain, menometrorrhagia, and a negative beta-HcG test undergoes uterine dilatation and curettage. The pathology report on the endometrial curettings states, "Compatible with decidualized gestational hyperplasia, no chorionic villi present." The next step or steps would be to

(1) repeat the beta-HcG test
(2) discharge the patient
(3) consider ectopic pregnancy
(4) consider appendicitis

359. An 18-month-old infant is evaluated for generalized tissue edema and ascites. Urinalysis shows numerous hyaline casts and lipid droplets. Total plasma protein and albumin are markedly decreased, whereas total lipids are increased. A light micrograph of a renal biopsy glomerulus is shown below. Statements applicable to this disorder include that

(1) the problem is hepatic, not renal
(2) electron microscopy is diagnostic
(3) hepatic ultrasound is diagnostic
(4) exacerbations are not uncommon

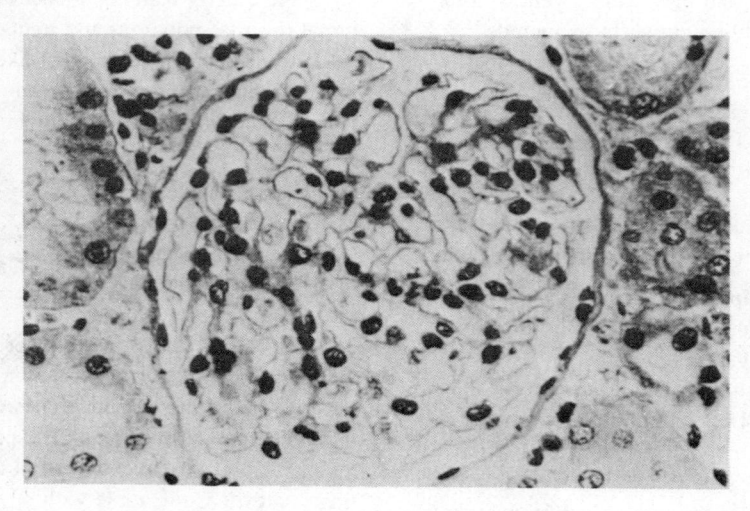

360. A female patient is being treated with penicillin for acute salpingitis and pelvic inflammatory disease without benefit. Which of the following organisms should now be considered in the differential diagnosis?

(1) *Bacteroides* species
(2) *Neisseria gonorrhoeae*
(3) *Chlamydia trachomatis*
(4) Adenoviruses

361. Cystic hyperplasia of the endometrium

(1) occurs at or just before menopause
(2) occurs in association with increased estrogen administration or production
(3) usually results in excessive uterine bleeding
(4) is associated with secretory cells lining the cystically dilated glands

362. Neoplasms that have been reported in increased incidence in homosexual men include

(1) cloacogenic carcinoma
(2) malignant lymphoma
(3) Kaposi's sarcoma
(4) Bowen's disease

363. A major role in the exclusion of albumin from the ultrafiltrate in the normal human glomerulus is played by

(1) sodium-potassium ATPase
(2) parietal epithelium
(3) endothelial fenestrations
(4) proteoglycans

364. Choriocarcinoma of the uterus

(1) is a malignancy of trophoblastic cells
(2) responds poorly to chemotherapy
(3) may arise in a hydatidiform mole
(4) never follows a normal pregnancy

365. A significant role in vascular permeability, particularly in the renal glomerulus, is played by

(1) desmin
(2) fibronectin
(3) podocytes
(4) polyanions

366. Uterine leiomyomas are colloquially known as "fibroids" and

(1) never become calcified
(2) may increase in size during pregnancy
(3) frequently metastasize
(4) are common tumors

367. A granulosa cell tumor of the ovary may produce excess estrogen and cause

(1) menstrual irregularities
(2) endometrial hyperplasia
(3) precocious puberty
(4) uterine enlargement

368. Ascites and pleural effusion have been detected in a woman with a primary ovarian neoplasm. These findings

(1) always mean that the tumor has metastasized and is thus inoperable
(2) are strong presumptive evidence that a granulosa cell tumor is present in an ovary
(3) indicate that the patient should receive intrapleural administration of methotrexate and actinomycin D
(4) may occur with a benign ovarian fibroma

369. The well-differentiated, superficial squamous cells shown in the photomicrograph below were the predominant cell type seen in a Papanicolaou smear of the lateral vaginal wall. The patient probably is

(1) postpartum
(2) being treated for cervical carcinoma
(3) receiving androgens
(4) premenopausal

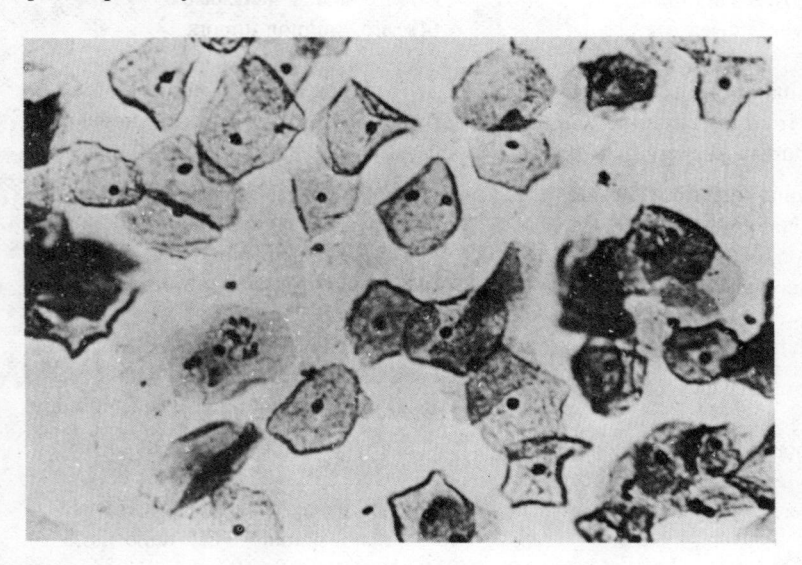

370. Which of the following at the present time can be considered to be conclusive evidence of coitus if found in vaginal fluid?

(1) alkaline phosphatase
(2) acid phosphatase
(3) prostatic acid phophatase
(4) p30

371. Mumps orchitis generally

(1) is bilateral
(2) results in sterility
(3) occurs simultaneously with parotid swelling
(4) occurs in adults

372. The botryoid (grapelike) neoplasm shown in the photograph below has developed in the urinary bladder and

(1) may contain malignant rhabdomyoblasts
(2) is most likely a papillary carcinoma
(3) may also arise in the vagina
(4) has a good prognosis

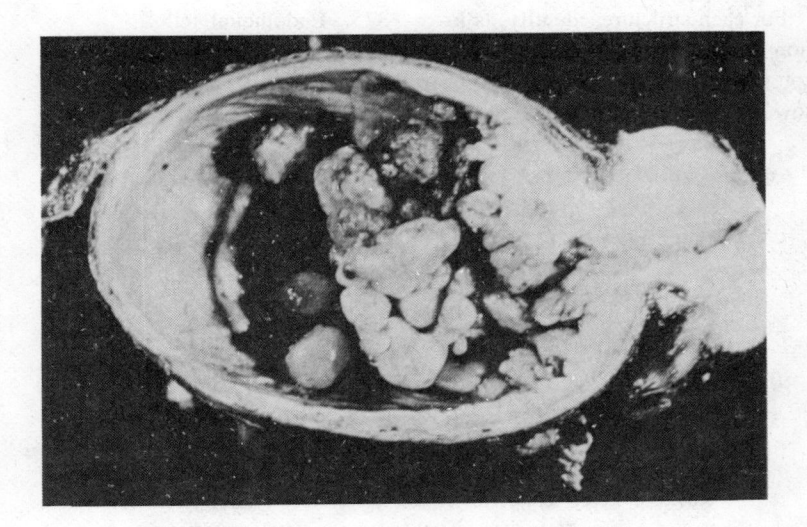

---

373. A gravida 2, para 0, 34-year-old woman is receiving prenatal care in the second trimester of her second pregnancy, and her Pap smear report comes back as "class III." Cervical biopsies then show cervical intraepithelial neoplasia, grade III (carcinoma-in-situ, severe dysplasia), with condylomatous change (warty atypia) at 3 o'clock only. The appropriate course of action now is to

(1) perform a hysterectomy
(2) perform cervical conization
(3) abort the fetus
(4) confer with the patient

Pathology

DIRECTIONS: The groups of questions below consist of lettered choices followed by several numbered items. For each numbered item select the **one** lettered choice with which it is **most** closely associated. Each lettered choice may be used once, more than once, or not at all.

Questions 374-378

For each structure, identify its location by letter in the electron micrograph of a renal glomerulus shown below.

374. Basement membrane
375. Endothelial cell
376. Epithelial cell foot process
377. Capillary lumen
378. Bowman's space

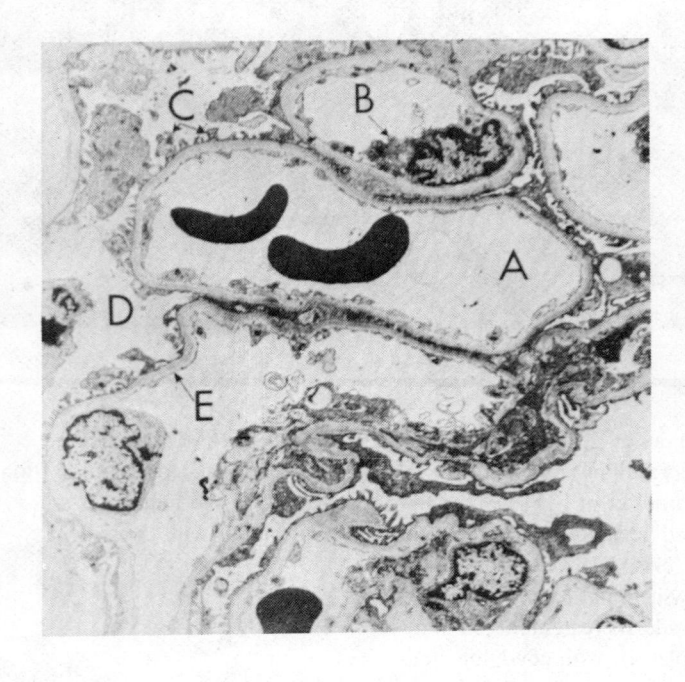

Questions 379-381

Match the renal disorders with the pathologic findings with which they are most likely to be associated.

(A) Hyalinized glomeruli
(B) Glomerular basement membrane splitting
(C) Diffuse capillary wall thickening
(D) Glomerular hypercellularity and leukocytes
(E) Glomerular epithelial crescents

379. Membranoproliferative glomerulonephritis

380. Membranous glomerulonephritis

381. Goodpasture's syndrome

Questions 382-384

Choose the disease in which each pathologic finding is most characteristic.

(A) Malignant hypertension
(B) Systemic lupus erythematosus
(C) Chronic thyroiditis
(D) Addison's disease
(E) Diabetic nephropathy

382. Hyperplastic arteriolar nephrosclerosis

383. Nodular or intercapillary glomerulosclerosis

384. Necrotizing papillitis

Questions 385-388

Match the following.

(A) Nephroblastoma
(B) Neuroblastoma
(C) Both
(D) Neither

385. Malignant tumor capable of metastasis

386. Metastases characteristically found in bones

387. Histologic sections may show embryonal rhabdomyoblasts (primitive skeletal muscle)

388. Lesions usually arise in adolescents

Genitourinary System Answers

318. The answer is C. *(Robbins, ed 3. pp 1056-1057.)* Wilms' tumor is the second most common visceral tumor of children under the age of 10 years. This tumor probably arises from the primitive renal blastema and may contain a variety of cell and tissue components of mesodermal origin. Wilms' tumors are usually unilateral and may grow to huge size.

319. The answer is A. *(Robbins, ed 3. p 1053. Stanbury, ed 5. pp 199-200.)* Primary hyperoxaluria results in overproduction of oxalic acid and consequent precipitation of insoluble calcium oxalate salt in the renal parenchyma. The resulting nephrolithiasis and nephrocalcinosis lead to chronic renal failure and early death from uremia. Unless this rare hereditary disorder is present, the amount of oxalates contributed to calcium oxalates is insignificant.

320. The answer is B. *(Robbins, ed 3. pp 265-266, 1123-1128.)* The photomicrograph depicts the presence of condylomatous cervicitis and shows the characteristic clear cell change with crinkling and hyperchromatism of the nuclei (koilocytosis) in several layers of the mucosa. Despite these changes no clones or clusters of dysplastic cells of similar appearance are seen in any layer. This koilocytosis is usually viral in nature. Recent in situ hybridization studies have shown that the human papilloma virus (HPV) type 16, while not absolutely proven to be the etiologic agent in carcinoma of the cervix, does correlate closely with the development of that disease. Since no dysplastic cells are seen, the appropriate Pap smear classification in the photomicrograph would be class II, which means atypical cells are present—in this case associated with condylomatous cervicitis. A class II classification suggests that the Pap smear should be repeated after therapy or after an appropriate period in which healing may be expected. Class III designation means dysplasia in any form whether mild, moderate, or severe. Class IV means carcinoma in situ, and class V means absolute diagnosis of carcinoma, and invasion may be present.

321. The answer is C. *(Robbins, ed 3. pp 745-746, 1010-1011.)* In Goodpasture's syndrome, circulating antibodies reactive with the glomerular basement membrane will bind in a linear pattern along the entire length of the glomerular basement membrane, which is their specific antigen. IgG is deposited in the basement membrane, along with complement. There are focal interruptions of the glomerular basement membrane as well, along with deposits of fibrin, as seen with electron microscopy.

322. The answer is D. *(Rosai, ed 6. pp 764-765.)* In a patient with a surgically correctable lesion of the renal artery, the corresponding kidney, which is potentially the least damaged one, should be saved. The contralateral kidney may be severely affected with arteriolonephrosclerosis and could perpetuate the hypertension if not removed. In a patient with parenchymal renal disease leading to hypertension, such as pyelonephritis, removal of the affected kidney may relieve the hypertension.

323. The answer is D. *(Robbins, ed 3. pp 185-186, 1021-1022.)* The thickening of the basement membrane in systemic lupus erythematosus and membranous glomerulonephritis is thought to result from deposition of immune complexes. The pathogenesis of this same lesion in diabetes mellitus and renal vein thrombosis is unknown. Electron-dense deposits are classically seen in a subendothelial position on the glomerular basement membrane but may be subepithelial as well in some cases.

324. The answer is B. *(Rosai, ed 6. pp 760, 781-785.)* It may be difficult to distinguish grossly between chronic glomerulonephritis and chronic pyelonephritis. However, chronic glomerulonephritis typically involves both kidneys and does not cause deformation of the pelvis and calyces. Microscopically, virtually all glomeruli are affected in chronic glomerulonephritis, whereas in pyelonephritis the changes may be patchy. Inflammation of the pelvis may also be recognized microscopically in chronic pyelonephritis.

325. The answer is C. *(Robbins, ed 3. pp 1004-1013.)* Glomerular injury caused by circulating antigen-antibody complexes is a secondary effect from a nonprimary renal source. Numerous clinical examples exist of a serum sickness-like nephritis picture as a consequence of systemic infection, with classical clinical models such as syphilis, hepatitis B, malaria, and bacterial endocarditis leading to renal disease. Immune complexes to antigens from any of these sources are circulating within the vascular system and become entrapped within the filtration system of the glomerular basement membranes. This can be seen as granular bumpy deposits by immunofluorescence within the basement membranes of the glomerulae. Liner fluorescence, on the other hand, is seen in primary antiglomerular basement membrane disease, wherein antibodies are directed against the glomerular basement membrane itself. Plasma cell interstitial nephritis is seen in immunologic rejection of transplanted kidneys. Nodular glomerulosclerosis is an effect of diabetes mellitus. The presence of red blood cell cases in the urine nearly always indicates that there has been glomerular injury, but is not specific for any given cause. Glomerular basement membrane thickening caused by subepithelial immune deposits is seen in membranous glomerulonephritis. While the morphology of membranous glomerulonephritis is different from that of nephritis caused by circulating antigen-antibody complexes (immune complexes), there are similarities in the pathogenesis in that both disorders may be a consequence of or in association with infections such as hepatitis B, syphilis, and malaria. Other causes for membranous glomerulonephritis include reactions to penicillamine, gold, and certain malignancies such as malignant melanoma.

326. The answer is A. *(Robbins, ed 3. pp 1000-1001.)* Polycystic kidney disease is a serious renal disorder that is inherited in two forms. The adult form is autosomal dominant with high penetrance of nearly 100 percent involvement of progeny who live to be older. The childhood polycystic form is autosomal recessive in inheritance. In the adult form one-third of the patients have cysts within the liver, while nearly all the childhood cases have hepatic cysts. Congenital hepatic fibrosis is associated with childhood polycystic kidney disease. In the adult form bilateral renal involvement is nearly invariable. One third of patients with the adult form of polycystic kidney disease succumb to renal failure, while death occurs in another third as a consequence of hypertension.

327. The answer is D. *(Robbins, ed 3. pp 293, 1078-1079.)* Nonspecific urethritis may actually be the most common cause of dysuria in sexually active males, although gonorrhea should always be excluded by laboratory examination. Causes of nonspecific urethritis include some bacteria, such as *Escherichia coli* and streptococci, but recent evidence implicates chlamydiae of the TRIC group as being perhaps the most common offending agents. The organism may take up residence in the prostate, producing chronic and active prostatitis. Prostatic hypertrophy, epididymitis, orchitis, and renal stones may cause urinary symptoms but also produce other signs and symptoms that distinguish them from nonspecific urethritis.

328. The answer is A. *(Anderson, ed 8. pp 1491-1493.)* "Fibroids" of the uterus are among the most common abnormalities seen in uteri surgically removed in the United States in women of reproductive age. They arise in the myometrium, submucosally, subserosally, and midwall, both singly and several at a time. Sharply circumscribed, they are benign, smooth muscle tumors that are firm, gray-white, and whorled on cut section. Their malignant counterpart, leiomyosarcoma of the uterus, is quite rare in the de novo state and arises even more rarely from an antecedent leiomyoma. Whereas cell pleomorphism, tissue necrosis, and cytologic atypia per se are established criteria in assessing malignancy in tumors generally, they are important to the pathologist in uterine fibroids only if mitoses are also present. Regardless of cellularity or atypicality, if 10 or more mitoses are present in 10 separate high-power microscopic fields, the lesion is leiomyosarcoma. If 5 or fewer mitoses are present in 10 fields with bland morphology, the leiomyoma is going to behave in a benign fashion. Problems arise when the mitotic counts range between 3 and 7 per 10 fields with varying degrees of cell and tissue atypicality. These equivocal lesions should be regarded by both pathologist and clinician as "gray-area" smooth muscle tumors of unpredictable biologic behavior. Fortunately, the "gray-area" leiomyoma of the uterus is rarely seen. Thus mitoses are the most important criteria in assessing malignancy in smooth muscle tumors of the uterus.

329. The answer is E. *(Robbins, ed 3. pp 244, 1085-1086.)* Of all the choices given, human papilloma virus-induced (HPV) condyloma without dysplasia is the only lesion that can be histologically discriminated from the others. The typical HPV condyloma has hyperplastic squamous mucosa that shows progressive maturation from the stratum germinativum to the surface that is often parakeratotic, without cells of dysplasia or malignancy. There often are vacuolated squamous cells in several layers of the mucosa. However condylomas, whether arising in the female or the male genital areas, may have atypia, dysplasia, or even be associated histologically with carcinoma. If present, these features must be commented upon in a pathology report. Condyloma, not otherwise specified, indicates that none of these disorders of growth are present along with it. Bowen's disease and erythroplasia of Queyrat are different clinical forms of squamous cell carcinoma in situ. Erythroplasia of Queyrat is a specialized form of squamous carcinoma in situ or severe dysplasia occurring on the glans penis mainly. It is characterized by a moist macular spreading red surface. It usually occurs in males of advanced age. Bowen's disease is also squamous carcinoma in situ but may have an association with malignancies of the viscera. Bowenoid papulosis refers to multiple, small, banal-appearing clinical papules on the vulvar or penile surfaces; it histologically shows features of Bowen's disease, and for all practical purposes cannot be distinguished from that disease on histologic grounds only. It is a rather new entity, histologically similar to carcinoma in situ, and it behaves as a self-healing and reversible lesion. Bowenoid papulosis usually occurs in young patients and is often associated with condylomas.

330. The answer is E. *(Robbins, ed 3. pp 1125-1127.)* Although the cervical intraepithelial neoplasia (CIN) system is not accepted by all workers in gynecology, many large centers are now using it for reporting cervical dysplasias. The system was created to circumvent and alleviate interpretation difficulties for pathologists, because cervical dysplasia includes a spectrum of diseases that, in many cases, eventuate in in-situ carcinoma followed by a stage of microinvasion. The squamous mucosa is examined for atypical squamous cells and the thickness of the total mucosa occupied by them. CIN-1 represents less than one-third thickness (mild dysplasia); CIN-2 represents one-third to two-thirds thickness (moderate dysplasia); CIN-3 represents two-thirds to the entire thickness occupied by abnormal cells (severe dysplasia, carcinoma-in-situ). It should be remembered that not all forms of cervical dysplasia inevitably go on to the next higher stage of disease, because some are reversible.

331. The answer is B. *(Robbins, ed 3. pp 1091-1093.)* The risk of developing a malignant germ cell tumor within a cryptorchid testis is definitely greater than the normal risk but has not been shown to be as high as the stated risks in the older literature. Recent studies show that the risk is somewhere between 2.5 and 8.8 rather than 60 times higher. Any malplacement of the testis leads to an increased risk of developing a malignant tumor, but the risk in inguinal placement is several times less than that in placement within the abdominal cavity. Furthermore the contralateral testis, even if it is in the normal position within the scrotal sac, is at greater risk of developing a malignant tumor. Black males, whether they reside in the United States or elsewhere, do not appear to have as high a risk as white males of developing malignancy in a malplaced testis. Reasons for this are not known, even though cryptorchidism also occurs in black patients. The standard recommendation for orchiopexy is to perform it prior to the patient's reaching 6 years of age.

332. The answer is E. *(Anderson, ed 8. pp 300, 1068-1069.)* Malacoplakia is an unusual inflammation that may occur in the urinary tract, prostate, testes, epididymides, or even the lower intestinal tract. The etiology of malacoplakia is not clear, but it is commonly associated with *Escherichia coli* infections. Gross appearance may simulate a tumor, but microscopic evaluation can facilitate accurate diagnosis. The lesions found on the mucosal surface of the bladder, for example, are generally described as yellow (or yellow-gray to brown) plaques that in histologic examination are observed to contain massive collections of large histiocytes. With either hematoxylin and eosin or periodic acid-Schiff reaction staining techniques, the granular cytoplasm and extracellular regions can be seen to contain Michaelis-Guttmann bodies, which are believed to be mineralized products of bacterial decomposition.

333. The answer is D. *(Robbins, ed 3. pp 1133-1139.)* Endometrial adenocarcinoma appears to be increasing in frequency in the United States, especially in younger women. It is now accepted that a high estrogen to progestin ratio predisposes to the development of this tumor. At menopause, estrogen in the form of estrone continues to be produced in the adrenal glands, and the amounts are directly proportional to body fat. This continues in a milieu in which progesterone is at a minimum because of noncycling. These factors explain why obese women are at an increased risk during and after menopause. Diabetes and hypertension also are associated factors, but they are more likely effects of obesity than isolated risk factors for developing cancer. Endometrial adenocarcinoma is nearly always preceded by endometrial hyperplasia in some form. This, of course, is not always documented in every case, because not every patient has had a diagnostic dilatation and curettage of the endometrium prior to development of the carcinoma. Furthermore, endometrial hyperplasia does not always lead to adenocarcinoma.

334. The answer is D. *(Anderson, ed 8. pp 521-524.)* Benign cystic teratomas constitute about 10 percent of cystic ovarian tumors. The cysts contain greasy sebaceous material mixed with a variable amount of hair. The cysts' walls contain skin and skin appendages, including sebaceous glands and hair follicles. A variety of other tissues, such as cartilage, bone, tooth, thyroid, respiratory tract epithelium, and intestinal tissue, may be found. The presence of skin and skin appendages gives the tumor its other name, "dermoid" cyst. Dermoid cysts are benign, but in less than 2 percent, one element may become malignant, most frequently the squamous epithelium.

335. The answer is C. *(Robbins, ed 3. p 1019.)* Many diseases involve hematuria, and a few diseases occur in the setting of an upper respiratory infection or of upper respiratory signs and symptoms (streptococcal glomerulonephritis, Henoch-Schönlein purpura, Wegener's granulomatosis, and bacterial endocarditis with embolism), but when the hematuria follows within 1 to 1½ days after onset of an upper respiratory infection without skin lesions in a young patient, IgA nephropathy (Berger's disease) should be considered. This disease involves the deposition of IgA in the mesangium of the glomeruli. Light microscopic examination may suggest the disease, but renal biopsy immunofluorescence must be performed to confirm it. This disorder is not at all uncommon and may become recurrent, with proteinuria that may approach nephrotic syndrome proportions. Serum levels of IgA may be elevated. A small percentage of patients may progress to renal failure over a period of years.

336. The answer is C. *(Robbins, ed 3. pp 1120-1121.)* Adenocarcinomas of the vagina and cervix have existed for years, but have increased in young women whose mothers had received diethylstilbestrol (DES) while they had been pregnant. DES was used in the past to terminate an attack of threatened abortion and thereby stabilize the pregnancy. However, a side effect of this therapy proved to be a particular form of adenocarcinoma called clear cell carcinoma. This phenomenon was elucidated by Herpses and Scully in 1970. This unique adenocarcinoma was discovered in daughters between the ages of 15 and 20 of those women who had received DES. The tumor, which carries a poor prognosis, has at least three histologic patterns. One is a tubulopapillary configuration, followed by sheets of clear cells and glands lined by clear cells, and solid areas of relatively undifferentiated cells. Many of the cells have cytoplasm that protrudes into the lumen and produces a "hobnail" (nodular) appearance. Prior to the development of adenocarcinoma, a form of adenosis consisting of glands with clear cytoplasm that resembles that of the endocervix can be seen. This has been termed vaginal adenosis and may be a precursor of clear cell carcinoma. Clinically adenosis of the vagina is manifested by red, moist granules superimposed on the pink-white vaginal mucosa.

337. The answer is A. *(Robbins, ed 3. pp 1143-1155.)* Malignant tumors of the ovary most commonly occur between the ages of 40 and 64. These, in the main, arise from the surface epithelium, which takes its origin from cells of the müllerian system. These cells are also referred to as surface or coelomic epithelium. The müllerian system has the ability to form lining cells of the fallopian tubes, endometrium, and endocervical gland epithelium. Hence, many malignant tumors that take their origin from the surface coelomic epithelium of the ovary resemble these structures. Examples include the borderline serous tumor, serous cystadenocarcinoma, serous cystadenofibrocarcinoma, borderline mucinous tumor, mucinous cystadenocarcinoma, endometrioid carcinoma, undifferentiated carcinoma, malignant Brenner tumor, and clear cell adenocarcinoma. Stem cells from the urogenital ridge can give rise to any genitourinary structure. Hilar cells represent small clusters and cords of androgen-producing cells. These presumably give rise to sex cord and Sertoli-Leydig cell tumors. Stromal cell tumors include granulosa cell tumors, theca cell tumors, thecomas, and fibromas. Germ cell tumors give rise to malignant and benign teratomas, including the cystic form (dermoid cyst), dysgerminoma, endodermal sinus tumor, choriocarcinoma, and mixed germ cell tumors.

338. The answer is C. *(Rosai, ed 6. pp 1025-1031.)* Ovarian cystadenomas are common neoplasms that are bilateral in 15 to 40 percent of patients and are frequently papillary. The less malignant lesions tend to be more papillary. Ovarian cystadenomas originate in surface epithelial cells from the müllerian system. The papillae may show complex arborization with an increase in cell layers without stromal invasion; in such cases, the tumors are classified as borderline malignant because of their less aggressive clinical course. Unlike in the case of true cystadenocarcinomas, the presence of peritoneal dissemination in cystadenomas of borderline malignancy does not appear to influence the clinical course.

339. The answer is A. *(Rosai, ed 6. pp 1057-1058.)* The eponym "Krukenberg's tumor" designates a bilateral ovarian neoplasm that is almost always metastatic from cancer of the gastrointestinal tract, particularly the stomach. This type of tumor is characterized microscopically by a diffuse infiltration of signet-ring cells containing abundant mucin and by areas of mucoid degeneration. The Krukenberg tumor designates a metastatic carcinoma to the ovary that is, at cursory examination, deceptively bland.

340. The answer is B. *(Anderson, ed 8. pp 802-806.)* Most malignant germ cell tumors of the gonads, specifically the testis, typically occur in the younger male between the ages of 22 and 35. The seminoma has several types, most of which are found also within the younger ages. The classic seminoma is populated by differentiated seminiferous tubule-type epithelium with intervening lymphocytes, while the anaplastic seminoma contains an increase in mitoses and a moderate degree of anaplasia. The spermatocytic seminoma, however, occurs in older patients, often between 55 and 65, and is a soft, yellowish, sometimes mucoid tumor that microscopically has several cell types: classic intermediate-sized germ cells, smaller secondary spermatocytic-type cells, and large mononuclear and multinuclear giant cells. Polyembryoma and embryonal carcinoma are related, occur in the younger patient, and are less common than the seminomas. The most malignant germ cell tumor of the testis is the choriocarcinoma, which is characterized by large cytotrophoblastic and syncytiotrophoblastic cells. Teratocarcinomas are tumors of more than one histologic type that may contain seminomatous and/or embryonal components.

341. The answer is E. *(Robbins, ed 3. pp 1144-1146.)* Primary ovarian tumors have a rather high degree of bilateral involvement as compared with tumors of other bilateral organs. Bilaterality could reflect either concurrent simultaneous primary tumors or vascular and lymphatic spread from one side to the other. The ovarian tumor having the highest rate of bilaterality (70 percent) is the serous cystadenocarcinoma. Serous cystadenomas have a 30 percent rate of bilaterality, while mucinous cystadenomas are bilateral in about 5 percent of cases. In contrast, mucinous cystadenocarcinomas are bilateral in 20 percent of cases, and endometrioid carcinoma is a little higher at about 45 percent. There is a higher probability of extension of endometrioid carcinoma outside of the ovaries when it presents with bilaterality.

342. The answer is B. *(Robbins, ed 3. pp 1104-1107.)* In nearly 75 percent of cases, carcinoma of the prostate arises within the posterior lobe of the gland, almost always in subcapsular location. This location occurs early in the development of prostatic carcinoma, and diagnosis may be difficult to make by usual means, including needle biopsy. Benign nodular hyperplasia of the prostate is, however, most often confined to the inner regions of the gland. Sufficient enlargement to cause decreased patency of the urethral lumen or to interfere with the internal sphincter must occur before the classic micturition disturbances become manifest.

343. The answer is C. *(Anderson, ed 8. pp 289, 313-315. Tam, N Engl J Med 310:1146, 1984.)* At least 50 percent of the infections of the uterine cervix in women in the United States today are caused by *Chlamydia trachomatis*, which is an intracellular obligate bacterium that can be identified by direct immunofluorescence using monoclonal antibodies. In addition to venereal transmission, *Chlamydia* also may cause psittacosis, trachoma, and neonatal infections. *Campylobacter* causes intestinal infections with diarrhea syndromes, while *Calymmatobacterium* causes granuloma inguinale, a venereally transmitted disease consisting of painful ulcers, which histologically shows granulomas with coccobacillary microorganisms within macrophages. The organism is antigenically related to *Klebsiella*. The gonococcus of the *Neisseria* genus causes gonorrhea but is less common than *Chlamydia*.

344. The answer is E (all). *(Robbins, ed 3. pp 1025, 1032-1033, 1037.)* Necrotizing papillitis is a serious form of specialized pyelonephritis in which the renal medullary papillary tips undergo necrosis, often in association with bacterial organisms, with subsequent sloughing of the distal papillae into the urine. Among the classic causes, consisting of analgesic abuse (acetoaminophen, aspirin, and phenacetin in combination), sickle cell anemia, and diabetes, can be found cases of obstructive uropathy, especially bladder neck obstruction caused by prostatic hypertrophy. Patients with appropriate causative factors who develop severe anemia, headache, and hypertension should be suspected of having this condition. A high index of suspicion is especially warranted if the sloughed necrotic papillae are seen on urine sediment examination. The disease is fatal if untreated.

345. The answer is E (all). *(Anderson, ed 8. pp 741-742.)* The photomicrograph shows focal glomerulonephritis with crescent formation and focal hypercellularity involving only one portion of the glomerulus. Focal glomerulonephritis involves some glomeruli, but not all, and may involve the entire glomerulus (global) or only parts of the glomerulus (segmental). The photomicrograph demonstrates focal segmental glomerulonephritis, which may be seen in systemic diseases as well as disorders affecting only the kidney. Hypercellularity involved several mesangia with proliferation of epithelial cells lining Bowman's capsule near the damaged capillary loops. This process is referred to as crescent formation. The disease may be seen in bacterial endocarditis and other systemic infections. Immunologic disorders causing focal segmental glomerulonephritis may include IgA focal glomerulonephritis, systemic lupus erythematosus, polyarteritis nodosa, and Schönlein-Henoch purpura (anaphylactoid purpura). IgA focal glomerulonephritis, also known as Berger's disease, has deposits of IgA and some IgG in the involved mesangium as demonstrated by immunofluorescence. Alport's syndrome is a hereditary form of chronic renal disease that may be associated with neural deafness with death at an early age, usually less than 30. Large collections of foam cells are also seen in the renal cortex in these patients. Electron microscopy shows splitting of the glomerular basements accompanied by small electron-dense granules.

346. The answer is B (1, 3). *(Robbins, ed 3. pp 1007-1009.)* Acute poststreptococcal glomerulonephritis usually affects children 5 to 30 days after a streptococcal infection. It is associated with decreased serum complement and increased ASO titer. Immune complexes seen as electron-dense deposits are bound within the glomerular basement membrane on the epithelial side. Ninety-five percent of affected patients recover without sequelae.

347. The answer is D (4). *(Anderson, ed 8. 755, 756.)* The pathologic picture presented is that of the hemolytic-uremic syndrome. Lupus erythematosus is virtually unknown in very young children. Acute poststreptococcal glomerulonephritis occurs in an older pediatric population, is a proliferative lesion pathologically, and is not usually associated with hemolytic anemia or fibrin deposition. Lipoid nephrosis shows no glomerular changes with light microscopy.

348. The answer is A (1, 2, 3). *(Robbins, ed 3. pp 1048-1049.)* Steroids and anticoagulation therapy have produced equivocal results at best in hemolytic-uremic syndrome. The hyaline thrombi material in the glomerular capillary loops in hemolytic-uremic syndrome appears to contain complement (C_3), fibrinogen, and IgM and fibrin. Although an infectious agent has not been reproducibly isolated, evidence for an infectious etiology lies in the fact that there are epidemics of the disease, multiple case outbreaks within families, and an apparent viral-like prodrome period. The disease appears to be endemic in specific geographic regions, including the western United States, Argentina, and the Netherlands.

349. The answer is B (1, 3). *(Anderson, ed 8. pp 768-770. Rosai, ed 6. pp 801-806.)* The neoplasms of renal cell carcinoma are produced as spheres that have diameters ranging from 3 to 15 cm and have been described as tissues that are bright or golden yellow, gray, tan in areas of low lipid content, white in areas of fibrosis and coagulative necrosis, or any combination of these colors. Renal cell carcinomas commonly arise from the upper pole, characteristically invade the renal veins, and then may metastasize unpredictably, slowly, or explosively to the lungs, bone, brain, regional lymph nodes, liver, adrenals, eye (sometimes), and vagina, or any one of these. The metastases often proceed asymptomatically and, when detected, may be diagnosed as a tumor of the lung or some other affected organ or tissue instead of as primary renal cell carcinoma. In the "solid cell" type of tumor, cytological detail persists and cells are cuboidlike; in the "clear cell" type, although cytoplasm is completely vacuolated, cell membranes remain intact.

350. The answer is E (all). *(Robbins, ed 3. pp 1023-1025.)* Capillary basement membrane thickening is a universal finding in diabetic kidney disease and consists of diffuse thickening of the capillary basement membrane as is seen in vasculopathy in other organ sites in diabetes. This has to be verified by ultrastructural examination by EM and is accompanied by widening of the mesangium as well. Additionally, tubular basement membranes also thicken in diabetes. Thickening is produced by hyalinelike material, which reacts with the PAS stain. This may have resulted from glycosylation of the basement membrane proteins. Thickening is probably also contributed by an increase in collagen type 4, as well as the basement membrane glycoprotein, laminin; however, the polyanionic proteoglycans are decreased. This may contribute to the increased permeability and consequent leakage of cationic proteins into the urine. Diffuse glomerulosclerosis results from an increase in the mesangial matrix as well as an increase in mesangial cells. This increase in matrix will also react with the PAS stain. Eventually, with continuing disease the glomerular tufts will become obliterated and yield a sclerosed, acidophilic tuft. At this stage the afferent and probably efferent arterioles will also be thickened and appear hyalinized.

Nodular glomerulosclerosis (Kimmelstiel-Wilson disease, intercapillary glomerulosclerosis) appears as laminated hyaline nodules at the peripheries of the glomerulus covered by what appears to be patent capillary loops. This may resemble amyloid and if present amyloid stain should be done to exclude it. Not always present, but highly characteristic of diabetic glomerulopathy are fibrin caps and capsular drops. The fibrin cap is a deposit that overlies a peripheral capillary within the glomerulus and consists of acidophilic deposits between the basement membrane and the endothelial cells. Capsular drops are PAS-positive proteinaceous foci that compose a thickening of the parietal layer of Bowman's capsule, giving the appearance of being free within the urinary ultrafiltrate.

351. The answer is A (1, 2, 3). *(Robbins, ed 3. pp 1011-1018.)* While many varieties of glomerulonephritis can produce the nephrotic syndrome, a few disorders will virtually always produce it. Included in the latter group are focal (segmental) glomerulosclerosis, membranous glomerulonephritis (GN), lipoid nephrosis, membranoproliferative glomerulonephritis, systemic diseases (such as amyloidosis and systemic lupus erythematosus), some tumors, hepatitis B, syphilis, drugs such as penicillamine, and certain allergies. Light microscopy shows very little change in glomeruli in lipoid nephrosis, and a diffuse absence of glomerular epithelial foot processes is noted with electron microscopy. Membranoproliferative GN is characterized by an increase in mesangial cellularity accompanied by splitting of the glomerular basement membranes ("double contour"). Membranous GN shows electron-dense deposits of immunoglobulin in the subepithelial portion of the basement membrane. The nephrotic syndrome includes massive albuminuria with significant loss of protein (more than 3 to 5 g of protein) in 24 hours, consequent reduced plasma albumin (less than 3 g/dl), hyperlipidemia, and anasarca (generalized edema).

352. The answer is E (all). *(Rosai, ed 6. pp 764-771.)* Many pathologic processes affecting the kidney can lead to hypertension. The three main categories are renovascular, renal parenchymal, and urinary tract obstruction. The renin-angiotensin system has been implicated in renovascular hypertension but has not been proved to be of etiologic importance in the other two categories. The most common parenchymal diseases leading to hypertension are pyelonephritis and hydronephrosis.

353. The answer is E (all). *(Robbins, ed 3. pp 1153-1154.)* Cells containing lipid may often yield a yellow color on cut surfaces macroscopically and include a wide variety of cell types throughout the gamut of human neoplasms. Cut surfaces of large ovaries, when solid, may include Krukenberg's tumor, thecomas, fibromas, and solid tumors arising from sex cord cells and stromal cells. Of all these the ones most likely to be yellow are thecomas and cells with a high content of lipid including hilus cell (Leydig) tumors, lipid cell tumors, luteomas, and carcinoid. Secondary involvement of the ovaries from a carcinoid often results from a primary adenocarcinoid, a special form of carcinoid with mucinous gland features that originates from the appendix. Stromal tumors that have a high content of collagen and fibroblasts (fibroma and thecoma-fibroma, with a high component of fibrous tissue), will appear white.

354. The answer is D (4). *(Robbins, ed 3. pp 1007, 1012-1015, 1022-1025.)* Ultrastructural studies reveal dense deposits in the mesangium of the glomerulus in addition to deposition of IgG, IgA, IgM, and complement (C_3), as seen by immunofluorescence microscopy. With light microscopy, fibrin and platelets also appear to be present. IgA is the immunoglobulin most commonly found in anaphylactoid purpura glomerulonephritis and may be associated with elevated serum levels of IgA.

355. The answer is D (4). *(Robbins, ed 3. pp 1125-1126.)* Cervical carcinoma in the United States has been the subject of a moderate success story, in that the mortality has dramatically dropped, owing to early diagnosis through use of Pap smears and colposcopy and to treatment of early lesions with cryotherapy, conization, and simple hysterectomy. Whereas the frequency of occurrence of cervical carcinoma is increasing in young women, the incidence of invasive carcinoma has been dramatically reduced in the United States, largely owing to early diagnosis and effective treatment. There appears to be a real but not severe risk of development of endometrial adenocarcinoma after exogenous estrogen exposure. However, the risk of developing squamous carcinoma of the cervix has not been similarly correlated to such exposure. Black women living in the ghetto show a greater incidence of the disease when age-matched with affluent white women, but this is due to socioeconomic factors rather than to racial differences. Women with a history of coitus at an early age, frequent coitus, multiple sexual partners, and multiple pregnancies have been shown to be at greatly increased risk of developing the disease. Attention is being given to herpes 2 virus and human papilloma virus type 16 as causative factors.

356. The answer is C (2, 4). *(Robbins, ed 3. pp 1104-1107.)* Carcinoma of the prostate typically arises in the posterior lobe. Invasion of the capsule, blood vessels, and perineural spaces is a helpful diagnostic sign. Metastatic carcinoma usually causes an elevation of the serum acid phosphatase level, but it is not known whether the elevation is due to the greater amount of neoplastic tissue present or to the more ready absorption of the enzyme into the bloodstream from the bony metastases. Tumor growth is not estrogen-dependent but may be inhibited by estrogen administration.

357. The answer is E (all). *(Robbins, ed 3. p 1077.)* Bladder neck obstruction from any cause will lead to urinary retention within the bladder with consequent bladder dilatation and an inability to empty the bladder completely on micturition. The patient may complain of having marked nocturnal frequency owing to a combination of a sense of urgency caused by being in the recumbent position with a "full" bladder and the inability to empty the bladder completely because of the obstruction. This leads to urinary stasis, which provides a potential culture medium for bacteria, especially such gram-negative coliform bacilli as *Proteus, Klebsiella*, and *Escherichia*. There is a potential hazard of developing gram-negative septicemia from this focus. The chronic retention and dilatation lead to bladder muscle hypertrophy with trabeculation of the submucosa and mucosa. Causes are usually prostatic in the male (benign prostatic nodular hyperplasia or carcinoma) and extrinsic pressure in the woman exerted by masses in the cervix or rectum. Early surgery is imperative.

358. The answer is B (1, 3). *(Robbins, ed 3. p 1158.)* Ectopic pregnancy is a potentially life-threatening condition if it is not treated by removal before rupture and hemorrhage with fatal exsanguination. The most common location for extrauterine implantation is the fallopian tube (more than 85 percent of cases), with rare implantation in the ovary or abdomen. If the tubal implantation has existed from 1 to 4 weeks, the beta-HcG test result is likely to be negative; thus a negative result does **not** exclude pregnancy. It is always worthwhile to repeat a laboratory test when the result is unexpected. Tubal pregnancy is not uncommon and should always be considered if endometrial curettings suggest gestational change without chorionic villi.

359. The answer is C (2, 4). *(Anderson, ed 8. pp 743-744.)* There are several causes of nephrotic syndrome (NS), including immune complex diseases, diabetes, amyloidosis, toxemia of pregnancy, and such circulating disturbances as bilateral renal vein thrombosis, but NS occurring in small children (under 3 years of age) should suggest the possibility of the renal disease known as minimal change nephropathy, which is synonymous with "foot process" disease or nil disease. This peculiar entity presents clinically as insidious nephrotic syndrome, characteristically occurring in younger children, but also seen in adults (rarely), with hypoalbuminemia, edema, hyperlipidemia, massive proteinuria, and lipiduria. The glomeruli are known for their rather normal appearance on light microscopy—at worst, there is mild and focal sclerosis. Electron microscopy is necessary for demonstrating characteristic attenuation and flattening of the foot processes of the podocytes attached to the Bowman's space side of the glomerular basement membrane. The podocytes may revert to normal (with steroid immunosuppressive therapy), or the foot-process attenuation may persist to some extent, in which case the proteinuria also persists. To date, no immune complex deposits or abnormalities of the glomerular basement membrane or mesangium have been demonstrated ultrastructurally.

360. The answer is B (1, 3). *(Anderson, ed 3. pp 1493-1494.)* *Neisseria gonorrhoeae* is a very common bacterium that causes acute pelvic inflammatory disease with salpingitis in this country as a result of venereal infection. Tuboovarian abscesses may develop from this bacterium, as well as other bacteria, but these organisms are susceptible to penicillin therapy. In the presence of unresponsiveness to penicillin, consideration should be given to *Bacteroides* species, which are important anaerobic gram-negative bacilli and are generally refractory to penicillin. These anaerobic bacteria may produce serious infections if uncontrolled. Chlamydia, while considered to be nongonococcal in origin, are nevertheless important agents in venereal transmission and often are contracted at the same time that *Neisseria* species are. When the gonococcus is adequately treated with penicillin, and symptoms continue, there may have been concurrent infection with chlamydia that is not responsive to penicillin but is sensitive to tetracycline. Adenoviruses are responsible for keratoconjunctivitis, tracheobronchitis, pneumonia in children, acute gastroenteritis, and occasionally hemorrhagic cystitis, but are not ordinarily causative in pelvic inflammatory disease.

361. The answer is A (1, 2, 3). *(Robbins, ed 3. pp 1133-1134.)* Cystic endometrial hyperplasia refers to the abnormal growth of endometrium associated with either an absolute or a relative estrogen excess. These are common findings at the time of menopause and in conditions causing an absolute excess of estrogen—e.g., Stein-Leventhal syndrome, functioning granulosa and thecal cell ovarian tumors, and the exogenous administration of estrogenic substances. The microscopic findings in an endometrial biopsy are dominated by the marked dilatation of the endometrial glands, giving the tissue section the appearance of Swiss cheese. The glands are lined by benign columnar epithelium that is nonsecretory.

362. The answer is A (1, 2, 3). *(Gottlieb, Ann Intern Med 99:208, 1983. Reichert, Am J Pathol 112:357, 1983.)* The most common tumor being seen in homosexual men with acquired immunodeficiency syndrome is Kaposi's sarcoma either locally in the skin or disseminated. Other tumors in this population being seen with increasing frequency are lymphomas, including those in the central nervous system, and solid tumors of the oral and anal regions. The latter have included squamous cell carcinomas, especially of the oropharynx but also of the perianal skin. The cloacogenic carcinoma of the anal rectal region is a deep tumor arising in the junction of the squamocolumnar mucosa, which may have a poor prognosis if composed predominantly of undifferentiated small cells.

363. The answer is D (4). *(Robbins, ed 3. pp 992-999.)* The unique structure and composition of the glomerular basement membrane and associated cells account for the formation of the plasma ultrafiltrate referred to as urine. The glomerular basement membrane is approximately 320 nm wide in the normal human with a central electron-dense lamina densa and electron-lucent lamina rara interna and externa with fenestrated endothelial cells immediately adjacent to the capillaries and the visceral epithelial cells (podocytes). Glomerular basement membrane is made up of collagen type 4, with laminin especially concentrated on both laminae rarae. Clustered also on both laminae rarae are polyanionic proteoglycans (especially heparan sulfate), which are thought to play a major role in the exclusion of albumin in the urinary filtrate by a mechanism of charge dependence restriction. This is based on the electronegative charge of the proteoglycans and the anionic charges of albumin. The mechanism is based on different isoelectric points. Thus it is felt that the glomerulus, because of these proteoglycans, may be able to discriminate materials passing through the glomerulus according to electronegative charge. Glomerular basement membrane does function by exclusion of materials based on size. Mesangial cells, by nature of their contractility, are thought to control intraglomerular blood flow under neurohormonal stimulation. Mesangial cells are not thought to function in filtration per se. The parietal cells lining the Bowmen's membrane may function as a barrier but do not participate in the ultrafiltration. The fenestrated endothelial cells and podocytes are part of the filtering membrane but probably play a minor role compared with the glomerular polyanion barrier.

364. The answer is B (1, 3). *(Robbins, ed 3. pp 1160-1162.)* Choriocarcinomas occur with the following incidence: 50 percent arise in moles, 25 percent follow abortions, approximately 22 percent arise in normal pregnancies, and the remainder arise in ectopic pregnancies and genital and extragenital teratomas. They also occur in teratomas in males. A cure rate of up to 80 percent may be obtained with chemotherapy.

365. The answer is D (4). *(Robbins, ed 3. pp 43, 993.)* It has been recently shown that polyanionic molecules at sites on the luminal endothelial cells retard anions by electronegativity forces, aiding the transport of cationic proteins. They may greatly increase vascular permeability, especially in the renal glomerulus. The glomerular basement membrane contains the glycoprotein entactin, fibronectin, collagen type IV, laminin, and polyanionic proteoglycans (heparan sulfate) found at sites on both laminae rarae. The glomerular filtration barrier is made possible by these polyanions. The podocyte is attached to the lamina rara externa on the epithelial (urine filtrate) side of the glomerular basement membrane. Desmin is an intermediate filament protein found in fibroblasts and muscle cells. Bowman's capsule epithelial cells line the inner side of the glomerulus and are bathed in urinary ultrafiltrate. Fibronectin, a connective tissue protein formed by endothelial cells, fibroblasts, and macrophages, stabilizes endothelial cell attachments and functions in wound healing.

366. The answer is C (2, 4). *(Robbins, ed 3. pp 1136-1137.)* Leiomyomas (fibroids) are benign smooth muscle tumors and are the most common tumors in women. They may proliferate and enlarge during pregnancy and become necrotic and calcified postmenopausally. They may cause symptoms owing to acute intratumor hemorrhage (pain) or to their proximity to the endometrium (menometrorrhagia). While uterine leiomyomas are excessively common, uterine leiomyosarcomas are extraordinarily rare. Uterine leiomyomas are usually spherical and firm, and the cut surface appears gray-white and whorled.

367. The answer is E (all). *(Rosai, ed 6. pp 1045-1048.)* The signs of hyperestrogenism produced by ovarian neoplasms, such as the granulosa cell tumor or a thecoma, are most obvious clinically as precocious puberty in a child or menstrual abnormalities and endometrial hyperplasia in a postmenopausal woman. These tumors may produce uterine enlargement as a result of muscle hypertrophy and marked endometrial hyperplasia.

368. The answer is D (4). *(Rosai, ed 6. pp 1048-1051.)* Meigs' syndrome is a benign ovarian fibroma associated with ascites and occasionally with pleural effusion, usually right-sided. After the fibroma is removed, the ascites and pleural effusion will normally disappear. Since the pleural space does not contain neoplastic cells in Meigs' syndrome, intrapleural administration of chemotherapeutic agents is not required therapy.

369. The answer is D (4). *(Koss, ed 3. pp 182-190.)* The vaginal epithelium responds to hormonal stimuli in three ways: by proliferation, maturation, and exfoliation. During the proliferative phase of the menstrual cycle, superficial squamous cells with pyknotic nuclei predominate. These cytologic changes are all represented in the photomicrograph and occur as a result of estrogen stimulation. During the secretory phase, numerous intermediate cells with vesicular nuclei are seen as a result of progesterone. An atrophic postmenopausal vaginal smear will contain few, if any, well-differentiated mature squamous cells, reflecting the lack of estrogen stimulation.

370. The answer is D (4). *(Graves, N Engl J Med 312:338, 1985.)* Measuring acid phosphatase intracellularly by the immunohistochemical method for in situ cells as in a needle biopsy is specific for prostate source, as is the same determination for prostatic specific antigen. Circulating plasma levels of prostatic acid phosphatase are elevated in circumstances of metastatic prostate adenocarcinoma. Alkaline phosphatases are found within the liver, placenta, and bone. Measurement of a recently described protein in semen is highly specific for seminal fluid, and the detection of the presence of p30 antigen in vaginal fluid is conclusive evidence that coitus has taken place. The test is an ELISA determination.

371. The answer is D (4). *(Robbins, ed 3. p 1084.)* Mumps orchitis rarely occurs before puberty. Testicular involvement, most often unilateral, commonly begins between the fifth and tenth days of illness during subsidence of parotid swelling. Some degree of atrophy, caused by pressure necrosis, occurs in about one-third to one-half of the cases of orchitis. The involvement of the testis is usually spotty, however, and seldom results in sterility.

372. The answer is B (1, 3). *(Robbins, ed 3. pp 1076, 1121.)* Sarcoma botryoides is composed of all the various mesodermal cell types and usually has an extremely poor prognosis, especially in adults. The predominant cell type is a small-celled embryonal rhabdomyoblast that contains thick and thin intracellular myofilaments ultrastructurally. Tumor cell infiltrate can be found tightly hugging the immediate basement zone of overlying epithelium "cambrium" or tree bark layer. The tumor is characteristically found in infants, in children, and in the second decade of life in the urogenital region, in the head and neck, and, rarely, in the biliary system.

373. The answer is D (4). *(Anderson, ed 8. pp 1474-1477.)* Although hysterectomy, radiotherapy, and therapeutic abortion all play a role in treatment of cancer of the uterus, the most appropriate course of action when dealing with noninvasive cervical carcinoma versus severe dysplasia (the definition of CIN, grade III) in a woman who may have a strong motivation for bringing a concurrent pregnancy to term is to confer with the patient. The patient and her spouse should be informed of the biology of the noninvasive states of cervical dysplasia and their risks. For example, although many invasive squamous carcinomas of the cervix are preceded by the various CIN dysplasia grades, not all CIN dysplasias will invariably yield to invasive carcinoma, and those that do may not do so for years. About 20 percent of cases of CIN-III go on to invasive carcinoma within 5 years, and about 40 percent follow this course within 20 years. Thus a patient who has CIN grade III at only one focus who is strongly desirous of having children may be willing to take a risk of 4 to 5 months to complete the pregnancy before undergoing definitive treatment. Cervical conization (cone biopsy) is acceptable treatment for CIN-II to CIN-III lesions, but such treatment in pregnancy would likely result in cervical incompetence with attending miscarriage.

374-378. The answers are: 374-E, 375-B, 376-C, 377-A, 378-D. *(Anderson, ed 8. pp 730-731.)* The ribbonlike basement membrane separates Bowman's space from the glomerular capillary lumen, which is lined by endothelial cells. The basement membrane is the site of deposits of immune complexes that circulate in plasma and then find their way to the membrane. The deposits appear ultrastructurally as electron-dense lumps and aggregates. In poststreptococcal glomerulonephritis (GN) the deposits are within the basement membrane or on the epithelial side. In membranous GN the deposits are subepithelial. In membrano-proliferative GN the deposits are either subendothelial (type I) or mainly located in the lamina densa (type II, or dense-deposit disease), whereas in lupus nephritis there are more deposits of immune complexes in a subendothelial position in the basement membrane. Splitting and lamination with regular thickening of the basement membrane occur characteristically in Alport's syndrome. Alport's syndrome is a form of hereditary nephritis associated with hematuria and nerve deafness.

The endothelial cells lining the capillaries (which contain erythrocytes in the electron micrograph shown) can be distinguished from epithelial cells by the lack of foot processes.

Foot processes come into direct contact with the basement membrane and represent extensions of the epithelial cells lining Bowman's space. In certain diseases these processes fuse. The foot process fusion in lipoid nephrosis probably is not true fusion. Current views favor the concept of podocytic foot processes as flattened, attenuated, or compressed in lipoid nephrosis.

The capillary lumen is easily distinguished from Bowman's space by the presence of erythrocytes and other cellular blood elements. Bowman's space can be distinguished from the capillary lumen by the adjacent foot processes, which are part of the glomerular epithelial cells.

379-381. The answers are: 379-B, 380-C, 381-E. *(Robbins, ed 3. pp 1009-1022.)* Membranoproliferative glomerulonephritis occurs in two types. Type I, which is associated with nephrotic syndrome, is immune complex driven; type II is associated with hematuria and chronic renal failure and in addition to immune complexes involves alternate complement activation. In either type there is mesangial proliferation accompanied by thickening of the glomerular basement membranes, and a special finding that often supports the diagnosis of membranoproliferative glomerulonephritis is the presence of actual splitting of the glomerular basement membranes. In type I there are subendothelial deposits of IgG, C3, C1, and C4. In type II there are dense deposits of (dense-deposit disease) C3 with or without IgG and no C1.

Membranous glomerulonephritis, on the other hand, rather than being driven by an immune complex is antibody-mediated and results in diffuse glomerular capillary wall thickening by subepithelial deposits of IgG and C3 in a diffuse involvement of the glomeruli. These deposits are seen by fluorescence as granular deposits. Membranous glomerulonephritis is also associated with the nephrotic syndrome.

Goodpasture's syndrome is an acute serious disease often heralded by pulmonary hemorrhages and remarkable hemoptysis accompanied by acute glomerulonephritis that often is of the rapidly progressive form. Antiglomerular basement membrane antibodies are seen in Goodpasture's syndrome, which would result in IgG linear deposits along the glomerular basement membranes. Also seen are marked and dramatic epithelial cell crescent formations accompanied by infiltrates of monocytes and neutrophils with fibrin deposition and necrosis of epithelial and endothelial cells. Unlike in membranoproliferative glomerulonephritis there is no accompanying glomerular basement membrane fragmentation.

Glomerular hypercellularity with ingress of neutrophils characterizes poststreptococcal glomerulonephritis, while hyalinized ("dropped-out") glomeruli may be seen in any terminal glomerulonephritis but are best seen in the conditions of chronic renal failure caused by chronic glomerulonephritis.

382-384. The answers are: 382-A, 383-E, 384-E. *(Robbins, ed 3. pp 1022-1025, 1032-1033, 1037, 1046-1047.)* Renal arteriolar changes in malignant hypertension include fibrinoid necrosis of arterioles and hyperplastic arteriolonephrosis. Hyperplastic arteriolonephrosis is recognized by a proliferation of smooth muscle cells and fibrocytes and lamination of fibrinoid material with the blood vessel wall, producing a concentric and laminated appearance. This condition differs from the lesion of hyaline nephrosclerosis, in which the arterioles demonstrate hyaline thickening only, without a proliferative cell component. The clinical course of malignant hypertension reflects the necrotizing and proliferative nature of the renal arteriolar changes in the disease, which can occur in a spectrum of underlying conditions, such as nephrosclerosis, pyelonephritis, glomerulonephritis, and progressive systemic sclerosis.

Diabetic glomerulosclerosis (DG; diffuse or nodular or intercapillary glomerulosclerosis), or Kimmelstiel-Wilson disease, yields a characteristic mesangial matrix increase with peripheral, glomerular-tuft, sclerotic, round nodules. There is usually no mesangial cell increase, as is seen in the membranoproliferative glomerulopathies. DG may resemble amyloid glomerulopathy, however, and in doubtful cases the PAS-positive nodules of DG should not produce green birefringence under polarization after staining with Congo red. Other forms of diabetic nephropathy are hyaline arteriosclerosis, pyelonephritis, and necrotizing papillitis—a variant of pyelonephritis.

385-388. The answers are: 385-C, 386-B, 387-A, 388-D. *(Anderson, ed 8. pp 768-770, 1920-1921.)* The majority of neuroblastomas arise in the adrenal gland in the pediatric age group. Some may, however, arise extraadrenally. Occasional examples of neuroblastomas are also seen in adolescents. Neuroblastomas are recognized by a pattern of primitive, small blue cells arranged in a sheetlike fashion with varying pseudorosettes. Subjected to electron microscopy, neuroblastomas will show tangles of neurite filaments. A neuroblastoma may differentiate and mature into ganglion cells, in which case the course of the condition becomes more favorable. If a neuroblastoma spreads to the liver, it becomes a unique entity for which there have been reported cases of spontaneous remission. Neuroblastomas frequently metastasize to bones, but nephroblastomas rarely do.

The prognosis of nephroblastoma, or Wilm's tumor, can now be predicted on the basis of histologic differentiation—that is, on the basis of how close it comes to reproducing primitive glomeruli and renal tubules. The poorly differentiated forms contain a cellular, atypical, spindle-cell stroma, as found in soft tissue sarcomas. The poorly differentiated forms tend to be more rapidly growing, with early pulmonary metastases. Heterologous mesenchymal structures and components of cartilage, bone, fat, fibrous tissue, and striated muscle cells may be present. These tumors are notorious for producing large masses that distend the abdomen.

Aggressive combined chemotherapy and radiotherapy have markedly improved the outlook for victims of this disease and are indicated in all cases, even in the presence of distant metastasis, because nephroblastoma, like neuroblastoma, still can metastasize widely and kill.

Nervous System

DIRECTIONS: Each question below contains five suggested answers. Choose the **one best** response to each question.

389. There appears to be some hazard in handling such tissues as brain and corneal tissue obtained from patients with Creutzfeldt-Jakob disease. Which of the following is considered adequate for inactivating the transmissible agent?

(A) Formalin
(B) Ultraviolet light
(C) Bleach
(D) Hexachlorophene
(E) Benyalkonium chloride

390. A 9-year-old boy who had been suffering from a gait disturbance for several weeks was found to have a posterior fossa mass on CT scan. The most likely cause for these findings is

(A) a berry aneurysm
(B) astrocytoma
(C) medulloblastoma
(D) oligodendroglioma
(E) pseudotumor cerebri

391. Subdural effusion may occur in infants with any form of meningitis but is most commonly seen in connection with meningitis caused by

(A) streptococci
(B) staphylococci
(C) pneumococci
(D) *Hemophilus influenzae*
(E) tubercle bacilli

392. A 55-year-old woman is suspected of having a brain tumor because of the onset of seizure activity. Computerized tomograms (CT scan) and skull x-rays demonstrate a mass in the right cerebral hemisphere that is markedly calcific. A high index of suspicion should exist for

(A) oligodendroglioma
(B) astrocytoma
(C) cerebral lymphoma
(D) metastatic carcinoma
(E) brown tumor

393. Type 1 G_{M2} gangliosidosis is a fatal disease that classically first becomes evident in 4- to 6-month-old children and is characterized by

(A) blindness, associated with a cherry-red spot in the retina
(B) enlargement and coloration of the tonsils
(C) enlargement of the liver and spleen
(D) the appearance of tuberous xanthomas
(E) dark coloration of the urine

394. Which of the following central nervous system cell populations is the most rapidly affected by ischemia?

(A) Axis cylinders
(B) Neuronal nerve cell bodies
(C) Astrocytes
(D) Microglia
(E) Oligodendroglia

395. All the following have been commonly associated with pyogenic brain abscesses EXCEPT

(A) congenital heart disease
(B) sinusitis
(C) lung abscess
(D) liver abscesss
(E) mastoiditis

396. Subdural hematomas occur most frequently in the

(A) supracerebellar region
(B) infracerebellar region
(C) cerebellopontine angle
(D) pituitary region
(E) cerebral hemisphere convexities

397. Select the one disorder below that has some clinicopathologic features in common with postvaccinal encephalomyelitis.

(A) Metachromatic leukodystrophy
(B) Multifocal leukoencephalopathy
(C) Guillain-Barré syndrome
(D) Hypoxic encephalopathy
(E) Hypertensive encephalopathy

398. Which of the following tumors is characterized by pseudopalisading, necrosis, endoneurial proliferation, hypercellularity, and atypical nuclei?

(A) Schwannoma
(B) Medulloblastoma
(C) Oligodendroglioma
(D) Glioblastoma multiforme
(E) Ependymoma

399. A young patient is found comatose in an automobile with the engine running. Death ensues within 3 days and an autopsy is performed. Sections through the brain would show

(A) subdural hematoma
(B) epidural hematoma
(C) basilar hemorrhage
(D) brainstem hemorrhages
(E) hemorrhages of the lenticular nuclei

400. Which of the following tumors is most likely to "seed" through the nervous system?

(A) Medulloblastoma
(B) Oligodendroglioma
(C) Pinealoma
(D) Choroid plexus papilloma
(E) Meningioma

401. Angiomyolipofibromas of the kidney and benign myocardial tumors occur in which of the following disorders?

(A) Tuberous sclerosis
(B) Hippel-Lindau disease
(C) von Recklinghausen's disease
(D) Sturge-Weber syndrome
(E) Pemphigus vegetans (Neumann type)

402. Extragonadal germ cell tumors have been described in such sites as the mediastinum and the

(A) corpus callosum
(B) hippocampus
(C) choroid plexus
(D) pineal gland
(E) olfactory bulb

403. The form of motor neuron disease in which there is weakness and atrophy of muscles, without corticospinal tract dysfunction, is known as

(A) amyotrophic lateral sclerosis
(B) progressive muscular atrophy
(C) Werdnig-Hoffmann syndrome
(D) primary lateral sclerosis
(E) Charcot-Marie-Tooth disease

404. A retinoblastoma is most similar to a

(A) fibroma
(B) pheochromocytoma
(C) neuroblastoma
(D) astrocytoma
(E) angioma

405. Transection of a peripheral nerve will result in all the following EXCEPT

(A) loss of the entire Schwann sheath proximal to the point of the cut
(B) dissolution of the Nissl substance in the nerve cell body
(C) degeneration of the nerve fiber distal to the cut
(D) proliferation of the Schwann sheath from the proximal nerve segment
(E) degeneration of the axons from 1 to 3 nodes of Ranvier proximal to the cut

DIRECTIONS: Each question below contains four suggested answers of which **one** or **more** is correct. Choose the answer:

A	if	**1, 2, and 3**	are correct
B	if	**1 and 3**	are correct
C	if	**2 and 4**	are correct
D	if	**4**	is correct
E	if	**1, 2, 3, and 4**	are correct

406. True statements about meningiomas include which of the following?

(1) They constitute 15 percent of all brain tumors
(2) They are more common in children than in adults
(3) They are more common in women than in men
(4) They usually are not amenable to surgical therapy

407. Differentiation into mature ganglion cells in the midst of more primitive cells may occur in

(1) oligodendroglioma
(2) neuroblastoma
(3) retinoblastoma
(4) medulloblastoma

408. Important causes of cerebral infarction include

(1) arteriosclerotic vascular disease
(2) acute lead poisoning
(3) cerebral embolization
(4) equine encephalitis

409. Hypertensive hemorrhage is common in which of the following anatomic sites?

(1) Internal capsule-basal ganglia
(2) Pons
(3) Cerebellum
(4) Medulla

410. A known alcoholic is brought to the emergency room following an altercation in a local bar. The intern observes respiratory irregularity, coma, and papilledema. Emergency surgery is planned in order to prevent

(1) brain herniation
(2) cerebellar herniation
(3) Duret hemorrhages
(4) death of the patient

411. Development of bilirubin encephalopathy depends on the

(1) plasma albumin level
(2) type of hyperbilirubinemia
(3) status of acid-base balance
(4) degree of hyperbilirubinemia

412. A preadolescent male with a history of epilepsy (seizures) and mental slowness has facial skin lesions that have become more prominent in the last several years. On the basis of this information, what other abnormalities have been described?

(1) Cardiac rhabdomyoma
(2) Subependymal gliosis
(3) Renal angiomyolipoma
(4) Periungual fibroma

413. Idiopathic parkinsonism is characterized by which of the following?

(1) Cerebral edema
(2) Depigmentation and loss of neurons in the substantia nigra
(3) Neurofibrillary tangles
(4) Lewy bodies

414. Which of the following tumors may be found arising within the pineal gland?

(1) Pineoblastomas
(2) Embryonal carcinoma
(3) Choriocarcinoma
(4) Craniopharyngioma

415. Diseases that are classified as demyelinating include

(1) multiple sclerosis
(2) Arnold-Chiari syndrome
(3) postinfectious encephalomyelitis
(4) myasthenia gravis

416. Tabes dorsalis causes

(1) bilateral degeneration of dorsal nerve roots
(2) a positive Romberg sign
(3) severe impairment of vibratory sense
(4) progressive sensitivity to pain

417. Of unknown pathogenesis, amyotrophic lateral sclerosis commonly occurs in midlife and

(1) is not always fatal
(2) causes sensory loss secondary to dorsal nerve root involvement
(3) produces spasticity of all affected muscles
(4) causes weakness, atrophy, and fasciculations of hand muscles

418. Syringomyelia, once regarded as an inflammatory reaction, is characterized by

(1) softening around the central canal of the cervical spinal cord
(2) loss of pain and temperature sense with segmental distribution
(3) sensory dissociation
(4) degeneration extending to the posterior funiculi

419. Subacute combined degeneration

(1) is associated with pernicious anemia
(2) usually affects the gray matter of the spinal cord
(3) causes posterior funiculi injury
(4) usually does not cause motor impairment

420. Alzheimer's disease is characterized by

(1) dementia
(2) neurofibrillary tangles
(3) diffuse general neuronal loss in the cortex, usually accentuated in the frontal and occipital lobes
(4) senile plaques

421. The lesion shown in the photomicrograph below was removed from a patient's nasal cavity. With no age given and at this low magnification, possible diagnoses include

(1) extramedullary plasmacytoma
(2) nasal glioma
(3) olfactory neuroblastoma
(4) nasopharyngeal angiofibroma

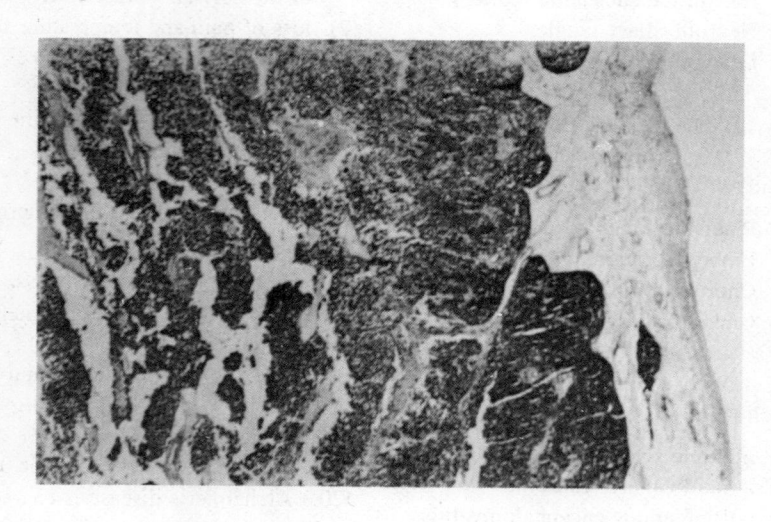

DIRECTIONS: The groups of questions below consist of lettered choices followed by several numbered items. For each numbered item select the **one** lettered choice with which it is **most** closely associated. Each lettered choice may be used once, more than once, or not at all.

Questions 422-426

For each of the following conditions, choose the most appropriate description.

(A) Herniation of the meninges alone
(B) Herniation of meninges and brain parenchyma
(C) Developmental bone defect
(D) Herniation of meninges and a portion of the spinal cord
(E) Herniation at the roof of the mouth

422. Cranium bifidum

423. Meningocele

424. Meningoencephalocele

425. Spina bifida

426. Meningomyelocele

Questions 427-433

For each of the following diseases, choose the sign with which it is most likely to be associated.

(A) Cowdry A intranuclear inclusion body
(B) Disseminated focal demyelination
(C) Diffuse general demyelination
(D) Motor neuron disease
(E) Status spongiosus

427. Creutzfeldt-Jakob disease

428. Kuru

429. Subacute sclerosing panencephalitis

430. Krabbe's disease

431. Multiple sclerosis

432. Amyotrophic lateral sclerosis

433. Metachromatic leukodystrophy

Questions 434-439

For each disease, choose the sign with which it is most likely to be associated.

(A) Neurofibrillary tangles
(B) Lewy bodies
(C) Cowdry A intranuclear inclusion bodies
(D) Corpora amylacea
(E) Small, "carrot-shaped" cells

434. Idiopathic parkinsonism

435. Postencephalitic parkinsonism

436. Herpes simplex encephalitis

437. Alzheimer's disease

438. Medulloblastoma

439. Nonspecific postmortem finding not linked to a known disease process

Nervous System Answers

389. The answer is C. *(Robbins, ed 3. pp 1387-1388.)* The transmissible agent found in Creutzfeldt-Jakob disease (CJ) produces a spongioform (Swiss-cheese) encephalopathy with multiple clear spaces and vacuoles of the cerebral cortex. There are very few, if any, inflammatory cellular elements or abnormal-appearing astrocytes, as are seen in progressive multifocal leukoencephalopathy (PML). The disease has characteristics of kuru (New Guinea) in that the spongiosis is similar, but CJ is better identified with earlier forms of dementia and shows more involvement of the cerebral cortex than kuru does, with kuru involving more of the cerebellar cortex. Two recorded cases document the transmission of contaminated tissue from one patient to another. The transmissible agent is thought to be a virus, but it is not visible with electron microscopy and exhibits alarming resistance to drying, radiation, ultraviolet light, formalin, and most antiseptic soaps. It is inactivated by solutions of hypochlorite (bleach) and autoclaving.

390. The answer is C. *(Robbins, ed 3. pp 1406-1407.)* Astrocytomas are not at all uncommon in the younger age group, but when a child presents with clinical symptomatology pointing to the intracranial posterior fossa, a cerebellar medulloblastoma should be suspected, especially if the child has no prior history of leukemia or neuroblastoma. Medulloblastomas occur predominantly in childhood and usually arise in the midline of the cerebellum (the vermis). They do occur (less commonly) in adults, in whom they are more apt to arise in the cerebellar hemispheres in a lateral position. They grow by local invasive growth and may block cerebrospinal fluid circulation (CSF block) by compression of the fourth ventricle. Recent aggressive treatment with the combined modalities of excision, radiotherapy, and chemotherapy have improved survival.

391. The answer is D. *(Robbins, ed 3. pp 1378-1380.)* Persistent vomiting, bulging fontanelles, convulsions, focal neurologic signs, and persistent fever are often indicative of subdural effusion in an infant with *Hemophilus influenzae* meningitis. *Hemophilus* is one of the two common causes of meningitis in childhood and infancy—the other is meningococcus. *Hemophilus* meningitis is characterized by a heavy, plasticlike, fibrin-rich exudate that collects about the base of the brain and brainstem. Because of the localization, the foramina and aqueducts may be obstructed, producing a progressive internal hydrocephalus.

392. The answer is A. *(Robbins, ed 3. pp 1403-1404.)* Although several lesions within the brain may be associated with dystrophic or metaplastic calcification, the presence of a calcified tumorlike mass lesion in the cerebral hemispheres should arouse suspicion of oligodendroglioma. Oligodendrogliomas are often slow-growing gliomas composed of round cells with clear cytoplasm ("fried-egg appearance"), occurring in the fourth and fifth decades. However, some oligodendrogliomas do proliferate in a rapid and aggressive fashion and may be associated with a malignant astrocytoma component. The brown tumor associated with hypercalcemia of hyperparathyroidism is associated with osteitis fibrosa cystica of bone. Some metastatic carcinomas may show microcalcifications in the form of psammoma bodies, as do some meningiomas. Papillary carcinomas of the thyroid and ovary are the best examples of such lesions, but the calcifications found in papillary carcinomas are rarely of the degree and magnitude of those found in some oligodendrogliomas.

393. The answer is A. *(Anderson, ed 8. pp 102, 106, 1898-1899.)* Type 1 G_{M2} gangliosidosis, or Tay-Sachs disease, results in blindness associated with a cherry-red spot in the retina. Affected individuals also demonstrate developmental retardation, paralysis, and dementia. The disease is usually fatal by the age of 3 to 4 years.

394. The answer is B. *(Robbins, ed 3. pp 1388-1391.)* Neurons in the central nervous system are most vulnerable to anoxia. The cells affected earliest are those in Sommer's sector of the hippocampus, followed by the Purkinje cells of the cerebellum. The primary motor areas and receptive areas are relatively spared in contrast to the severe involvement of the association areas.

395. The answer is D. *(Anderson, ed 8. pp 1901-1903.)* Pyogenic brain abscesses may have a number of possible sources, but the origin can often be determined from the location and number of abscesses in the brain parenchyma. Isolated lesions in the frontal lobes often arise from extension of sinus infections. In the temporal lobe or cerebellum, an isolated lesion may have the middle ear or mastoid as the primary site. Multiple lesions, especially in the superior aspects of the cerebrum, are seen with hematogenous dissemination, often from lung infection or in association with the lesions of congenital heart disease.

396. The answer is E. *(Rosai, ed 6. pp 1563-1566.)* When blood enters the potential space between the arachnoid and dura, a subdural hematoma forms. Subdural hematomas are most commonly located over the cerebral hemisphere convexities. The traditional explanation for the formation of subdural hematomas has been tearing of the bridging veins that pass from the cortical surface to the superior sagittal sinus. Blood may also leak from lacerated cortical vessels or arachnoidal vessels ruptured by a meningeal tear.

397. The answer is C. *(Robbins ed 3. pp 1424, 1429-1431.)* Guillain-Barré (GB) syndrome (acute inflammatory polyradiculoneuropathy) is similar to postinfectious (or postvaccinal) encephalomyelitis in that both cause a process of demyelination and show perivascular infiltrates of lymphoid cells (in the brain and brainstem in encephalomyelitis and in the craniospinal nerve, roots, and ganglia in Guillain-Barré syndrome). In addition, the anterior horn cells in GB syndrome may be degenerative. GB syndrome manifests clinically as lower limb weakness and paralysis with varying sensory disturbances, such as hypesthesiae of the lower limbs. The disease may progress to involvement of the musculature of the upper body, including the muscles of respiration, which can lead to respiratory arrest in the absence of mechanical ventilatory assistance. GB syndrome was identified in some individuals who were vaccinated with influenza vaccines during the late 1970s.

398. The answer is D. *(Rosai, ed 6. pp 1431-1434, 1574-1581.)* Schwannomas generally appear as extremely cellular, spindle cell neoplasms, sometimes with metaplastic elements of bone, cartilage, and skeletal muscle. Medulloblastomas occur exclusively in the cerebellum and microscopically are highly cellular with uniform nuclei, scant cytoplasm, and, in about one-third of cases, rosette formation centered by neurofibrillary material. Oligodendrogliomas, which are marked by foci of calcification in 70 percent of cases, commonly show a pattern of uniform cellularity and are composed of round cells with small dark nuclei, clear cytoplasm, and a clearly defined cell membrane. Ependymomas are distinguished by ependymal rosettes, which are ductlike structures with a central lumen around which columnar tumor cells are arranged in a concentric fashion.

399. The answer is E. *(Anderson, ed 8. pp 214-216.)* Incomplete combustion of any carbon fuel will lead to accumulation of carbon monoxide gases. Oxygen deprivation results from the formation of carboxyhemoglobin, which displaces the normal oxyhemoglobin and interferes with oxygen exchange. In addition to small petechial hemorrhages of serosa and white matter of the cerebral hemispheres, patients who have lived for several days following exposure will have gross lesions in the brain that consist of hemorrhagic necrosis of the basal ganglia that is bilaterally symmetrical, especially in the globus pallidus, and the hippocampus.

400. The answer is A. *(Robbins, ed 3. pp 1406-1407.)* Medulloblastoma, more than any other glioma, has a tendency to seed through the subarachnoid space to involve brain and spinal cord. Midline medulloblastomas expand into the fourth ventricle and produce ventricular obstructive symptoms. The other tumors listed may disseminate through the cerebrospinal pathways but do so less commonly than the medulloblastoma.

401. The answer is A. *(Anderson, ed 8. pp 1875, 1631.)* Tuberous sclerosis, an autosomal dominant disease with dysplastic development of the central nervous system ectodermal cells, may be associated with developmental abnormalities in multiple organs. Sturge-Weber syndrome consists of angiomas of the skin, meninges, and brain and is characterized by epilepsy, hemiplegia, glaucoma, and intracranial calcifications. Neurofibromatosis is known as von Recklinghausen's disease. Hippel-Lindau disease is the eponym given to cystic angiomas of the cerebellum associated with angioma of the retina and polycystic kidneys. The Neumann type of pemphigus vegetans is characterized by marked acanthosis and by bullous lesions that usually first appear in the mucous membranes of the mouth or on the skin of the trunk.

402. The answer is D. *(Anderson, ed 8. p 1921.)* Germ cell tumors do occur as primary neoplasms outside of and apparently without relation to the ovaries or the testicles; such tumors are designated "extragonadal germinomas." Examples include tumors in midline sites of the body, such as the pineal gland (seminoma), mediastinum, and sacrum (teratoma). Every germ cell neoplasm that is primary in the testis has at one time or another been reported as occurring in the male mediastinum. Whereas not all researchers agree that the germinoma arising in the pineal gland is of germ-cell origin, its histologic appearance is strikingly similar to that of classic seminoma.

403. The answer is B. *(Robbins, ed 3. pp 1306, 1309.)* Motor neuron disease is a progressive disorder of the motor neurons in the cerebral cortex, brainstem, and spinal cord and occurs in different forms, depending on the involvement of one or more of these anatomic sites. In progressive muscular atrophy, there is predominant involvement of anterior horn cells, with remittent weakness and atrophy of muscles but no evidence of the corticospinal tract dysfunction that is a finding in amyotrophic lateral sclerosis. However, the basic pathologic processes of these two diseases are similar.

404. The answer is C. *(Robbins, ed 3. p 1247.)* The neuroblastoma is a highly malignant tumor that occurs most frequently in children and young adolescents. About 50 percent of neuroblastomas are found in the adrenal gland, and most of the remainder occur in association with the sympathetic chain. When these tumors develop in the retina, they are called retinoblastomas. The tumor cells form rosettes, with nerve fibrils growing into the center of each rosette.

405. The answer is A. *(Robbins, ed 3. pp 1428-1429.)* The axonal reaction that occurs when a peripheral nerve is cut includes a number of striking changes. In the cell body, swelling and dissolution of the Nissl substance are apparent within 24 to 48 hours after transection. The axon and covering myelin or Schwann sheath distal to the lesion first degenerate and undergo resorption. In addition, the axis cylinder and Schwann sheath degenerate proximal to the cut over the distance of a few nodal segments. Regeneration occurs when the Schwann cells proliferate from the proximal portion to form a hollow myelin sheath through which the axons grow again.

406. The answer is B (1, 3). *(Robbins, ed 3. pp 1407-1409.)* Meningiomas are more common in adults than in children and occur nearly twice as often in women as in men. The tumors apparently arise from fibroblastic elements normally found in arachnoidal tissue. Because meningiomas occur outside the brain parenchyma and grow slowly, they are uniquely amenable to surgical treatment. Meningiomas are typically discrete and encapsulated, so that symptoms occur as the growing tumor displaces and compresses normal brain parenchyma.

407. The answer is C (2, 4). *(Robbins, ed 3. pp 1247-1248.)* Neuroblastoma may be primary in the cerebral hemisphere in children, although it is more likely to arise in the adrenal gland. Like its counterpart in the adrenal, cerebral neuroblastoma may show areas of differentiation into mature ganglion cells. Medulloblastoma, another childhood tumor of primitive neuroblastic-type cells, may also form foci of ganglion cells. Medulloblastoma and cerebral neuroblastoma also have other similarities. These include small, dark-staining cells with primitive nuclei; rosette formation; and the capability to spread through the central nervous system by seeding the cerebrospinal fluid.

408. The answer is B (1, 3). *(Robbins, ed 3. pp 1389-1391.)* The major causes of cerebral infarction are cerebral arteriosclerosis, cerebral arteritis, and cerebral embolism. In arteriosclerotic vascular disease, thrombi may form on atheromatous plaques or in stenotic regions. Emboli to cerebral vessels come chiefly from the heart, either from thrombi formed in the fibrillating left atrium, from mural thrombi overlying a myocardial infarct, or from valvular material associated with endocarditis.

409. The answer is A. *(Robbins, ed 3. p 1395.)* Hypertensive hemorrhages occur nearly 80 percent of the time in the cerebral hemispheres. They affect, in decreasing order, the putamen and claustrum, the thalamus, and the white matter (rare). Approximately 10 percent of hypertensive hemorrhages occur in the pons or midbrain, and the remaining 10 percent occur in the cerebellum.

410. The answer is E. *(Robbins, ed 3. pp 87-88, 1398-1399.)* The clinical constellation of altered sensorium and papilledema should call to mind the presence of intracranial pressure, regardless of the cause, which can be due to cerebral edema, tumor mass, or, more commonly, intracranial bleeding with hematoma formation. If the pressure is severe enough, downward displacement of the cerebellar tonsils into the foramen magnum may occur, producing further compression on the brainstem with consequent hemorrhage into the pons and midbrain (Duret hemorrhages). This is nearly always associated with death, since the vital centers, including respiratory control, are located in these regions. Subdural as well as epidural hemorrhages are sufficient to cause critical downward displacement of the cerebellar tonsils. The situation can be remedied with appropriate neurosurgical intervention. In this situation, the downward displacement could be due to hemorrhage-hematoma formation into the posterior intracranial fossa, caused by either a direct (coup) or an indirect (contracoup) blow to the occiput.

411. The answer is E (all). *(Anderson, ed 8. pp 1143-1144, 1900.)* Kernicterus is a neurologic complication of severe, unconjugated hyperbilirubinemia that may develop in a jaundiced newborn. Normally, the binding of unconjugated bilirubin by albumin restricts pigment diffusion into tissue cells. However, when the unconjugated bilirubin concentration exceeds the albumin-binding capacity, the lipid-soluble, unconjugated bilirubin is free to diffuse through the blood-brain barrier. Depression of the plasma albumin level; administration of drugs that bind to albumin, displacing bilirubin; and metabolic acidosis all predispose to kernicterus. The bile pigments are noted to discolor the globi pallidi, subthalamic nuclei, hippocampi, dentate nuclei, and inferior olivary nuclei most commonly.

412. The answer is E (all). *(Robbins, ed 3. p 1428.)* Tuberous sclerosis is an important autosomal, dominantly inherited disorder characterized by the triad of epilepsy, mental retardation, and skin lesions. The skin lesions are protean, appear unrelated histologically, and consist of multiple angiofibromas (misnamed adenosebaceum) over the forehead, eyelids, and cheeks. Other lesions are "ash leaf" spots, shagreen patches on the trunk, and periungual fibromas. Periungual fibromas are very characteristic of the disease, if not almost pathognomonic. Visceral involvement may include benign cardiac tumors (rhabdomyoma), angiomyolipoma of the kidney, and a peculiar gliosis occurring around the ventricles of the brain. Because of its unique macroscopic waxy appearance, this unusual gliosis has been called "candle drippings."

413. The answer is C (2, 4). *(Robbins, ed 3. pp 1417-1418.)* The pathology of Parkinson's disease remains controversial as to the significance of the observed lesions. In this disease, there is a reduction of pigment in the substantia nigra and nerve cell loss and degeneration. Nigral cells may show rounded intracytoplasmic inclusions that are termed Lewy bodies. A small lenticular nucleus and atrophy of the ansa lenticularis have also been observed.

414. The answer is A (1, 2, 3). *(Robbins, ed 3. pp 1200, 1253-1254.)* Primary tumors of the pineal gland are very uncommon but are of interest, especially in view of the mysterious and relatively unknown functions of the pineal gland itself. The gland secretes neurotransmitter substances such as serotonin and dopamine, with the major product being melatonin. Tumors of the pineal gland include germ cell tumors of all types including embryonal carcinoma, choriocarcinoma, teratoma, and various combinations of germinomas. Germ cell tumors may arise extragonadally within the retroperitoneal space and the pineal gland, with the only commonality being that these structures are in the midline. Primary tumors of the pineal gland occur in two forms: the pineoblastoma and the pineocytoma. Pineoblastomas occur in young patients and consist of small tumors having areas of hemorrhage and necrosis with pleomorphic nuclei and frequent mitoses. Pineocytomas occur in older adults and are slow-growing; they are better differentiated and have large rosettes. Craniopharyngiomas occur not in the pineal gland but above the pituitary gland in the hypothalamus and are thought to arise from structures related to Rathke's pouch.

415. The answer is B (1, 3). *(Robbins, ed 3. pp 1410-1413.)* Demyelinization occurs in many pathologic processes of the central nervous system, but the demyelinating diseases are those in which loss of myelin without proportionate loss of axis cylinders is the major manifestation. Only three important diseases fall within this strict definition: postinfectious encephalomyelitis, multiple sclerosis, and progressive multifocal leukoencephalopathy. Postinfectious encephalomyelitis can follow measles, chickenpox, smallpox, and inoculation for smallpox or rabies. The etiology of multiple sclerosis is unknown.

416. The answer is A (1, 2, 3). *(Robbins, ed 3. p 1381.)* Tabes dorsalis causes bilateral degeneration of dorsal nerve roots and the posterior funiculi. During the early phase of the disease, there are sharp attacks of pain because of irritation of the dorsal nerve roots, but later there is a progressive loss of sensitivity to pain, vibration, and proprioceptive stimuli. The interruption of the stretch reflex may result in a positive Romberg sign. The pathogenesis of tabes dorsalis is controversial. Etiologic postulates include focal leptomeningeal inflammation of the dorsal roots, such factors as changes in the structure of the dorsal root ganglia, and a toxic product or metabolic disorder rather than tissue infestation by *Treponema*.

417. The answer is D (4). *(Robbins, ed 3. p 1419.)* Amyotrophic lateral sclerosis is a disease of unknown etiology that may have a prolonged course but is eventually fatal. Destruction of motor neurons occurs in the anterior gray horns, together with bilateral degeneration of the pyramidal tracts, and thus the clinical deficit is mixed upper and lower motor neuron disease. Weakness, atrophy, and fasciculations occur in some muscles, usually in the hands, and spasticity and hyperreflexia in others, usually in the legs. Amyotrophic lateral sclerosis, progressive spinal muscular atrophy, and progressive bulbar palsy differ from one another only in the distribution of the lesions.

418. The answer is A (1, 2, 3). *(Robbins, ed 3. p 1427.)* Syringomyelia is a disease in which there is softening and cavitation around the central canal of the spinal cord. The lateral spinothalamic tracts are interrupted as they cross ventral to the canal, resulting in loss of pain and temperature sense in a segmental distribution (the long tracts are not disturbed). The cause of syringomyelia remains unknown. At autopsy, the spinal cord is found to contain a cyst surrounded by scar tissue and filled with fluid. The overlying leptomeninges are often thickened. The extent of spinal cord degeneration depends on the size of the cyst and the amount of resulting gliosis.

419. The answer is B (1, 3). *(Robbins, ed 3. pp 634, 1421.)* Subacute combined degeneration is a disease often associated with pernicious anemia or with other nutritional disturbances. The posterior funiculi and pyramidal tracts undergo degeneration, but the gray matter is only rarely affected. Motor weakness with spasticity is the characteristic result. The degeneration is clearly related to B_{12} deficiency, as partial correction of the associated megaloblastic anemia with folic acid does not improve the myelopathy.

420. The answer is E (all). *(Robbins, ed 3. pp 1414-1416.)* Alzheimer's disease is said to be the major cause of organic mental change in elderly patients. If the syndrome of parenchymal lesions of cortical atrophy, neuron loss, neurofibrillar degeneration, and senile plaques occurs earlier in life, the resultant clinical picture is termed presenile dementia. Progression usually results in complete dementia.

421. The answer is B (1, 3). *(Anderson, ed 8. pp 990-991, 997. Askin, Cancer 43:2438, 1979.)* The photomicrograph (at low magnification) shows an intact overlying mucosa with a subjacent highly cellular neoplasm composed of small dark-staining cells ("tumor of small blue cells"). In the child, small blue cell tumors comprise lymphoma, neuroblastoma, cerebellar medulloblastoma, undifferentiated nephroblastoma (Wilm's tumor), retinoblastoma, embryonal rhabdomyosarcoma, and Ewing's sarcoma. In the adult, anaplastic, small-cell carcinomas of the lung, pancreas, uterine cervix, and anorectum (cloacogenic carcinoma); plasmacytomas; and neuroectodermal tumors of thoracopulmonary origin are also included. In addition to the age of the patient and the organ site, certain structures visible at higher magnification, such as rosettes (retinoblastoma) and pseudorosettes (anaplastic small-cell carcinoma, neuroblastoma) aid in the differential diagnosis. In the example given, the lesion is too cellular to be either nasal glioma (large, pale glial cells) or nasopharyngeal angiofibroma (vascular structures). The olfactory neuroblastoma (the tumor depicted in the photomicrograph) arises from the olfactory placode of the stem cell referred to as the esthesioneuroblast. The cells populating the tumor are round or oval neuroepithelial cells occurring in clusters and associated with a fibrillary intercellular matrix.

422-426. The answers are: 422-C, 423-A, 424-B, 425-C, 426-D. *(Robbins, ed 3. pp 1426-1427. Rosai, ed 6. pp 1556-1557.)* Developmental anomalies of the central nervous system occur under genetic and environmental influences or sporadically during a critical phase in gestation. Various trisomies are examples of genetic mishaps. Environmental factors include drugs (both therapeutic and illegal), ionizing radiation, infections (rubella, syphilis, toxoplasmosis), malnutrition, and circulatory insufficiency.

When the bony spinal cord fails to close, multiple errors, occurring sporadically as single entities or in association with other central nervous system anomalies, are possible. Spina bifida, the most common developmental defect that occurs in the neural tube, involves the failure of the vertebral arches to close completely. Meningomyelocele is herniation of part of the spinal cord tissue and the meninges through such a defect. In spina bifida occulta the neural tube closure defect is covered by skin and dermis, with only a pinpoint sinus or hair-covered depression marking the site. Bacterial meningitis, or meningomyelitis, is the major potential risk in these patients.

A developmental defect in the skull bones similar to spina bifida is cranium bifidum, which is regarded as a congenital cranial cleft. Meningocele is herniation of the meninges alone through a cranium bifidum.

Meningoencephalocele includes herniation of meninges and brain substance in the region of the occipital bone. Meningoencephalocystocele, a herniation at the roof of the mouth, together with cranial meningocele and cranial meningoencephalocele, occurs less frequently than the herniations associated with spina bifida.

The Arnold-Chiari malformation consists of herniation of the cerebellum and fourth ventricle into the foramen magnum, skull base flattening, and cerebral aqueduct stenosis with hydrocephalus and meningomyelocele. Various combinations of the above abnormalities exist, and it is not necessary for all of them to be uniformly present for the disease to qualify as Arnold-Chiari malformation. In all cases, however, the clinical course is reflected by the degree of hydrocephalus.

427-433. The answers are: 427-E, 428-E, 429-A, 430-C, 431-B, 432-D, 433-C. *(Robbins, ed 3. pp 1410-1412, 1413, 1424-1425.)* Creutzfeldt-Jakob disease, kuru, and subacute sclerosing panencephalitis (SSPE) are diseases caused by slow viruses with incubation periods measured in years. Krabbe's disease (globoid leukodystrophy), metachromatic leukodystrophy, multiple sclerosis, and amyotrophic lateral sclerosis are connected in various ways with demyelination. Krabbe's disease and metachromatic leukodystrophy are leukoencephalopathies thought to result from congenital defects in formation or maintenance of myelin, the material sheathing medullated nerve fibers. These fibers are the main components of the white matter. Multiple sclerosis is also a disease of the white matter, but its pathogenesis is not yet known.

Creutzfeldt-Jakob disease and kuru are both examples of subacute spongiform (spongiosis) encephalopathy. The spongiotic changes in the brain involve vacuoles that are membrane-bound in neuronal processes. Personality changes, visual incoordination, progressive marked dementia, and myoclonus characterize the clinical course of Creutzfeldt-Jakob disease. Kuru is a disease of the Fore tribe of New Guinea that has been linked to transmission by cannibalism of diseased brains.

SSPE is characterized histopathologically by a perivascular mononuclear cell infiltrate, neuronophagia and neuron dropout, and fibrillary gliosis, but its distinguishing feature is Cowdry A intranuclear inclusion bodies—measles virus particles found in the oligodendrocytes and cortical neurons, as seen with electron microscopy. The cell lysis may be caused by immunologic reaction to the persistent virus particles.

Krabbe's disease, or globoid leukodystrophy, is a deficiency of galactoside-β-galactosidase with diagnostic multinucleate giant histiocyte cells situated around cerebral vessels. Electron microscopy reveals intracytoplasmic hollow tubular structures.

In metachromatic leukodystrophy, demyelination is quite extensive in the cerebrum as well as in the peripheral nervous system and is inherited as an autosomal recessive condition. It is a sulfatide lipidosis that results from a deficiency of aryl sulfatase-A. Sulfatides accumulate pathologically in lysosomes. These accumulations, then, are PAS-positive and stain metachromatically with cresyl violet (hence the disease's name). The sulfatides accumulate in other organs and can be demonstrated in sloughed renal epithelial cells and macrophages in the urine with cresyl violet.

The demyelinating plaques of multiple sclerosis are widespread in both gray and white matter. More than in any of the other demyelinating disorders, however, they have a propensity for occurring around the corners of the lateral ventricles and hence are known as periventricular plaques.

Amyotrophic lateral sclerosis has as its fundamental pathologic process degeneration of corticospinal or corticobulbar pathways and degeneration of motor nerve cells of the spinal cord and brainstem. The disease demyelinates the corticospinal tracts of the dorsolateral columns of the spinal cord as well as the cranial nerves.

434-439. The answers are: 434-B, 435-A, 436-C, 437-A, 438-E, 439-D. *(Robbins, ed 3. pp 1383-1385, 1406-1407, 1414-1415, 1417-1418.)* Parkinson's disease has several clinical pathologic forms. Classic Parkinson's disease presents between the sixth and ninth decades, is progressive, and results in degeneration of the striatonigral pathway, with diminution of dopamine in the corpus striatum. The amount of dopamine deficiency correlates with the severity of the clinical symptoms.

In idiopathic parkinsonism, Lewy bodies, rounded intracytoplasmic inclusions in the cells of the substantia nigra, can be found in the brain.

Postencephalitic parkinsonism (von Economo's disease), one of the complications of encephalitic lethargia, has the same effects on the striatonigral pathway and amount of dopamine in the corpus striatum as classic parkinsonism, but it occurs earlier and is not progressive. In postencephalitic parkinsonism, neurofibrillary tangles result from an alteration of the neurofibrillar apparatus so that the fibrils appear thickened and tortuous, forming a tangled skein within the cytoplasm.

Alzheimer's disease also shows neurofibrillary tangles within areas of neuronal loss. The tangles are neurofilaments stainable by silver and are demonstrated within neurons. "Senile" silver-stainable plaques are also present in the gray matter of the hippocampus in Alzheimer's disease. Alzheimer's differs from Pick's disease in its progressive atrophy of the entire brain; Pick's is associated with a striking atrophy of the frontal lobes and some loss of the temporal lobes.

Herpes simplex encephalitis has a high mortality rate (65 to 80 percent) if untreated with adenine arabinoside-A (ARA-A). The disease causes necrotizing lesions with Cowdry A intranuclear inclusion bodies in oligodendroglia and occasional neurons. In addition to the nonspecific perivascular mononuclear infiltrates, characteristic hemorrhagic necrosis is present in the temporal and frontal lobes, especially the orbital gyri.

Classically, in microscopic examination, medulloblastoma is characterized by the presence of many small carrot-shaped cells that contain oval or elongated nuclei.

Corpora amylacea are small hyaline-appearing masses of degenerated cells that are found in a number of tissues and are not thought to be specific for any known disease.

Musculoskeletal System

DIRECTIONS: Each question below contains five suggested answers. Choose the **one best** response to each question.

440. The most common tumor that involves bone is

(A) a metastatic tumor from an extraosseous site
(B) osteogenic sarcoma
(C) multiple myeloma
(D) chondrosarcoma
(E) a giant-cell tumor

441. Pott's disease (tuberculosis of the spine) most commonly involves

(A) cervical vertebrae
(B) cervical and thoracic vertebrae
(C) thoracic and lumbar vertebrae
(D) the sacroiliac region
(E) all regions of the vertebral column equally

442. The part of a long bone initially involved in hematogenous osteomyelitis is the

(A) metaphyseal region
(B) diaphysis
(C) epiphysis
(D) area around the entrance of the nutrient artery
(E) medullary cavity

443. Which of the following phrases describes the organisms associated with gas gangrene?

(A) Facultative anaerobic, gram-positive bacilli
(B) Facultative anaerobic, gram-negative bacilli
(C) Strictly anaerobic, gram-positive bacilli
(D) Strictly anaerobic, gram-positive cocci
(E) Strictly anaerobic, gram-negative cocci

444. Arthritic involvement of only the distal interphalangeal joints is characteristic of

(A) rheumatoid arthritis
(B) Still's disease
(C) ankylosing spondylitis
(D) Reiter's disease
(E) psoriatic arthritis

445. The most common location for development of an osteochondroma is the

(A) scapula
(B) spinous process of a vertebral body
(C) rib
(D) metaphysis of the femur
(E) skull

446. The lesion illustrated in the photomicrograph below is most likely
(A) a rheumatoid nodule
(B) myositis ossificans
(C) necrotizing panniculitis
(D) polymyositis
(E) fat necrosis

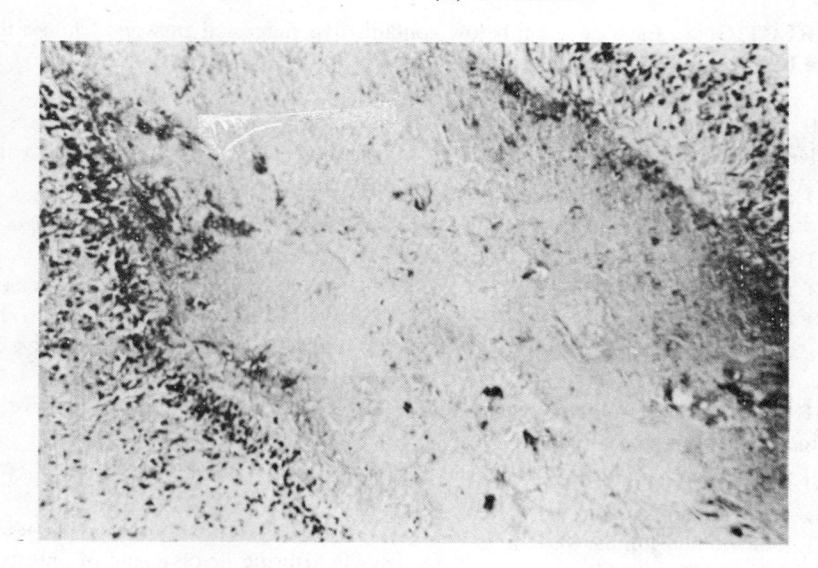

447. In comparison with the general population, workers using radium-containing paints have a higher incidence of
(A) osteogenic sarcoma
(B) carcinoma of the bladder
(C) carcinoma of the lung
(D) carcinoma of the skin
(E) leukemia

448. Osteomalacia has been shown to be the result of
(A) osteosarcoma
(B) excess vitamin D
(C) excess parathormone
(D) vitamin D deficiency
(E) vitamin A deficiency

449. Osteogenesis imperfecta involves
(A) defective synthesis of organic bone matrix
(B) defective intestinal calcium absorption
(C) bone marrow aplasia
(D) absence of osteoblasts
(E) osteoclastic hyperactivity

450. In radiologic evaluation, Ewing's sarcoma has been described as
(A) "onion skin"
(B) "figure of eight"
(C) "soap bubble"
(D) "signet ring"
(E) "double bubble"

451. The specimen shown in the photomicrograph below is from a mass removed from the thigh of a 58-year-old man. Using the current nomenclature, this lesion is compatible with

(A) nodular fasciitis
(B) rhabdomyosarcoma
(C) myositis ossificans
(D) osteogenic sarcoma
(E) malignant fibrous histiocytoma

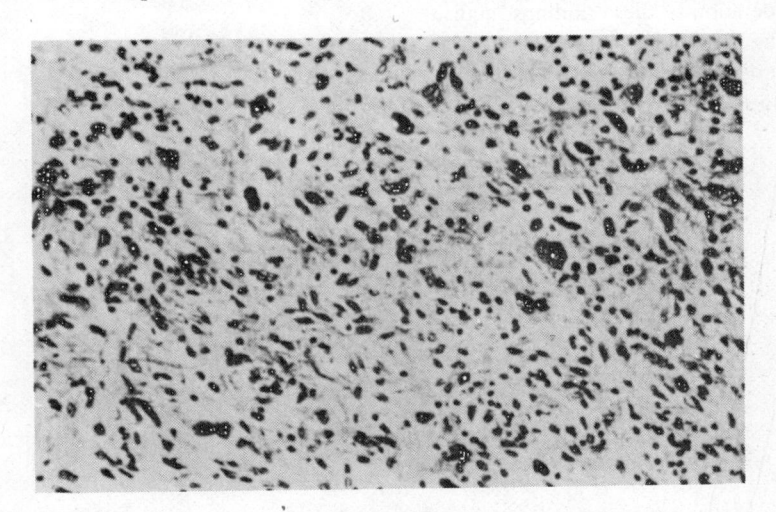

452. Which of the following fibroosseous bone disorders is most likely to be associated with skin lesions?

(A) Osteoid osteoma
(B) Albright's syndrome
(C) Nonossifying fibroma
(D) Polyostotic fibrous dysplasia
(E) Monostotic fibrous dysplasia

453. Which of the following disorders has an X-linked recessive pattern of transmission?

(A) Childhood muscular dystrophy
(B) Congenital adrenal hyperplasia
(C) Sphingomyelin lipidosis
(D) Renal tubular acidosis
(E) Hereditary spherocytosis

454. A patient has enlargement of the skull and bowing of the tibias and femurs. Radiologic evaluation provides confirmation of bone enlargement and evidence of increased radiolucency. In consideration of these findings, signs, and the bone biopsy shown in the photomicrograph below, the most likely diagnosis is

(A) osteomalacia
(B) osteoporosis
(C) Paget's disease
(D) dyschondroplasia
(E) osteogenesis imperfecta

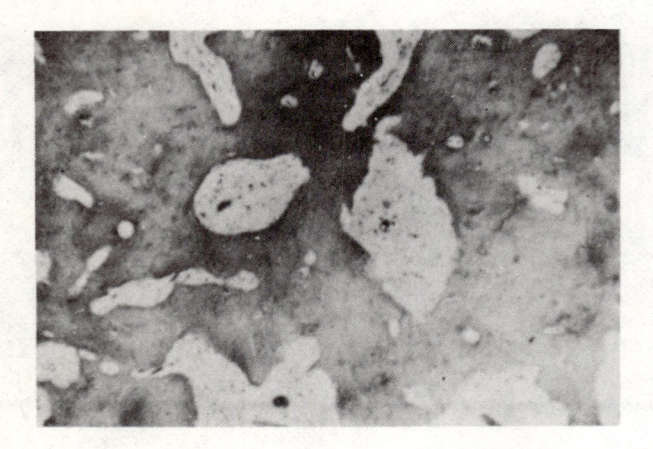

455. A perivascular inflammatory infiltrate in skeletal muscle, as shown in the photomicrograph below, is likely to be seen in all the following EXCEPT

(A) hypersensitivity angiitis
(B) polymyositis
(C) polyarteritis nodosa
(D) cystic medial necrosis
(E) systemic sclerosis

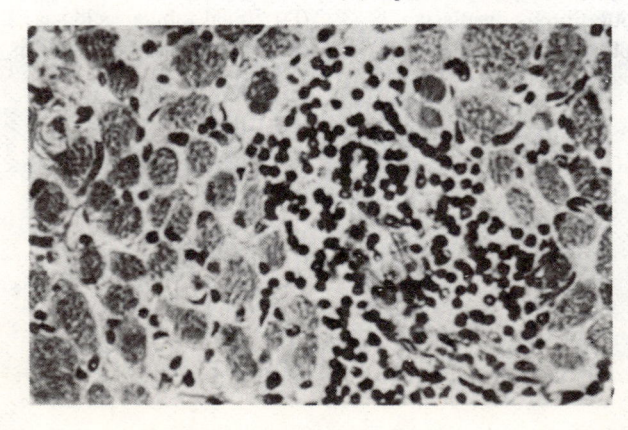

456. The atypical rhabdomyoblasts illustrated in the photomicrograph below may be seen in all the following lesions EXCEPT

(A) sarcoma botryoides
(B) myositis ossificans
(C) mixed heterologous müllerian tumor of the uterus
(D) adult pleomorphic rhabdomyosarcoma
(E) embryonal rhabdomyosarcoma

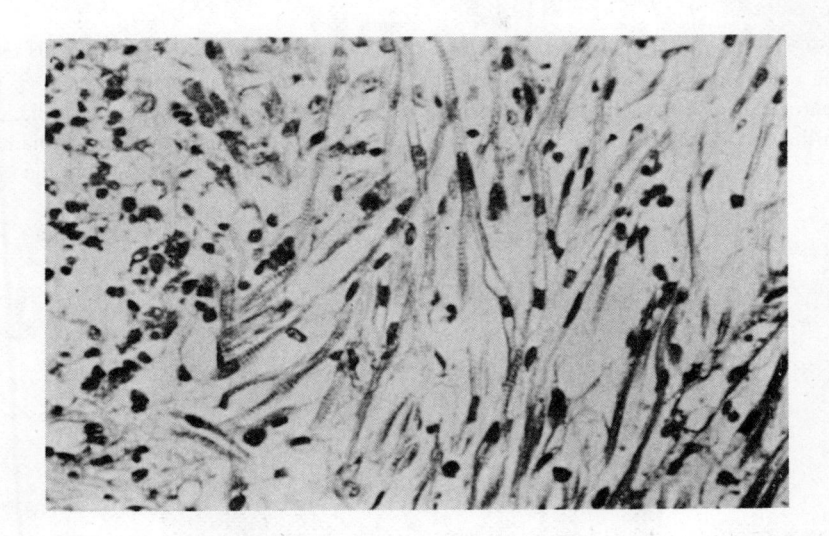

DIRECTIONS: Each question below contains four suggested answers of which **one** or **more** is correct. Choose the answer:

A	if	**1, 2, and 3**	are correct
B	if	**1 and 3**	are correct
C	if	**2 and 4**	are correct
D	if	**4**	is correct
E	if	**1, 2, 3, and 4**	are correct

457. In the radiograph reproduced in the photograph below, the juxtacortical (parosteal) osteosarcoma shown arising in the distal tibia

(1) may be confused with myositis ossificans
(2) is primarily composed of cartilage
(3) has a much better prognosis than osteosarcoma arising within the bone shaft
(4) is usually secondary to trauma

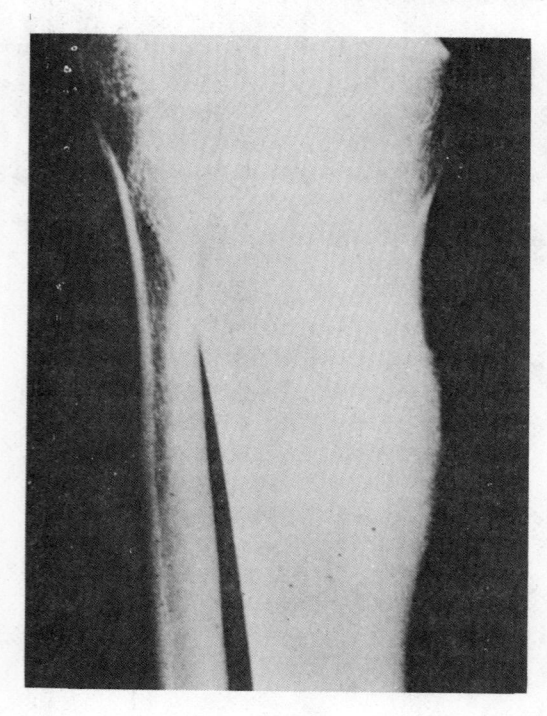

458. Osteogenic sarcoma, shown below in a photograph of an x-ray of a hemisected tibia,

(1) is the most common type of bone cancer in the young
(2) may be associated with Paget's disease in the elderly
(3) may have a sun-burst appearance on x-ray
(4) has a 5-year survival rate of 50 percent

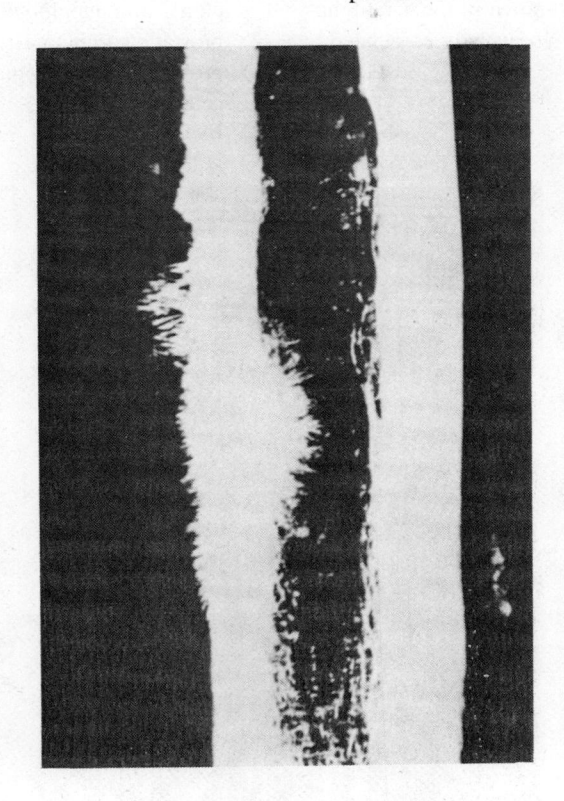

459. Likely sites for liposarcoma include which of the following structures?

(1) Retroperitoneum
(2) Eyelid
(3) Buttock
(4) Ankle

---

460. Multiple, focal osteolytic lesions in the skull, as shown in the x-ray photograph below, are usually associated with

(1) increased production of monoclonal immunoglobulin
(2) prostatic carcinoma
(3) proliferation of neoplastic plasma cells
(4) Ewing's tumor

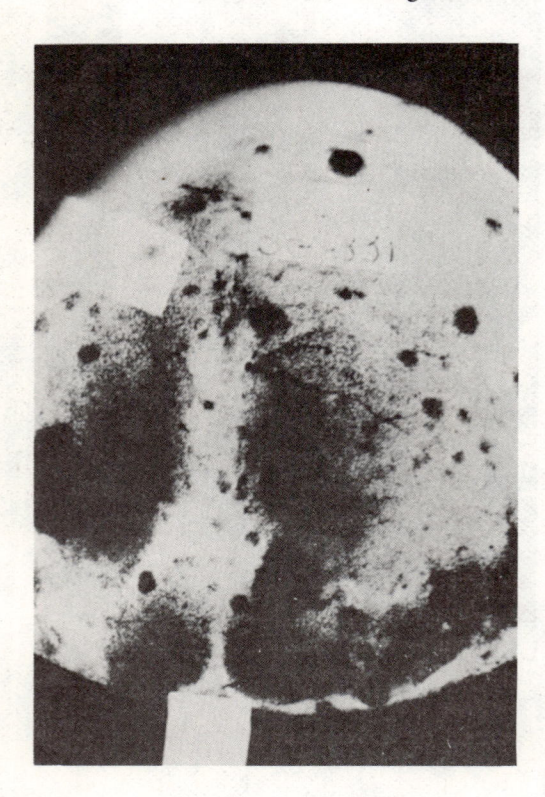

Musculoskeletal System

DIRECTIONS: The groups of questions below consist of lettered choices followed by several numbered items. For each numbered item select the **one** lettered choice with which it is **most** closely associated. Each lettered choice may be used once, more than once, or not at all.

Questions 461-465

For each disease choose the artist's representation of a microradiogram, shown below, with which it is most likely to be associated. Answer "E" if the disease is not associated with any of the microradiograms.

461. Osteosarcoma
462. Primary hyperparathyroidism
463. Vitamin D-resistant rickets
464. Osteoporosis
465. Paget's disease

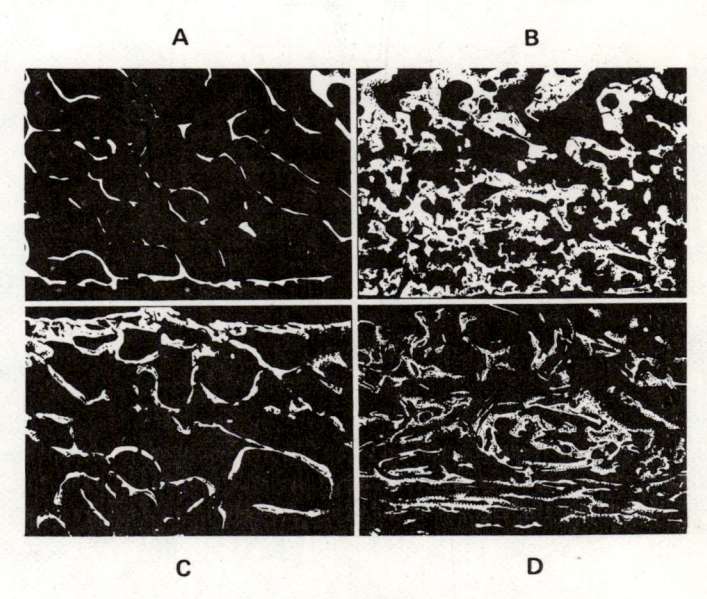

A

B

C

D

E None of the above

Questions 466-470

For each bone lesion, select the lettered location and general configuration with which it is most likely to be associated in the diagram below.

466. Giant cell tumor of bone (osteoclastoma)
467. Unicameral (solitary) bone cyst
468. Osteochondroma
469. Osteoid-osteoma
470. Nonossifying fibroma of bone

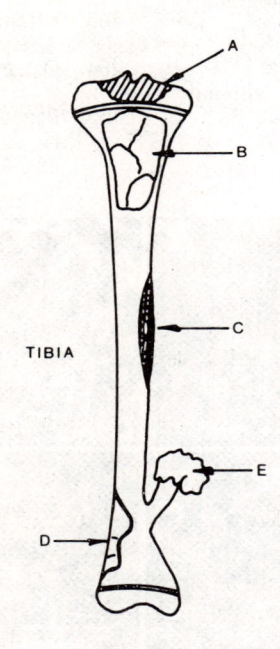

Musculoskeletal System Answers

440. The answer is A. *(Rosai, ed 6. pp 1365-1367.)* Metastases account for the majority of bone tumors, followed in frequency by multiple myeloma and osteogenic sarcoma. Common carcinomas that metastasize to bone include lung, thyroid, breast, prostate, and renal cell carcinomas. Whereas most metastatic carcinomas to bone produce osteocytic radiologic lesions, prostate carcinoma tends to produce osteoblastic metastases. The serum calcium and alkaline phosphatase may be elevated in osseous metastases.

441. The answer is C. *(Anderson, ed 8. p 1764.)* Pott's disease is described as tuberculosis of the spine. The lower thoracic and lumbar vertebrae and their corresponding disks are involved in more than 50 percent of cases of tuberculosis of bone and joints. The progressive bone destruction leads to vertebral body collapse, which may progress to kyphosis. The incidence of osseous tuberculosis is linked to the transmission of bovine tuberculosis to humans. Although its prevalence in the Western world has declined, osseous tuberculosis is still the most common extrapulmonary form of tuberculosis.

442. The answer is A. *(Rosai, ed 6. pp 1312-1317.)* Nutrient arteries to long bones divide to supply the metaphyses and diaphyses. In the metaphyses, the arteries become arterioles and finally form capillary loops adjacent to epiphyseal plates. This anatomic feature allows bacteria to settle in the region of the metaphysis and makes it the site initially involved in hematogenous osteomyelitis. As a consequence of vascular and osteoclastic resorption, the infected bone is replaced by fibrous connective tissue. Persistent chronic osteomyelitis is often associated with sequelae that include amyloidosis and the appearance of malignant tumors in old sinus tracts within the damaged bone.

443. The answer is C. *(Anderson, ed 8. pp 283-285.)* The bacteria that cause gas gangrene belong to the genus *Clostridium*, a genus that also includes the organisms causing tetanus and botulism. All are gram-positive bacilli, and three members—*C. welchii (perfringens)*, *C. novyi*, and *C. septicum*—all cause gas gangrene and are strictly anaerobic. All form spores, which may be introduced into wounds involving soil and begin to germinate in the absence of oxygen deep within the wounds. With large numbers of gram-positive bacilli, muscle fibers undergo necrosis and may liquify. The gas-forming clostridia cause the emission of toxins, which range from lecithinase to hemolytic toxins.

444. The answer is E. *(Anderson, ed 8. pp 1836-1837.)* The most common pattern of joint involvement seen in psoriatic arthritis is a scattered, asymmetrical involvement of the interphalangeal joints of the hands and feet. Much less common, but characteristic of psoriatic arthritis, is the exclusive involvement of distal interphalangeal joints. The joint involvement is often morphologically indistinguishable from the changes of rheumatoid arthritis. The clinical course and features warrant the separation of these entities.

445. The answer is D. *(Rosai, ed 6. pp 1338-1339.)* Osteochondromas are the most common benign tumors of bone. Because these tumors often develop as sessile or stalked protuberances, the term "osteocartilaginous exostosis" is quite appropriate. Osteochondromas may arise in nearly any bone preformed in cartilage but are noted most frequently in the long limb bones, especially in the metaphyseal regions.

446. The answer is A. *(Anderson, ed 8. pp 1594-1595.)* Rheumatoid arthritis frequently affects the small joints of the hands and feet. The larger joints are involved later. Subcutaneous nodules, with a necrotic focus surrounded by palisades of proliferating cells, are seen in some cases. In the joints, the synovial membrane is thickened by a granulation tissue pannus that is infiltrated by many inflammatory cells. Nodular collections of lymphocytes resembling follicles are characteristically seen. The thickened synovial membrane may develop villous projections, and the joint cartilage is attacked and destroyed.

447. The answer is A. *(Robbins, ed 3. pp 1337-1340.)* The leading type of bone cancer in the young is osteogenic sarcoma. When it arises after the age of 40, it is usually associated with Paget's disease, prior irradiation, or exposure to radium-containing paints. The lesions usually occur in the long tubular bones with a large proportion occurring in the distal femur and proximal tibia. The metaphysis is most often the region involved with relative sparing of the epiphyseal growth plate. Better survival is being seen with conservative resection en bloc with multiagent chemotherapy.

448. The answer is D. *(Robbins, ed 3. pp 491, 409-411, 1329.)* Osteomalacia is characterized by inadequate mineralization of the bone matrix, resulting in an increase in the relative amount of osteoid tissue. Mineralization may lag behind osteoid synthesis by several weeks, rather than by the normal 6 to 10 days. Osteomalacia may be caused by vitamin D deficiency, hypophosphatemia with normal vitamin D intake, or conditions with normal calcium, phosphorus, and vitamin D intake, such as fluoride intoxication.

449. The answer is A. *(Robbins, ed 3. pp 1320-1321.)* Osteogenesis imperfecta is a hereditary trait characterized by defective synthesis of connective tissue, including bone matrix. The skeletal parts are thin and porous, with slender trabeculae. Fractures are common, and deafness may result from involvement of the bones of the middle ear.

450. The answer is A. *(Rosai, ed 6. pp 1353-1354.)* Ewing's sarcoma tends to be extensive, sometimes involving the entire shaft of a long bone. The tumor often begins in the diaphyseal marrow and, while growing through the cortex, may elevate the periosteum in sequential stages. The cortex may show only minimal destruction, whereas periosteal elevation may produce the multilayering of subperiosteal new bone formation that gives Ewing's sarcoma an "onion skin" or "sun ray" appearance in roentgen films.

451. The answer is E. *(Anderson, ed 8. pp 1653-1657.)* Malignant fibrous histiocytoma (MFH) is the current term used to designate sarcomatous growths of the deep soft tissues. This is principally a disease of the lower extremity and thigh in middle- to advanced-aged patients of both sexes, but it has also been reported as occurring in far-removed areas, such as the adventitia of the thoracic aorta and the ocular orbit. It has also occurred with some frequency years after irradiation. The tumor is composed of a background of spindle cells with varying amounts of collagen (hence, fibrous) and scattered giant, bizarre, xanthomatous and myoblasticlike cells (hence, histiocytic). In the past, many of these tumors were undoubtedly labeled as pleomorphic liposarcomas and pleomorphic adult rhabdomyosarcomas, both of which must be differentiated from MFH. This does not imply, of course, that pleomorphic liposarcomas and adult rhabdomyosarcomas do not exist simply because a new term has been introduced, but rather that strict histologic criteria should be adhered to in order to exclude MFH—namely, that unequivocal malignant myoblasts with cytoplasmic striations (rhabdomyosarcoma) and lipoblasts (liposarcoma) must be demonstrated. The prognosis is poor for MFH.

452. The answer is B. *(Robbins, ed 3. pp 1333-1337.)* Fibroosseous lesions of bone classically include fibrous dysplasia, nonossifying fibroma (fibrous cortical defect), and osteoid osteoma. Histologically, fibrous dysplasia shows a characteristic "Chinese-lettering" effect of the bony trabeculae, which are surrounded by a cellular, fibrous stroma, with osteoblasts and osteoclasts conspicuously decreased at the periphery of the entrapped woven bone. Histologically, nonossifying fibroma shows characteristic foam cell histiocytes within the lesions of the metaphysis. Osteoid osteomas are found within the diaphysis of long bones and contain osteoid trabeculae in a cellular, fibrous matrix, but unlike fibrous dysplasia, this disease demonstrates (singular) peripheral trabecular osteoblasts. Fibrous dysplasia (FD) produces radiolucent bone lesions involving long bones and thorax, skull, and facial bones. "Monostotic FD" refers to single-bone involvement, "polyostotic FD" refers to involvement of multiple lesions or bones, and "Albright's syndrome" refers to polyostotic bone lesions, endocrinopathy (hyperthyroidism, thyrotoxicosis, hyperpituitarism, Cushing's syndrome), precocious puberty in females, and café au lait spots on the skin. The pigmented, macular café au lait spots are usually more irregular (coast of Maine) in outline than the forms seen in neurofibromatosis. Monostotic FD is very rarely associated with the skin lesions.

453. The answer is A. *(Robbins, ed 3. pp 408, 616-617, 1241-1242, 1308-1310.)* The inheritance of childhood (Duchenne) muscular dystrophy is determined by an X-linked recessive trait. Muscular dystrophies are genetically determined myopathies characterized by alterations in individual myocytes leading to weakness in the affected muscles. The system of classification is based on specific patterns of muscle involvement; the pathologic changes in the individual muscle cells are nearly identical in all clinical patterns. The diseased muscle fibers may show an infiltrate of neutrophils, lymphocytes, and macrophages, early in the course of the disease. Isolated muscle fiber shrinkage, atrophy, and disappearance of cells are evident later. Finally, many muscle cells atrophy and fat cells accumulate and become interspersed between remaining muscle fibers.

454. The answer is C. *(Robbins, ed 3. pp 1331-1333.)* Paget's disease of bone is characterized by the replacement of normal bone by expanded, soft, poorly mineralized, osteoid tissue. The bones are enlarged but are soft and easily deformed by the stress of weight bearing. Long-standing Paget's disease of bone predisposes to a particularly aggressive form of osteosarcoma.

455. The answer is D. *(Robbins, ed 3. pp 137-138, 192-195, 520-522.)* Cystic medial necrosis is not inflammatory, but degenerative. Hypersensitivity angiitis primarily affects small vessels; polyarteritis nodosa affects small to medium-sized arteries. In addition to interstitial inflammation (often perivascular), patients with polymyositis have histologic evidence of muscle fiber death. Perivascular inflammation is one of the early skeletal muscle changes in scleroderma (systemic sclerosis).

456. The answer is B. *(Robbins, ed 3. pp 1140, 1312-1316.)* Myositis ossificans is a benign condition characterized by fibrous repair of a skeletal muscle tear with secondary cartilage formation, ossification, and calcification. The other lesions mentioned are malignant neoplasms that may contain a variety of mesodermal tissues. Many tumors diagnosed as rhabdomyosarcoma in the past would be classified as malignant fibrous histiocytoma today, although if cell striations are present in the cells, the lesions still qualify as rhabdomyosarcoma.

457. The answer is B (1, 3). *(Rosai, ed 6. pp 1335-1336.)* Juxtacortical (parosteal) osteosarcoma, an uncommon variant of osteosarcoma, usually has a less malignant-appearing stroma and may even be confused histologically with a benign condition such as myositis ossificans. Trauma does not usually precede juxtacortical (parosteal) osteosarcoma, which has a better prognosis than osteosarcoma of the shaft or medullary cavity.

458. The answer is A (1, 2, 3). *(Robbins, ed 3. pp 1337-1340.)* The characteristic sun-burst shown in the x-ray is due to calcified perpendicular striae of reactive periosteum adjacent to the growing tumor. Osteosarcoma, the most common bone cancer of children, can occur in the elderly, in whom the sarcoma is almost always associated with Paget's disease. The prognosis is extremely poor, with a 5-year survival rate of 5 to 20 percent.

459. The answer is B (1, 3). *(Anderson, ed 8. pp 1667-1673.)* Accounting for approximately 20 percent of all soft tissue sarcomas, liposarcomas constitute the most common primary malignant neoplasm in soft tissues. Liposarcomas have a recognized predilection for the deep structures of the thigh, leg, and buttocks and for the retroperitoneum. These tumors form bulky masses that infiltrate surrounding tissues and give rise to satellite lesions. A wide variety of histologic patterns is typical in liposarcomas, ranging from well-differentiated to highly anaplastic pleomorphic forms.

460. The answer is B (1, 3). *(Robbins, ed 3. pp 689-692.)* Metastatic lesions from carcinoma of the prostate are usually osteoblastic. Multiple osteolytic skull lesions are characteristic of multiple myeloma. Myeloma tumors typically produce gelatinous regions of osteolysis within the marrow cavities of involved bones. Coalescence of these foci may cause erosion of the cortical bone and occasionally will produce through-and-through defects. Histologic evidence of bone necrosis with new bone formation is very rare in myeloma lesions.

461-465. The answers are: 461-E, 462-C, 463-D, 464-A, 465-B. *(Anderson, ed 8. pp 1725-1726, 1730, 1749-1752, 1787-1793.)* Primary hyperthyroidism causes increased lacunae size in the trabeculae of the bones and is associated with increased levels of parathyroid hormones. Its early lesions consist of loss of calcium and demineralization. For this reason, primary hyperthyroidism is almost indistinguishable in the early stages from osteomalacia. Osteitis fibrous cystica and "brown tumors" resulting from hyperthyroidism are very rarely seen today.

Osteoporosis (essential bone loss) causes enlargement of the spaces of bone (the haversian canals), producing a porous appearance in the bones. The loss of bony substance results in a brittleness or softness in the bones. The disease results from either an increased rate of resorption or a decreased rate of bone formation. Osteoporosis can be a manifestation of aging or can be an underlying peripheral effect in a great variety of disorders. These include postmenopause; diabetes mellitus, malnutrition, malabsorption (protein, calcium, vitamin C, and vitamin D deficiencies), and almost all other forms of endocrinopathy; Ehlers-Danlos syndrome; Marfan's syndrome; alcohol abuse; heparin administration; methotrexate administration; immobility, such as confinement in bed; and acidosis.

Osteomalacia is demineralization of the osteoid matrix, which results in areas of decreased mineral density and loss of bone rigidity. Rickets is osteomalacia in infants and children. It is usually caused by dietary lack of vitamin D. Osteomalacia in adults is, as it were, vitamin D-resistant rickets. The defect in vitamin D resistance involves a failure of D to be converted to $1,25\text{-}(OH)_2D_3$, which is the metabolically active form of the vitamin. Other examples of this defect are advanced renal disease, or renal osteodystrophy, and congenital absence of 25-hydroxylase.

Paget's disease of bone, or osteitis deformans, is seen late in life. It is a benign neoplasia of bone characterized by increased skeletal remodeling. The skeletal remodeling is indicated by marked increases both in the amount of resorption activity present and in the amount of bone-formation activity. Specifically, there is progressive erosion of cancellous bone spicules, with fibroconnective tissue replacement and eventual concomitant osteoclastic bone resorption with osteoblastic bone formation. A mosaic pattern is seen in biopsy material, caused by persistence of visible osteoid seams.

Osteosarcoma, or osteogenic sarcoma, is a highly malignant tumor characterized by a fibroblastic sarcomatous stroma in which osteoblastic activity induces the formation of tumor osteoid and new bone. This lesion is not pictured in the microradiogram representation.

466-470. The answers are: 466-A, 467-B, 468-E, 469-C, 470-D. *(Anderson, ed 8. pp 1799-1801.)* Osteoclastoma, the giant-cell tumor of bone, usually produces a lytic lesion involving the epiphysis of long bones. The proximal tibia is a common site. Unicameral, or solitary, cysts are loculated, lytic lesions of bone that characteristically abut on the epiphyseal plate in older children and produce cortical irregularities. Regions involved in the benign lesion are prone to fracture. Osteochondromas are cauliflowerlike lesions that contain a core of cortical and medullary bone and a cartilage cap that decreases in width as age increases. Osteochondromas usually protrude from the metaphyses of long bones and may be multiple. Osteoid-osteomas occur most frequently in the cortex of the diaphysis of long limb bones, particularly the tibia. A small radiolucent nidus is usually surrounded by dense, sclerotic bone. Clinically, the lesion is often associated with pain. Nonossifying fibromas of bone, usually well-demarcated, eccentric, lytic metaphyseal lesions, most commonly occur in the tibia and femur. Nonossifying fibromas of bone are histologically identical to fibrous cortical defects and consist of a fibroblastic growth without concomitant bone formation.

There are many pitfalls involved in making a diagnosis of giant-cell tumor of bone. The main problem involves the difficulty of distinguishing the bone destruction that is a true neoplasm from bone destruction that is the result of various types of osteoclastic-osteoblastic activity. Direct communication with the radiologist and, preferably, the orthopedic surgeon is, therefore, nearly mandatory for the pathologist when making a diagnosis.

Skin and Breast

DIRECTIONS: Each question below contains five suggested answers. Choose the **one best** response to each question.

471. A 56-year-old woman has for 1 year's duration indurated plaques and nodules about the lower back and proximal thighs; the skin biopsy is seen below. What nuclear features are characteristic for this disorder?

(A) Markedly thickened nuclear membranes
(B) Unusually large nucleoli
(C) Folded, cerebriform nuclei
(D) Numerous mitotic figures
(E) Nuclear pyknosis

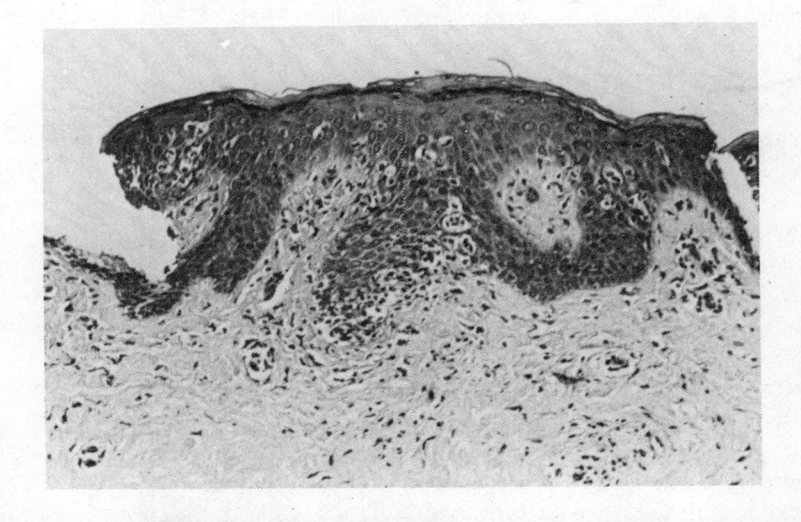

472. A menopausal woman is given a diagnosis of lobular carcinoma of the breast. What impact will this have on her clinical follow-up?

(A) The same impact as other types of carcinoma
(B) The impact depends on node involvement
(C) Biopsies of the contralateral breast are indicated
(D) Radiation should be administered
(E) A tylectomy is sufficient treatment

473. The clinical photograph below suggests that the patient

(A) has Leser-Trelat sign
(B) has multiple basal cell nevus syndrome
(C) is at risk for developing malignant melanoma
(D) has leopard syndrome
(E) has Torre's syndrome

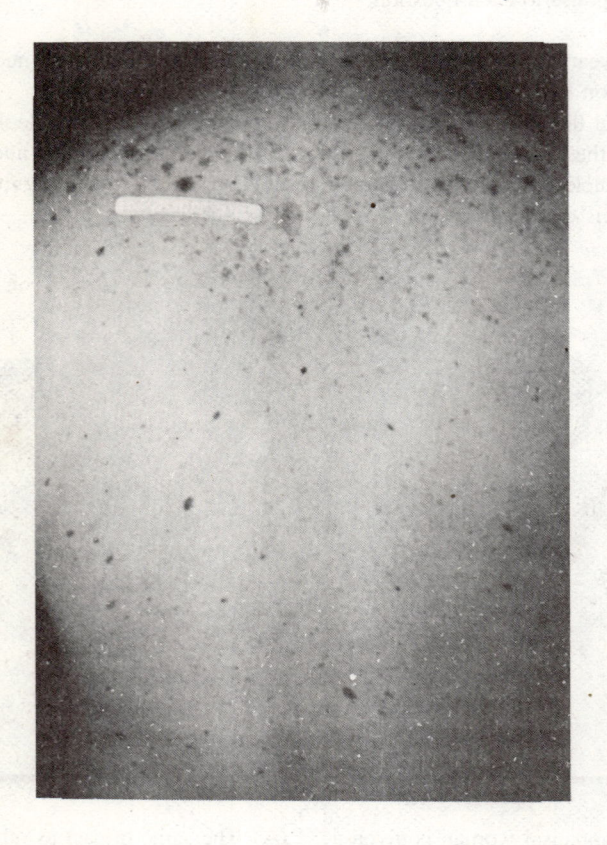

Skin and Breast

474. All the following forms of breast cancer belong in the same classification EXCEPT

(A) scirrhous carcinoma
(B) lobular carcinoma
(C) colloid or mucinous carcinoma
(D) medullary carcinoma
(E) ductal carcinoma

475. All the following malignant tumors of the breast have been known in some instances to have a deceptively bland histologic appearance and hence have at times been misdiagnosed as benign by the pathologist EXCEPT

(A) duct carcinoma
(B) tubular carcinoma
(C) angiosarcoma
(D) papillary carcinoma
(E) metastasizing mucinous carcinoma

Questions 476-477

A portion of an excisional biopsy taken from a nipple of a 42-year-old woman is shown in the photomicrograph below.

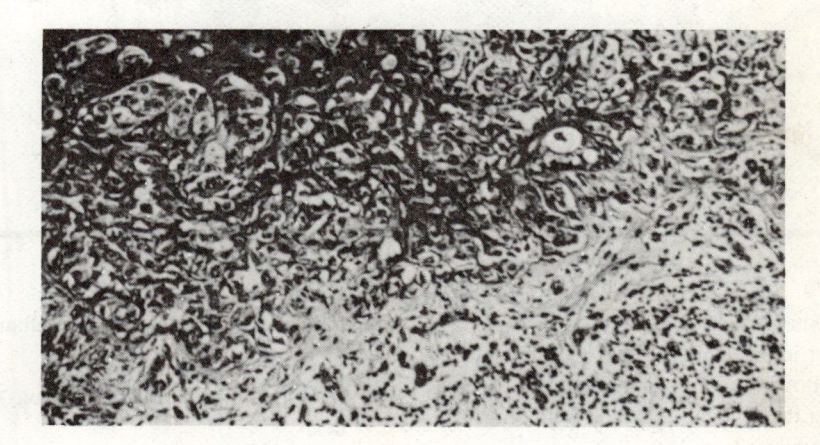

476. In consideration of the histologic character in the photomicrograph and the patient's complaint of bloody discharge from the nipple for 2 months, the diagnosis is most likely

(A) epidermoid carcinoma
(B) acanthosis nigricans
(C) verruca vulgaris
(D) chronic inflammation
(E) Paget's disease of the nipple

477. The superficial nipple lesion is almost invariably associated with

(A) gastrointestinal malignancy
(B) ductal adenocarcinoma of the breast
(C) multiple basal cell carcinomas
(D) collagen disease
(E) melanin production

478. The pigmented skin lesion shown in the photograph below should be

(A) excised and examined histologically
(B) fulgurated
(C) treated with topical 5-fluorouracil
(D) observed carefully
(E) treated with high-dose x-irradiation

479. The incidence of malignant melanoma of the skin appears to be increasing in the United States. Which of the following is most significant in predicting the clinical behavior following diagnosis?

(A) The degree of pigmentation
(B) The level and depth
(C) The amount of inflammation
(D) The degree of pleomorphism
(E) The state of nutrition

480. Which of the following statements most accurately describes inflammatory breast cancer?

(A) Inflammation improves the prognosis
(B) Inflammation is increased in Paget's disease
(C) Acute inflammatory cells are present
(D) Chronic inflammatory cells are present
(E) Lymphatic permeation is present

481. Which of the following pairs of disorders would most appropriately be considered in the differential diagnosis for the lesion seen in the photomicrograph below?

(A) Superficial spreading malignant melanoma in situ and Paget's disease
(B) Mycosis fungoides and metastatic carcinoma
(C) Psoriasis and lichen planus
(D) Lupus erythematosus and lupus vulgaris
(E) Leukemia and lymphoma

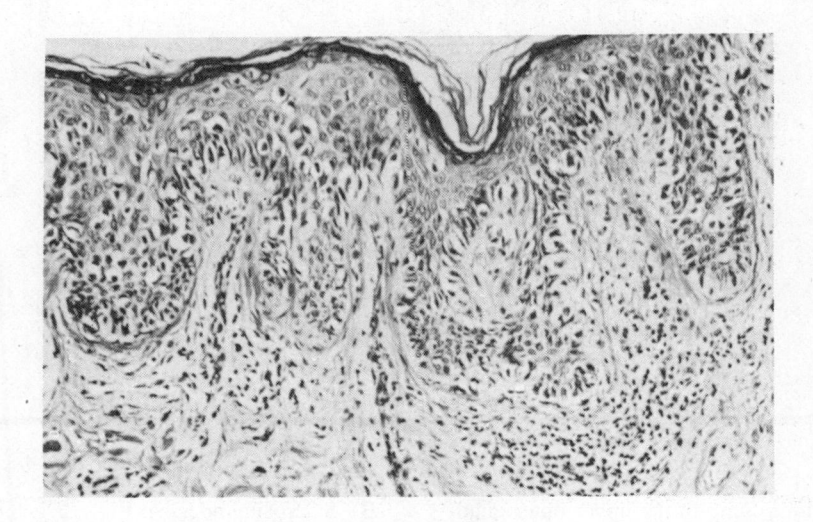

482. A 52-year-old woman undergoes a modified radical mastectomy for infiltrating duct carcinoma diagnosed by frozen section. Which of the following statements in the final pathology report is most important in predicting the clinical course in this patient?

(A) The tumor is in the outer quadrant
(B) Two axillary lymph nodes contain carcinoma
(C) One axillary lymph node is 3.0 cm in size
(D) There is apocrine metaplasia in the lower-outer quadrant
(E) There is fibrocystic disease in the upper-outer quadrant

483. A 16-year-old girl undergoes biopsy of a breast lump that shows the changes in the photomicrograph below. What is the most appropriate course of action to follow?

(A) Radiotherapy
(B) Local excision
(C) Radical mastectomy
(D) Modified radical mastectomy
(E) No further therapy

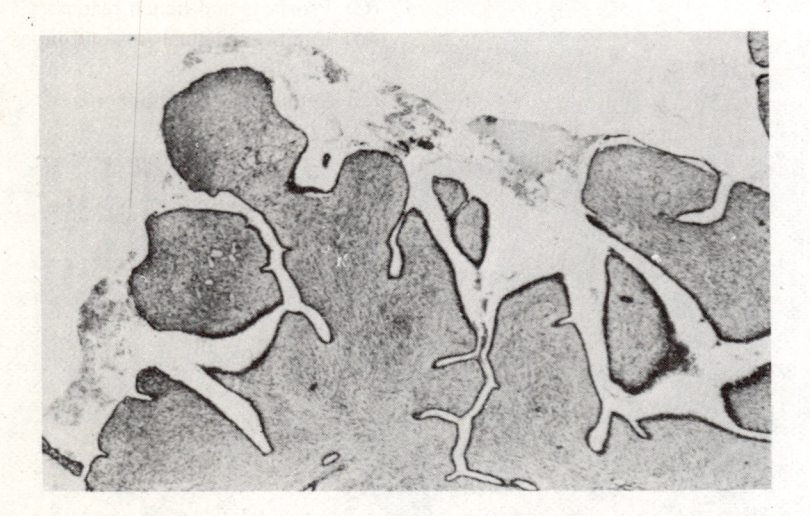

484. A 37-year-old woman presents with a lump in the upper outer quadrant of the left breast, which shows a wide spectrum of benign breast disease on pathologic examination. Which of the following is considered to indicate the greatest risk for subsequent carcinoma of the breast?

(A) Intraductal papillomatosis
(B) Sclerosing adenosis
(C) Florid papillomatosis
(D) Marked apocrine metaplasia
(E) Duct epithelial hyperplasia

DIRECTIONS: Each question below contains four suggested answers of which **one** or **more** is correct. Choose the answer:

A	if	**1, 2, and 3**	are correct
B	if	**1 and 3**	are correct
C	if	**2 and 4**	are correct
D	if	**4**	is correct
E	if	**1, 2, 3, and 4**	are correct

485. True statements about the condition seen in the photomicrograph below include which of the following?

(1) It is often misdiagnosed clinically as seborrheic dermatitis
(2) It may have associated otitis media
(3) It may involve multiple viscera
(4) Birbeck granules can be observed in the cells

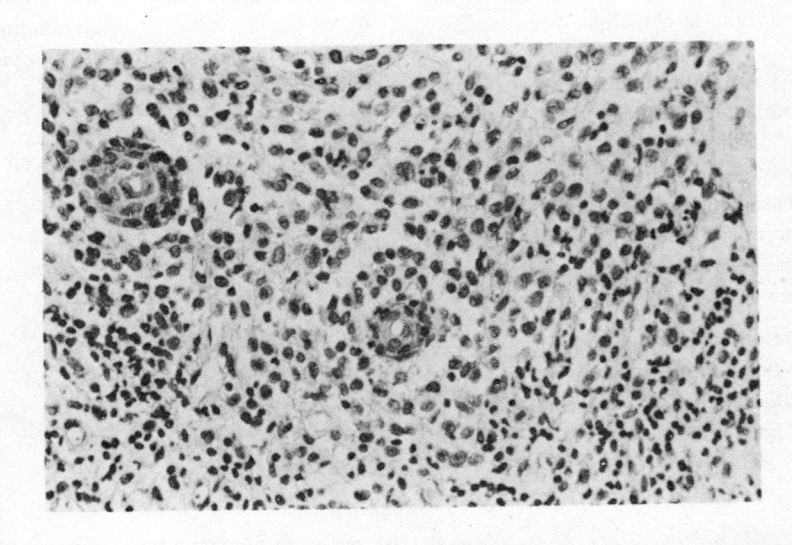

486. Leonine facies can be seen in which of the following?

(1) Onchocerciasis
(2) Leprosy
(3) Leishmaniasis
(4) Mycosis fungoides

487. Risk factors for breast carcinoma in women include

(1) first conception at a later age
(2) nulliparity
(3) diet low in protein and fat
(4) menarchy prior to age 13

SUMMARY OF DIRECTIONS				
A	B	C	D	E
1, 2, 3 only	1, 3 only	2, 4 only	4 only	All are correct

488. Fibromatosis is a term applied to an array of fibrous or collagen tissue abnormalities. Which of the following may be considered fibromatoses?

(1) Keloid
(2) Musculoaponeurotic desmoid
(3) Peyronie's disease
(4) Pseudosarcomatous fasciitis

489. An adult patient develops crops of bullae and vesicles in the mouth and later on the skin of the trunk. A skin biopsy is inconclusive but shows a suprabasal acantholysis of the overlying epidermis. Direct immunofluorescence of the skin can be used to identify which of the following?

(1) Bullous pemphigoid
(2) Pemphigus vulgaris
(3) Dermatitis herpetiformis
(4) Erythema multiforme

490. Characteristic histologic features of psoriasis include

(1) parakeratosis
(2) acanthosis
(3) elongation of the rete ridges and dermal papillae
(4) epidermal microabscesses containing polymorphonuclear neutrophilic leukocytes

491. A papillary lesion is seen in a biopsy from a 32-year-old woman who presented with sanguinous discharge from the nipple. Which of the following would be useful in differentiating benign intraductal papilloma from papillary adenocarcinoma?

(1) A cribriform pattern
(2) The presence or absence of cell uniformity
(3) Fibrovascular cores
(4) The age of the patient

Skin and Breast

492. The differential diagnosis of the lesion depicted below could include
(1) lupus erythematosus
(2) polymorphous light eruption
(3) pseudolymphoma
(4) malignant lymphoma

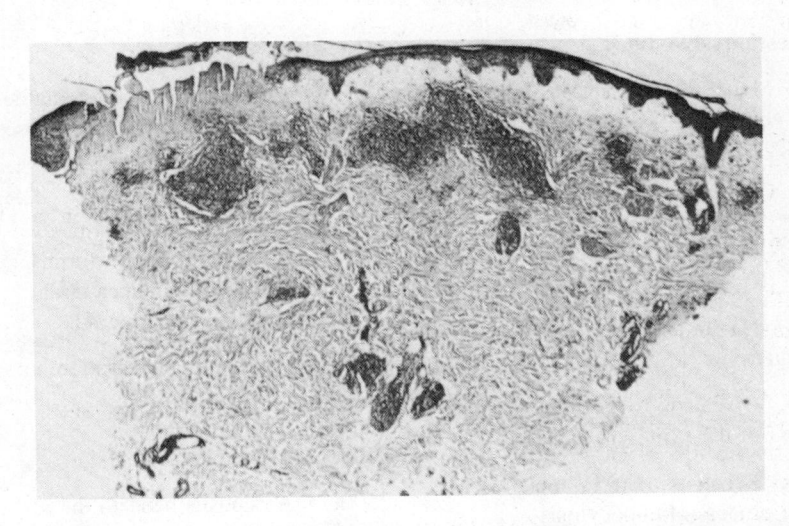

493. Marasmus is characterized by inelastic, wrinkled skin and loss of subcutaneous fat and muscle tissue. It is related to a dietary deficiency of
(1) carbohydrate
(2) lipid
(3) protein
(4) vitamins

DIRECTIONS: The groups of questions below consist of lettered choices followed by several numbered items. For each numbered item select the **one** lettered choice with which it is **most** closely associated. Each lettered choice may be used once, more than once, or not at all.

Questions 494-496

Match the descriptions below with the correct cell.

(A) Merkel's cell
(B) Langerhans cell
(C) Basal melanocyte
(D) Stratum basale cell
(E) Keratinocyte

494. Has Ia and T6 surface membrane antigens

495. Gives rise to trabecular carcinoma of the skin

496. Receives stage IV melanosomes by a process of endocytosis

Questions 497-500

Match each of the following descriptions of acantholytic dermatoses with the appropriate disorder.

(A) Pemphigus vulgaris
(B) Erythema multiforme
(C) Dermatitis herpetiformis
(D) Porphyria cutanea tarda
(E) Bullous pemphigoid

497. Related to malabsorption

498. Aggravated by sunlight

499. Positive Nikolsky's sign

500. IgA deposits beneath the epidermis

Skin and Breast Answers

471. The answer is C. *(Anderson, ed 8. pp 1631-1633.)* The characteristic features seen in mycosis fungoides cells consist of folded and enlarged nuclei producing a pattern that has been described as cerebriform or brainlike. At low-power magnification these cells may be missed because of their bland appearance, but at higher magnification the cerebriform, folded appearance is easily seen. Mycosis fungoides is actually an older term that is inappropriate in light of current knowledge of this lesion. The cells of mycosis fungoides are a T-cell lymphoma that manifests itself in the skin and that is slowly progressive over many years, pursuing a rather indolent clinical course. A few patients, however, have an accelerated form that can reach a lethal outcome within 1½ to 2 years. The disease is seen in a phase of parapsoriasis en plaque in the skin, which is nondiagnostic showing only epidermal acanthosis, and a mild to moderate perivascular and bandlike infiltrate in the papillary dermis. A very rare mycosis cell may be seen at this stage. The diagnostic stage is when tumor cells are in aggregates in a large packet in the epidermis, referred to as a Pautrier abscess.

472. The answer is C. *(Robbins, ed 3. pp 1184-1186.)* Lobular carcinoma comprises approximately 10 percent of all histologic types of breast cancer, with duct carcinoma being the most common (70 to 75 percent of the total). It presumably arises from the terminal duct epithelium of the lobule, and it carries a high propensity to multifocality and bilateral breast involvement. There is evidence that this form of breast cancer gives rise to multiple, separate primaries within both breasts. For this reason, breast therapists currently advocate biopsies of the contralateral breast when the tumor is diagnosed. The lobular architectural spectrum begins with lobular hyperplasia and may then progress to lobular neoplasia, atypical lobular neoplasia (lobular carcinoma in situ), and, finally, infiltrating lobular carcinoma. The therapy for lobular hyperplasia and even atypical lobular neoplasia is controversial and is different in various medical centers. If there is any degree of stromal infiltration, however, therapy should at least include a mastectomy; if this is not done, a modified radical mastectomy is required, since the clincal behaviors of infiltrating breast cancers of various histologic subtypes are similar. Some states have written legislation concerning the patient's option to have only excision of the tumor without mastectomy (tylectomy), since more aggressive conventional surgical therapy has not significantly altered total survival over the past 5 or 6 decades. This new approach should be regarded as controversial, however, and more study is needed before the superiority of alternative forms of therapy over more radical surgery is indicated. Early diagnosis still remains the best approach to cancer therapy.

473. The answer is C. *(Robbins, ed 3. pp 1262, 1265, 1278-1279.)* The clinical photograph depicts the presence of the dysplastic nevus syndrome, first decribed by Dr. Wallace Clark and his coworkers Drs. Mark Greene, David Elder and E. Bondi in Philadelphia during the mid 1970s. This valuable finding elucidated the presence of abnormal nevi that are at least a marker for the development of malignant melanoma. These nevi, while not malignant, have atypical features compared with those of normal nevi, such as irregular borders, a pink base, and irregular pigmentation. The Leser-Trelat sign refers to the development of multiple seborrheic keratoses over a short period of time in older patients who have visceral malignancy, while the basal cell nevus syndrome is dominantly inherited with the association of numerous basal cell carcinomas forming throughout life, bifid ribs, keratocysts of the mandible, unusual facies, and abnormalities of the central nervous system and reproductive system. Recently a familial occurrence of dysplastic nevus syndrome with basal cell nevus syndrome was elucidated at the 1985 meeting of the International Academy of Pathologists by Elliot Foucar. The leopard syndrome refers to multiple flat lentigines that are not premalignant for melanoma, in addition to cardiac abnormalities, and ocular hypertelorism. Recent studies have shown that the dysplastic nevus syndrome is not only familial, but may be sporadic in about 6 percent of the general population. The risk of developing melanoma in the dysplastic nevus familial situation is greatly increased over that in the general population. It has been stated that patients with dysplastic nevi belonging to a kindred of dysplastic nevus and familial malignant melanoma have a 100-fold risk of developing malignant melanoma over their entire lifetime.

474. The answer is B. *(Robbins, ed 3. pp 1178-1188.)* All the tumors mentioned except lobular carcinoma arise in the mammary duct epithelium. Lobular carcinoma presumably arises from terminal ductule cells. Lobular carcinomas, commonly found to be multicentric in origin within a single breast, tend to be bilateral far more often than ductal carcinomas and have a 20 percent chance of occurring in both breasts. The three main clinical evolutionary stages recognized for lobular carcinoma are lobular carcinoma in situ, lobular carcinoma in situ with infiltration, and infiltrative lobular carcinoma without an in situ component. The in situ forms are not clinically palpable and hence are usually found incidentally in mastectomy specimens.

475. The answer is A. *(Anderson, ed 8. pp 1568, 1564-1565, 1562-1564.)* The most notorious malignant tumor of the breast, presenting a deceptively inocuous histologic and cytologic appearance, is angiosarcoma, with its almost unrecognizable anastomosing clear channels lined by flattened and barely visible endothelial cells. If this combination is seen within unequivocal breast lobules and ducts, the pathologist must suspect angiosarcoma. Well-differentiated adenocarcinoma of the breast (tubular carcinoma) demonstrates a tumor that is rather benign in appearance, with small ducts lined by single and inocuous-appearing epithelial cells. Whereas the primary site of mucinous carcinoma of the breasts (colloid carcinoma), with its "cysts" filled with extracellular mucin and signet-ring cells, presents no problem in diagnosis, biopsies of metastatic lesions will not infrequently show sheets of bland granular cells with pinpoint nuclei resembling granular cell tumor of the skin, a benign lesion. Early intraductal papillary carcinomas have been misdiagnosed at times as benign intraductal papillomas, and the reverse error of papillomas being called carcinomas has also occurred. Infiltrating duct (scirrhous) carcinoma presents no diagnostic problem in either frozen or permanent section analysis for the average pathologist.

476. The answer is E. *(Anderson, ed 8. pp 1565-1566.)* In the nipple, an infiltrate of atypical, mucin-positive cells with clear cytoplasm is diagnostic of Paget's disease. The appearance of these cells is invariably associated with an underlying cancer of the breast, and the disease usually occurs in middle-aged women.

477. The answer is B. *(Anderson, ed 8. pp 1565-1566.)* Paget's disease of the nipple is almost invariably associated with an underlying ductal malignancy. Paget's disease arising in the vulva or other unusual places is not as frequently associated with underlying carcinoma. The "Paget" cells in the epidermis reflect upward spread of breast carcinoma in the case of the nipple. These cells resemble the cells of superficial spreading melanoma by routine H & E stains but are PAS positive-diastase resistant, unlike melanoma cells. Paget's disease of the anal-vulvar-perineal region may or may not be associated with an underlying carcinoma. However, total excision is necessary in those sites, because the disease may, if neglected, progress to invasive Paget's disease.

478. The answer is A. *(Robbins, ed 3. pp 1279-1282.)* Most pigmented skin lesions are benign. However, lesions with a suspicious clinical appearance must be biopsied to exclude malignant melanoma. The lesion illustrated is a malignant melanoma, and the prognosis depends in part on the depth of invasion. Lesions that have microscopically reached the subcutaneous fat have a very poor prognosis.

479. The answer is B. *(Robbins, ed 3. pp 1279-1282.)* Although malignant melanoma of the skin is not as common as squamous and basal cell carcinoma, it is an exceedingly important and somewhat mysterious tumor owing to its often devastating clinical course and occasionally unpredictable behavior. There appear to be strong immune factors that presumably account for some well-documented remissions, lengthy survival after distant metastasis, and rapid growth in renal transplant patients. However, most patients with this form of cancer pursue a course characterized by eventual distant and visceral metastasis, especially if the histologic type is either nodular or superficial spreading. The subtype called lentigo maligna melanoma, found in the sun-exposed skin of elderly patients, generally has a much more favorable outlook. The most important predictors of outcome are the level of penetration into the subepidermis and reticular dermis (Clark levels I through V—I, in situ; V, subcutaneous fat) and the actual depth of invasion, measured in millimeters with an ocular micrometer (Breslow depth). The survival at 5 years is 90 percent if the tumor is Clark I or II and 0.76 mm or less in depth, but survival falls to 40 to 48 percent if the tumor is level III or IV and greater than 1.9 mm in depth. While some melanoma cells may show cytologic pleomorphism, many aggressive melanomas exhibit uniformity and blandness. Recent work has shown that melanomas arising in the region of the shoulder, upper trunk, and back in men behave in an aggressive fashion.

480. The answer is E. *(Robbins, ed 3. p 1185.)* Inflammatory breast carcinoma is often misunderstood because of the qualifying adjective "inflammatory." The term does not refer to the presence of inflammatory cells, abscess, or any special histologic type of breast carcinoma; rather, it refers to more of a clinical phenomenon, in that the breast is swollen, erythematous, and indurated and demonstrates a marked increase in warmth. These changes are caused by widespread lymphatic and vascular permeation within the breast itself and in the deep dermis of the overlying skin by breast carcinoma cells. The clinical induration and erythema are presumably related to lymphatic-vascular blockage by tumor cells; if present, these findings mean a worse prognosis for the patient.

481. The answer is A. *(Robbins, ed 3. pp 182-187, 777-780, 1118-1119, 1271-1272, 1291-1293.)* The photomicrograph was taken from a patient with superficial spreading malignant melanoma, in situ, showing individual cells resembling Paget's disease invading the upper regions of the epidermis. The basement membrane zone is intact and there are lymphocytes in the underlying dermis. Cells with clear cytoplasm and malignant-appearing nuclei such as shown here resemble those of Paget's disease, from which they must be distinguished. Some cells of mycosis fungoides will resemble this, but they occur in nest formations called Pautrier's abscesses. Metastatic carcinoma can produce lesions that resemble malignant melanoma, but these are problems relating to the dermis. Leukemia-lymphoma infiltrates mainly involve the dermis, although the epidermis may become ulcerated and atrophic. Lupus erythematosus and lichen planus produce subepidermal lymphocytic infiltrates with no involvement of the epidermis itself. Psoriasis produces parakeratosis and elongated rete ridges but no abnormal cells in the epidermis.

482. The answer is C. *(Robbins, ed 3. pp 1178-1188.)* It is unfortunate that the outlook for survival in breast cancer in the United States has not improved significantly in the 50 years since the days of Halsted, despite newer techniques of xeromammography and ultrasound, greater public awareness, and attempts at early diagnosis. Perhaps hormonal manipulation based on the presence or absence of estrogen/progesterone receptors on the tumor cells will improve the 5- and 10-year survival rates, but at present the overall survival rate is an unacceptable 50 percent at 5 years.

If all axillary lymph nodes are negative for tumor on histopathologic examination in the mastectomy specimen, the survival is an optimistic 80 to 85 percent at 5 years, which dramatically falls to only 30 percent if more than three axillary lymph nodes are involved, if one or more nodes are fixed in the axilla, or if any nodes are greater than 2.5 cm in maximum dimension. Three or fewer positive lymph nodes only slightly correlate with a less favorable course. Recent work has shown that if metastatic breast cancer has grown out and spilled through the lymph node capsule, the prognosis also worsens. Breast cancer continues to be already systemic in at least 30 percent of afflicted patients coming to clinical attention.

483. The answer is B. *(Anderson, ed 8. pp 524, 1550-1551.)* The lesion depicted in the photomicrograph is that of a cellular fibroadenoma, a basically benign neoplasm of the breast. Mueller initially described cystosarcoma phyllodes in 1838 and named it for the resemblance of the lesion to leaves. In older women if the stroma is hypercellular with mitoses and peripheral infiltrative borders, it has the capacity to metastasize. In the adolescent female, cellular stroma of spindle cells, occasional mitoses, such as in this example, may not behave in a malignant fashion as in older women. There is only one documented case of death with dissemination caused by lesions of this type in young girls in the literature. Because most lesions like these behave in a benign fashion, conservative but total excision with a small rim of normal tissue surrounding the lesion is all that is necessary in the adolescent.

484. The answer is E. *(Robbins, ed 3. pp 1172-1178.)* The spectrum of benign breast disease includes fibrocystic disease, which is probably a misnomer; adenosis, both sclerosing and microglandular; intraductal papillomas and papillomatosis; apocrine metaplasia; fibrous stromal hyperplasia; and hyperplasia of the epithelial cells lining the ducts and ductules of the breasts. At one time or another each of the above was considered to be a forerunner of carcinoma; however, with extensive studies in the literature, none of these has been shown to necessarily correlate with a greater risk of developing carcinoma with the exception of duct epithelial hyperplasia. With any of the features, but especially duct epithelial hyperplasia, adding a positive family history of breast cancer in a sibling, mother, or maternal aunt markedly increases the risk for developing carcinoma of the breast in the given patient. Owing to the advances and technology of xeromammography, there has been an increased interest in calcifications, which are markers for carcinoma of the breast. These calcifications, however, do not necessarily occur within the cancerous ducts themselves and can be found frequently in either adenosis adjacent to the carcinoma or even in normal breast lobules in the region. Stipple calcification as seen by xeromammography is regarded as an indication for a biopsy of the region by some workers.

485. The answer is E (all). *(Robbins, ed 3. pp 694-695, 1272-1273.)* The photomicrograph demonstrates the presence of Langerhans cells in an infiltrated fashion into the upper dermis, showing reniform nuclei and crowding characteristic of the disorder previously referred to as a form of histiocytosis-X. These are now known to be disorders of Langerhans cells, which have surface membrane FC receptors and react with antibodies to thymocyte differentiation antigens (OKT6) and ultrastructural granules referred to as Birbeck granules. The Letterer-Siwe form arises in children, often in infants, and presents with cutaneous lesions that resemble seborrheic dermatitis (or cradle cap). Often these patients present with fever and otitis media or mastoiditis, which call attention to the disorder. If the disease disseminates it may involve organs of the mononuclear phagocyte system, including the spleen, liver, lymph nodes, bone marrow, and lungs. X-ray lesions are reflected by cystic radiolucent areas that can be seen in the skull, pelvis, and long bones. Patients often have anemia and thrombocytopenia, which can contribute to a terminal outcome owing to infections. The term Langerhans cell granulomatosis has been offered as an alternative designation to histiocytosis-X, Letterer-Siwe form. Many infants died from the disorder in years past, but with the use of chemotherapy and improvement of underlying hypoimmunity, there has been a reversal of the death rate.

486. The answer is E (all). *(Anderson, ed 8. pp 324, 411-412, 438, 1631-1633.)* Leonine facies is a characteristic abnormality induced by swelling, edema, and inflammation of the dermis and subcutaneous tissues of the face from multiple causes but especially microorganisms. The swelling and inflammation induce redundant folds, especially around the eyes and upper cheeks, yielding a facies having folds like that of the male lion. Among the microorganisms noted for this are those that cause onchocerciasis (*Onchocerca volvulus*), leishmaniasis (*Leishmania*), and lepromatous leprosy (*Mycobacterium leprae*). In the United States the cutaneous T-cell lymphoma mycosis fungoides may have a stage referred to as follicular mucinosis, which, if it involves the hair follicles of the face and forehead, will also produce a leonine facies.

487. The answer is D (4). *(Robbins, ed 3. pp 1178-1180.)* Breast cancer is continuing at a significant pace in Western society with the estimated number of new cases diagnosed being in the range of 112,000 to 116,000 per year with approximately 35,000 deaths. It is more prevalent in the West than in populations of third world countries or even advanced societies such as Japan and the Nationalist Republic of China. Correlating with an increased risk of breast cancer are diets that are high in fat and protein with accompanying obesity. Family history is significant as shown by studies indicating that if a mother and sister have had carcinoma of the breast before menopause, then a given woman will have an increased risk of 50 times that of controls. Early menarchy, especially before age 13, correlates with an increased risk of developing breast carcinoma, as does delayed menopause, such as that occurring after age 50. This suggests a greater period of hormonal exposure during the reproductive years. Women having their first child past the age of 30 are at increased risk as are women past the age of 50 generally. If a woman has had breast carcinoma in the past, she is at greater risk of developing contralateral breast carcinoma, especially of the lobular histologic type. Thus, hormonal factors plus a genetic disposition and diets high in fat and protein appear to be three strong indicators for carcinoma of the breast.

488. The answer is E (all). *(Anderson, ed 8. pp 1646-1647.)* All the entities listed are forms of fibromatosis. A keloid is a scar that can develop in the skin as a response to insect bites, burns, vaccinations, incisions, and other trauma. The histologic features include tissue hypertrophy and thickened bands of collagen mixed with active fibroblasts. Musculoaponeurotic desmoids arise from fascia and related structures to produce benign fibrous tumors, typically in skeletal muscle. These account for the majority of fibrous tumors of soft parts, excluding the skin. Pseudosarcomatous fasciitis (nodular fasciitis), also benign, is a tumorlike proliferation of fibroblasts that may resemble sarcomas histologically. This form of fibromatosis typically develops in subcutaneous fascia or in the deep fascia of underlying muscle sheaths. In Peyronie's disease (plastic induration), inflammatory hyperplasia develops in the deep (Buck's) fascia and the sheath of one or both corpora cavernosa of the penis.

489. The answer is A (1, 2, 3). *(Robbins, ed 3. pp 1284-1285, 1294-1297.)* Patients of either sex in the fourth to sixth decade who develop oral vesicles followed by disseminated bullae are likely to have pemphigus vulgaris, one of the blistering (bullous) dermatoses. The differential diagnosis in this setting is widespread and can include various forms of erythema multiforme (or Stevens-Johnson syndrome in the young), bullous pemphigoid, and pemphigus vulgaris. Common to most bullous dermatoses is the presence of epidermal cell separation, producing spaces and clefts (acantholysis) that are visible in ordinary tissue sections and specific to location within the epidermis. The bullae may be subcorneal, intraepidermal, suprabasal, or subepidermal, and multiple diseases can be grouped according to acantholysis location. To categorize the type of disease further, direct immunofluorescence testing can be done on a fresh skin lesion, using antibodies to immunoglobulins, fibrin, and complement. Pemphigus vulgaris shows a characteristic "basket-weave" pattern in the epidermis to IgG, IgA is found at the tips of the dermal papillae in dermatitis herpetiformis, and linear bands of IgG and complement are found in the subepidermal zones in bullous pemphigoid, whereas erythema multiforme has no immunofluorescent pattern.

490. The answer is E (all). *(Robbins, ed 3. pp 1291-1293.)* All the features mentioned, plus edema with clubbing of dermal papillae and dilatation of straight capillaries in the dermal papillae, are pathognomonic, histologic characteristics of psoriasis. The diagnosis of a lesion as "psoriasi-form dermatitis" indicates that some but not all of the six characteristics are present. A partial pattern is nondiagnostic and should not be taken to mean psoriasis, since it is a nonspecific histologic pattern that may be found in other conditions, including exfoliative dermatitis, seborrheic dermatitis, chronic contact dermatitis, and neurodermatitis.

491. The answer is A (1, 2, 3). *(Anderson, ed 8. pp 1551-1552, 1557.)* The histologic distinction between benign, cystic intraductal papillomas of the breast and papillary adenocarcinomas is based on multiple criteria. The age of the patient is not of immense importance, since papillomas occur in both younger and older women. Benign papillomas are structured with a complex arrangement of papillary fronds of fibrovascular stalks, covered by one or (usually) two types of epithelial cells. Papillary carcinomas are usually of one monotonous cell type and have either no fibrovascular stalks or only a few of them. Papillary carcinomas show a uniform growth of similar-appearing cells with enclosed tubular spaces, with the whole arrangement bridging across the entire lumen at times or simply lining the outer rim of the duct (cribriforming). Peripheral invasion of the stroma, if present at all, makes the diagnosis of carcinoma rather certain. There are lesions in which the differentiation is exceedingly difficult, even in the hands of renowned surgical pathologists. Many competent pathologists understandably prefer to defer the diagnosis on all papillary lesions of the breast on frozen section until well-fixed and optimally prepared permanent sections are available.

492. The answer is E (all). *(Anderson, ed 8. pp 1587-1589, 1633. Robbins, ed 3. pp 1300-1301.)* Dense lymphocytic infiltration of the skin carries with it a differential diagnosis that includes the five L's: Lupus, light, lymphoma, pseudolymphoma, and lymphocytic infiltration of the skin (Jessner) are all characterized by lymphoid hyperplasia of the dermis. Leukemic lymphomas are diagnosed by atypical sheets of lymphoblastic cells with mitoses; lupus erythematosus is characterized by lymphoid infiltration around the follicles and vessels of the dermis. Light eruptions are characterized by a lymphocytic perivascular inflammation on the skin of the face. A difficult differential diagnosis includes lymphocytic infiltration of the skin (Jessner), which often has an increase in dermal mucopolysaccharides that can be demonstrated by alcian blue stains.

493. The answer is E (all). *(Anderson, ed 8. pp 497-500.)* Marasmus is a chronic wasting disease of the tissues that occurs chiefly in children. It is characterized by growth retardation, loss of subcutaneous fat and muscle, and inelastic, wrinkled skin. A diet markedly deficient in proteins, carbohydrates, lipids, vitamins, and minerals (balanced starvation) is associated with the disease. Infectious diseases have also been postulated as precipitating factors. Marasmus is often considered to be related to kwashiorkor, though the latter disease is more specifically linked to protein deficiency.

494-496. The answers are: 494-B, 495-A, 496-E. *(Robbins, ed 3. pp 1258-1259.)* The skin should be regarded as a biologic unit, unique by function and structure, containing populations of cells with similarities to other organ cells, but having unique properties by location and function.

The Langerhans cell is a member of the mononuclear phagocyte system that is probably derived from bone marrow stem cells but spends much of its time within the epidermis itself. These fascinating cells are dendritic and have macrophage markers on their surfaces, including HLA-DR(Ia), T6 thymocyte differentiation antigen, and in some cases FC receptors. They function in processing foreign antigens and presenting the antigens to T lymphocytes. They contain unique ultrastructural granules, referred to as Birbeck granules, which may possibly be related to the surface membrane.

Merkel's cells are poorly understood cells in the upper papillary dermis that may function as neurotactile receptors. These cells are characterized ultrastructurally by dense core granules, which are situated in a circumferential manner around the nucleus and which, when neoplastic, give rise to the Merkel's tumor, otherwise referred to as trabecular carcinoma. These tumors may resemble lymphomas of the skin, from which they must be distinguished.

Basal melanocytes are situated in the stratum basale and are derived from the neural crest. They function in melanogenesis because they contain all the enzymes necessary for the production of melanin, including tyrosinase and dihydroxyphenylalanine. Melanocytes are thought to give rise to melanomas as well as differentiation into nevocellular cells of the dermis, which compose the ordinary mole. They are under the influence of hormones including MSH, ACTH, melatonin, and probably growth and sex hormones. Melanocytes contain the four stages of melanin-associated organelles referred to as melanosomes, which can be distinguished by their stages, ranging from stage I (nonmelanized) through stage IV (totally melanized). The melanosomes can be found on the dendrites that extend from the melanocyte and are in contiguity with cells of the epidermis, otherwise known as the keratinocytes. The melanosomes, especially stage III and stage IV, can be transferred from the dendrites of the basal melanocyte directly to the surrounding keratinocyte by endocytosis. In this manner, melanin is transferred from the melanocyte to the squamous cells, especially in response to sunlight (a process referred to as tanning).

The basal cell of the epidermis is the stratum basale cell, which functions in giving rise to keratinocytes.

497-500. The answers are: 497-C, 498-D, 499-A, 500-E. *(Anderson, ed 8. pp 1577-1582. Robbins, ed 3. pp 1284-1285, 1294-1297.)* Classification of vesiculobullous dermatoses is important, since treatment and prognosticating protocols depend on accurate identification. The cleavage planes under the stratum corneum include toxic epidermal necrolysis, bullous impetigo, and Reiter's disease. Occurring in the midepidermis are pemphigus foliaceous and vegetans, and examples of suprabasal acantholytic occurrence are Darier's disease, pemphigus vulgaris, Grover's disease, Hailey-Hailey disease, and actinic keratosis. Certain forms of erythema multiforme, dermatitis herpetiformis, porphyria cutaneous tarda, and bullous pemphigoid occur beneath the epidermis, at times separating it from the dermis.

Dermatitis herpetiformis manifests as papules and vesicles grouped in a symmetrical fashion on extensor surfaces of the shoulders, scapulae, forearms, and legs. Nestlike aggregates of neutrophils and eosinophils occur in the papillary dermis beneath the epidermis, along with deposits of IgA. This disorder may be associated with intestinal malabsorption in the form of gluten enteropathy. Removing wheat products from the diet improves both the malabsorption syndrome and the cutaneous lesions.

Pemphigus occurs in four clinicopathologic forms: p. vulgaris, p. erythematosus, p. vegetans, and p. foliaceous. All four have the same IgG deposition around individual epidermal cells, however. Because of the cleavage planes at different levels in the epidermis itself, gentle pressure from an examiner's thumb on the patient's skin will cause denudation (Nikolsky's sign).

Erythema multiforme (EM) may arise in protean fashions in young and old patients, precipitated as a result of viral-bacterial infection, toxins, and drugs, Stevens-Johnson syndrome is considered a variant of erythema multiforme. Classic lesions of EM may show circinate rings of erythema with pale centers (iris-target lesions). Bullous pemphigoid is distinguished from EM by a linear band of IgG seen beneath the epidermis by immunofluorescence microscopy. One of several types of porphyria, porphyria cutanea tarda is characterized by remissions and exacerbations of vesicular, erythematous lesions aggravated by sunlight exposure. Thus lesions are commonly seen on the backs of hands, where small scars documenting prior attacks with consequent healing may also be present. Biopsies show characteristic small knobs of papillary dermis protruding into the cleavage space beneath the epidermis. Less commonly seen are perivascular polysaccharide deposits in the underlying dermis.

Bibliography

Anderson WA, Kissane JM (eds): *Pathology*, 8th ed. St. Louis, CV Mosby, 1985.

Askin FB, Rosai J, Sibley RK, et al: Malignant small cell tumor of the thoracopulmonary region in childhood: a distinctive clinicopathologic entity of uncertain histogenesis. *Cancer* 43:2438–2451, 1979.

Davis BD, et al: *Microbiology*, 3rd ed. New York, Harper & Row, 1980.

Duray PH, Mark EJ, Barwick KW, et al: Congenital polycystic tumor of the AV node. *Arch Pathol Lab Med* 109:302, 1985.

Evatt BL, et al: Coincidental appearance of LAV/HTLV-III antibodies in hemophiliacs and the onset of the AIDS epidemic. *N Engl J Med* 312:483, 1985.

Gottlieb MS, Schroff R, Schanker HM, et al: *Pneumocystis carinii* pneumonia and mucosal candidiasis in previously healthy homosexual men: evidence of a new acquired cellular immunodeficiency. *N Engl J Med* 305:1425, 1981.

Gottlieb MS, et al: UCLA Conference: The acquired immunodeficiency syndrome. *Ann Intern Med* 99:208, 1983.

Graves HCB, et al: Postcoital detection of a male-specific semen protein. *N Engl J Med* 312:338, 1985.

Henry JB, et al (eds): *Todd-Sanford-Davidsohn Clinical Diagnosis and Management by Laboratory Methods*, 17th ed. Philadelphia, WB Saunders, 1984.

Hurst JW, et al (eds): *The Heart*, 5th ed. New York, McGraw-Hill, 1982.

International Symposium on Legionnaire's Disease. *Ann Intern Med* 90:491, 1979.

Isselbacher KJ, et al (eds): *Harrison's Principles of Internal Medicine*, 10th ed. New York, McGraw-Hill, 1983.

Koss LG: *Diagnostic Cytology and Its Histopathologic Bases*, 3rd ed. Philadelphia, JB Lippincott, 1979.

Moore JD, Thompson NW, Appelman HD, et al: Arteriovenous malformations of the gastrointestinal tract. *Arch Surg* 111:381–388, 1976.

Morris JG, et al: Cholera and other vibrioses in the United States. *N Engl J Med* 312:343, 1985.

Murray HW, et al: Impaired production of lymphokines and immune (gamma) interferon in the acquired immunodeficiency syndrome. *N Engl J Med* 310:883, 1984.

Nicholson WJ: Cancer following occupational exposure to asbestos and vinyl chloride. *Cancer* 39:1792, 1977.

Philips SC, Milduan D, William DC, et al: Sexual transmission of enteric protozoa and helminths in a venereal disease clinic population. *N Engl J Med* 305:603, 1981.

Postkanzer DC, Herbst AL: Epidemiology of vaginal adenosis and adenocarcinoma associated with exposure to stilbestrol in utero. *Cancer* 39:1982, 1977.

Reichert GM, et al: Special topic review. Autopsy pathology in acquired immune deficiency syndrome. *Am J Pathol* 112:357, 1983.

Robbins SL, Cotran RS: *Pathologic Basis of Disease*, 3rd ed. Philadelphia, WB Saunders, 1984.

Rosai J: *Ackerman's Surgical Pathology*, 6th ed. St. Louis, CV Mosby, 1981.

Rosai J, Dorfman R: Sinus histiocytosis with massive lymphadenopathy. *Arch Pathol* 87:63–70, 1969.

Rosen SH, Castleman B, Liebow AA: Pulmonary alveolar proteinosis. *N Engl J Med* 258:1123–1142, 1958.

Schwarz WB, Wolfe HJ, Pauker SG: Pathology and probabilities: a new approach to interpreting and reporting biopsies. *N Engl J Med* 305:917, 1981.

Stanbury JB, et al: *The Metabolic Basis of Inherited Disease*, 5th ed. New York, McGraw-Hill, 1983.

Stout J, Yu VL, Zuravleff J: Ubiquitousness of *Legionella pneumophila* in the water supply of a hospital with endemic Legionnaire's disease. *N Engl J Med* 306:466, 468, 1982.

Takahashi M: *Color Atlas of Cancer Cytology*, 2nd ed. Tokyo, Igaku-Shoin, 1982.

Tam R: Culture-independent diagnosis of *Chlamydia trachomatis* using monoclonal antibodies. *N Engl J Med* 310:1146, 1984.

Williams RH (ed): *Textbook of Endocrinology*, 6th ed. Philadelphia, WB Saunders, 1981.

Williams WJ, et al: *Hematology*, 3rd ed. New York, McGraw-Hill, 1983.

Wintrobe MM, et al: *Clinical Hematology*, 8th ed. Philadelphia, Lea & Febiger, 1981.